STRESS TESTED

UNIVERSITY OF CALGARY
LCR Publishing Services

STRESS TESTED

The COVID-19 Pandemic and Canadian National Security

EDITED BY
**Leah West, Thomas Juneau,
and Amarnath Amarasingam**

LCR Publishing Services
An imprint of University of Calgary Press
2500 University Drive NW
Calgary, Alberta
Canada T2N 1N4
press.ucalgary.ca

LIBRARY AND ARCHIVES CANADA CATALOGUING IN PUBLICATION

Title: Stress tested : the COVID-19 pandemic and Canadian national security / edited by Leah West, Thomas Juneau, and Amarnath Amarasingam.
Names: West, Leah, editor. | Juneau, Thomas, editor. | Amarnath Amarasingam, editor.
Description: Includes bibliographical references and index.
Identifiers: Canadiana (print) 20210320273 | Canadiana (ebook) 20210320311 | ISBN 9781773852430 (softcover) | ISBN 9781773852447 (Open Access PDF) | ISBN 9781773852454 (PDF) | ISBN 9781773852461 (EPUB)
Subjects: LCSH: National security—Canada. | LCSH: Intelligence service—Canada. | LCSH: COVID-19 Pandemic, 2020-—Canada.
Classification: LCC UA600 .S83 2021 | DDC 355/.033071—dc23

The University of Calgary Press acknowledges the support of the Government of Alberta through the Alberta Media Fund for our publications. We acknowledge the financial support of the Government of Canada. We acknowledge the financial support of the Canada Council for the Arts for our publishing program.

The editors gratefully acknowledge the support of the Social Sciences and Humanities Research Council Partnership Engage Grant and the Mobilizing Insights in National Defence and Security Targeted Engagement Grant.

Printed and bound in Canada by Marquis
♻ This book is printed on 57lb Enviro paper

Copyediting by Ryan Perks
Cover image: Colourbox 10514414
Cover design, page design, and typesetting by Melina Cusano

Contents

List of Figures and Tables

Introduction

Leah West, Thomas Juneau, and Amarnath Amarasingam

The role of Canada's intelligence and national security community has been widely debated since the onset of the COVID-19 pandemic. Some describe its emergence as an intelligence failure or a failure of early warning. Those in this camp argue that Canada should expand the mandates of its security and intelligence agencies to monitor and respond to global health threats. Others argue that the role of intelligence and national security in health matters is and should remain limited. Pandemics have traditionally been considered a public health issue with national security consequences, not a national security issue in and of itself. Tasking security and intelligence agencies with a health intelligence mandate might cause more problems than it solves, duplicating existing capabilities and overstating the utility of early warning to policy-makers.

While this debate continues, traditional defence and security threats have evolved rapidly during the pandemic. We have seen a rise in extremist violence, foreign interference, economic and political espionage, and civil unrest in Canada and around the world. What is more, conspiracy theories related to the pandemic, sometimes perpetuated or augmented by adversarial nations seeking to undermine democratic states, have made it harder to get the virus under control.

All of this raises important questions. How ought we prioritize national security threats during a public welfare emergency? Should Canadian intelligence agencies engage in "health intelligence"? Do our defence, security, and intelligence agencies have the appropriate tools and mandates to take on new roles or adapt their existing missions in a pandemic? How are threats evolving in response to the global crisis, and what are the challenges in countering them in a pandemic? What limits are Canadians willing to accept on their privacy, rights, and freedoms to counter those threats? How well did Canada's security and intelligence community balance the increased demands on its workforce tied to working in a pandemic environment, and did those demands compromise operational effectiveness?

Our collective effort to break down and answer these questions is the result of a Partnership Engage Grant funded by Canada's Social Sciences and Humanities Research Council. Additionally, the funding to ensure that this work is available in an open access format results from a Targeted Engagement Grant from the Department of National Defence's Mobilizing Insights in National Defence and Security (MINDS) program. We thank both organizations for their funding and support.

Our partner in this grant was the Privy Council Office's Intelligence Assessment Secretariat (IAS). The IAS is a central unit tasked with providing non-partisan, all-source analysis to the Prime Minister, cabinet, and the broader federal government. It produces intelligence assessments on a wide range of topics, including, since March 2020, those that help inform the government's response to the pandemic. The need for this research was obvious. Not only is Canada facing an unprecedented health and economic crisis, but when we started this project there was virtually no rigorous academic research explicitly focused on the role of the Canadian intelligence and security community in monitoring public welfare emergencies and managing their consequences. Furthermore, there is limited literature on health intelligence from national contexts other than the United States. This work seeks to add to this small body of literature, not only to expand its scope, but also to offer workable policy solutions for lawmakers and security and intelligence practitioners in Canada and across like-minded states.

In the summer and fall of 2020, the editors worked with the IAS to hold a roundtable with senior officials from across the national security and intelligence community to discuss the challenges they faced six months into the pandemic. Following this broad conversation, and as the situation evolved, several chapter authors continued the discussion with relevant government officials on a direct basis. Ultimately, these discussions spawned the research questions that each author set out to answer.

Not only is the interdisciplinary team of experts assembled in this text highly esteemed, but it is also rare to have such a diverse field of expertise analyze a single, timely, and relevant issue that has a direct impact on the lives of Canadians. Each author employs the methodology best suited to answer their specific research question, which is rooted in the project's overarching question: How well did Canada's national security and intelligence community respond to the COVID-19 pandemic? We are proud that this team is not only diverse in terms of the fields of study and academic lenses they bring to bear on their topics, but it is also gender-balanced and includes scholars from the Black, Indigenous, and People of Colour (BIPOC) community. Many of our contributors also had significant practical experience in the national defence, security, and intelligence community, whether in government or the private sector, before joining academia.

The result combines insights from intelligence studies, political science, international relations, sociology, public health, and law. Together, the chapters in this book provide a deeper understanding of how the intelligence and security community can improve and better integrate its capabilities into federal efforts to prepare, identify, manage, and respond to public health and welfare emergencies. By improving and refining the conceptual and methodological study of the links between security and public health, this work also represents a significant advancement in the broader security and intelligence studies literature.

Plan of the Book

We have arranged this book in two parts. The first contains four chapters and examines some of the new challenges facing those working in Canadian national security. The first chapter, by Argentino and Amarasingam, looks at the interplay between COVID-19 lockdowns, conspiracy theories, and political violence. Using social media data across multiple platforms, arrest records, and digital ethnographic research, they show the ways in which the pandemic has impacted individuals and movements, how they are mobilizing, and what future threat trajectories may look like. The second chapter, by Wilner and Babb, examines how established extremist and terrorist groups have become emboldened worldwide, including in Canada, finding opportunities to exploit the situation, incite hate, (re)mobilize, and promote their ideologies online in new and novel ways.

The following two chapters focus on the nexus between the national security and economic realms. The third chapter, by Stephanie Carvin and students from the Infrastructure Protection and International Security Program at Carleton University, explores the heavy strain placed on supply chains in Canada by the pandemic. They analyze the policies and market dynamics that guide the production and distribution of goods and essential components in Canada and find that supply chains are still not sufficiently resilient against future disruptions. Their chapter calls for Canada to re-examine its food, manufacturing, and distribution policies, and potentially reshape the landscape to improve resilience. The final chapter in part 1, by Momani and Bélanger, examines how the pandemic has shed light on the vulnerabilities related to Canada's critical infrastructure. They argue that the digitalization of critical infrastructure—including energy and utilities, the financial system, food systems, transportation, health systems, etc.—combined with the pressures of the pandemic expose these systems to cyber attacks and therefore needs added policy attention.

The second part of the book contains ten chapters and looks at how several sectors of the Canadian government responded to the pandemic. Davis and Corbeil, in chapter 5, examine the use of intelligence collection and surveillance techniques against the pandemic, and explore the ethics of this type of surveillance. They conclude by delving into the potential utility of a health intelligence priority for Canada. In the next chapter, Carvin examines how the pandemic and subsequent lockdowns impacted national security operations. Based on interviews with individuals who work in the intelligence community, Carvin explores how national security agencies managed the need to revolutionize the way they do business while facing an unprecedented surge in demand for security advice and assistance. She concludes by examining the lessons learned and the implications for the future. Robinson, in the next chapter, examines the impact of the pandemic on the Communications Security Establishment (CSE). One of the challenges, he notes, was the urgent task of ensuring the electronic security of the Government of Canada as public servants shifted overwhelmingly to working from home. Additionally, he describes how protecting the country's health system and research institutions from pandemic-related cyber threats became a top priority.

Moving on to the impact of the pandemic on the Canadian Armed Forces (CAF), Saideman, von Hlatky, and Hopkins compare and contrast domestic and international operations, noting that while the pandemic dramatically influenced how the CAF operates within Canada, the external effects varied based on the type of unit involved and what they were doing. They conclude the chapter by examining some of the implications for present and future CAF operations. Cox, in the next chapter, examines the Defence Intelligence Enterprise, which provides strategic and operational intelligence to deployed CAF military missions at home and abroad. With the pandemic, authorities imposed decisive health-care restrictions across the Department of National Defence and the CAF. Initially, defence intelligence activity was dramatically slowed and reduced. By the end of the summer, 2020, Cox argues, the Defence Intelligence Enterprise had found its "sea legs" and, thanks to several procedural and workforce adjustments, returned to a more comfortable, but no less hectic, level and pace of activity.

In the next chapter, Lee and Piper delve into the Global Public Health Intelligence Network (GPHIN), an initiative launched two years after the 2003 SARS outbreak. GPHIN, Lee and Piper argue, underwent political and financial challenges just when such a network was needed most. They identify key lessons learned and ways forward for reviving GPHIN's role as a critical component of Canada's core public health capacities and global health security. In the next chapter, West unpacks the debate about whether existing legal authorities and emergency legislation permit the Canadian government to retool state resources—especially the surveillance apparatus—to help with public health demands, such as contact tracing and enforcement of public health measures.

Nesbitt and Hansen, in the next chapter, take a close look at how the pandemic "stress-tested" the criminal justice system in Canada. The result, they argue, is that the system has been asked to show its capacity to respond to *increased* national security threats—be they foreign espionage and disinformation campaigns, politically or ideologically motivated extremism, and pandemic-specific enforcement actions—all while operating with a *reduced* capacity to respond and prosecute.

Next, Wallace looks at the impact of the pandemic on the Canada Border Services Agency. He argues that while the pandemic all but required a total suspension of the agency's deportation program, things will not simply go back to normal after the pandemic is over. According to Wallace, there are real legal and practical impediments to deportation that will emerge as the pandemic fades. In the last chapter, Rayes and Sahloul argue that should another large-scale disease threaten the health and safety of the global community, the national security apparatus of the United States must work closely with its Canadian counterparts as well as the global community at large to engage BIPOC communities. The goal, they argue, is to create best practices that reduce the disproportionate impacts of any disease, as such action is key to maintaining the economic strength and security of marginalized and vulnerable communities.

Finally, in the conclusion, Juneau provides an overview of the key questions this edited collection sought to answer: the extent to which Canada's national security and intelligence community was ready to face the pandemic at its onset; how the threat environment changed during the pandemic; how the community adjusted; and the longer-term implications.

Recommendations

We conclude this introduction with a series of recommendations for the Canadian national security and intelligence community on how it could better prepare for future public health emergencies. These recommendations, based on the more detailed analysis in the following chapters, are divided into three categories: threat assessments, tools, and lessons learned.

Threat Assessments

This collection demonstrates that many of the threats Canada faced during the pandemic were not new but rather arose from the intensification of pre-existing trends. This is especially true in the online space. Wilner and Babb thus recommend that Canada's national security and intelligence community should continue to pay close attention to online activities seeking to undermine the Government of Canada, to recruit new members to terrorist organizations and extremist groups, and to incite or motivate acts of violence. These threats are proliferating worldwide, and Canada is no exception.

The 6 January 2021 insurrection at the Capitol in Washington, DC, as well as multiple other acts of violence since March 2020, also make clear that the spread of disinformation and conspiracy theories represents a threat to national security. Canadian policy-makers should therefore consider how to take a more proactive approach to fostering critical thinking and digital literacy. Amarasingam and Argentino emphasize that the pandemic may, in hindsight, be a practice run for other disasters to come. As a result, they recommend that the government take an inventory of the lessons it has learned.

Critical infrastructure can be particularly vulnerable to cyber attacks. Of course, this exposure existed before 2020, but it intensified as the pandemic accelerated the shift to the digitalized world. As Momani and Bélanger explain, some of these risks are further complicated by the fact that Canada's critical infrastructure has shifted from public to private ownership and control, adding new actors to the equation. Momani and Bélanger therefore argue that there is a need for better coordination among these multiple actors, both public and private, since a lack of information sharing and co-operation often represents a vulnerable point in cyber attacks on critical infrastructure.

Additionally, the pandemic intensified pre-existing concerns about the security of supply chains and, more broadly, about the links between the economy and national security. Carvin and a group of her students thus raise the thorny question of the appropriate role of governments in protecting elements of the economy with strategic or national importance, especially the manufacturing of personal protective equipment and the security of food supplies. They argue that the federal government must do more to prepare supply chains for long-term global disruptions in an era of adversarial geo-economic strategies. In particular, they recommend that the government implement initiatives to increase the economy's resilience and self-sufficiency in specific sectors. More broadly, they recommend that, given the likelihood of future disruptions of the type seen during the pandemic, future national security discussions should give greater weight to concerns around the management of supply chains.

Tools

To date, Canada has not employed national security tools and practices to track the spread of COVID-19. However, the pandemic has provided further impetus for the national security and intelligence community to intensify a trend of recent years: increased collaboration with non-traditional partners elsewhere in the federal government, in sub-national levels of government, and in the private sector.

There has been much media attention on GPHIN in particular, a Canadian initiative to gather and disseminate epidemic intelligence. According to critics, including scientists within the federal government, GPHIN's role became steadily less prominent over the years until the Liberal government reallocated its resources in 2019. However, as the chapter by Lee and Piper explains, the pandemic demonstrated the need for renewed investment in an epidemic intelligence system. Moreover, they recommend that such a public health intelligence system be better integrated with the Canadian health system and other parts of the government, including the intelligence community.

Similarly, Davis and Corbeil argue that greater integration and information-sharing between the traditional security and intelligence community and the health intelligence community could produce earlier warning and, by extension, lead to better policy responses in future public health crises. Nevertheless, they remind us that there are real concerns with a possible expansion of the Canadian intelligence community's mandate to include health intelligence. These concerns include already existing resource shortages, the need to identify the right use of tools and technologies, and questions of proportionality and privacy. Therefore, they conclude that a wholesale adoption of health intelligence as a national security and intelligence priority might be premature, and they argue instead for better integration and information-sharing.

The chapter by Rayes and Sahloul explains how the pandemic has highlighted the public health, social, economic, and political challenges facing minority communities in the United States and Canada. They assess how these outcomes could have been mitigated with higher-quality data, and how data can be integral to preventing future national and global security threats. In this context, they recommend that the Canadian government engage in more thorough and transparent data collection on how public health emergencies affect minority communities.

Looking forward, the federal government should also reflect on the legal tools at its disposal. Two key debates that emerged during the pandemic were whether Canada's surveillance apparatus could be leveraged in a public health crisis and whether the federal government could mandate that individuals or telecommunication service providers share location data generated by wireless devices with health or security agencies. In her chapter, West argues that the answer in both cases is negative. Should lawmakers ultimately determine that it is appropriate to leverage the tools and techniques developed by CSIS and CSE to face future public health emergencies, West recommends, among other initiatives, that they consider amending the federal *Emergencies Act* to authorize the collection of information in a public welfare emergency or expanding CSE's assistance mandate to include provincial health authorities.

For their part, Nesbitt and Hansen explain how Canada's criminal justice system was put under significant stress by the pandemic, notably because of increases in certain types of criminal behaviour, such as cyber scams. In addition, Canada saw an increase in ideologically motivated extremism, particularly on the far right. As a result, they recommend the development of a strategy to better prioritize criminal investigations and prosecutions. This exercise should, in their view, include critical thinking on how to investigate and prosecute emerging threats, especially online criminality, financial crimes, fraud, and the spread of mis- and disinformation.

Lessons Learned

As the national security and intelligence community adapted to the pandemic, it learned useful lessons. Some of them, clearly, will be of limited value once the pandemic is over. Others, however, can be applicable, even if only partially, in the post-pandemic world to help the community improve its performance. At the very least, we therefore strongly recommend that the community commit to a serious lessons-learned exercise. This should provide an official record—some of which should be made public—of how the community adapted its operations, and where it succeeded and failed. To be most effective, this effort should be led by the

National Security and Intelligence Advisor and include participation from the heads of all relevant departments and agencies. The two main review and oversight bodies, the National Security and Intelligence Committee of Parliamentarians and the National Security and Intelligence Review Agency, should also consider examining the community's performance during the pandemic.

This lessons-learned exercise—similar to after-action reports prepared by the military—could include, in particular, how working from home can—and cannot, as the case may be—continue after the pandemic. As discussed in many chapters—notably by Carvin, Cox, and Robinson—there are some benefits to continuing this practice, albeit arguably in a limited form. Similarly, because so many of the intelligence community's employees have been working from home on at least a part-time basis, the pandemic has forced agencies to intensify their use of open-source information and analysis. Here, too, there are potential long-term benefits to incorporating these valuable lessons.

Finally, the pandemic forced difficult choices onto the community. Working at a reduced capacity, departments and agencies had to choose which activities they needed to stop or reduce. As discussed, for example, in the chapter on CAF operations by Saideman, von Hlatky, and Hopkins, the military was forced to determine which of its activities were vital priorities that could not be curtailed. The temptation here will often be to simply resume all or most of these activities as the pandemic subsides in 2021 and 2022. This would be a wasted opportunity. Vested interests and inertia often make it difficult for bureaucracies to jettison or significantly downsize programs. The gradual end of the pandemic presents a golden opportunity to engage in a comprehensive review of the community's priorities and to reallocate resources to tackle the next generation of security threats.

Acknowledgements

The editors would like to thank all of the contributors for agreeing to undertake this project during incredibly demanding times: your commitment to timely and relevant research is an inspiration. We are also grateful to the Privy Council Office's Intelligence Assessment Secretariat for partnering with us on this project. The organization's willingness to engage in this study made this work stronger and, we hope, more relevant for those in the national security and intelligence community. We also want to thank the Social Sciences and Humanities Research Council for awarding us a Partnership Engage Grant, as well as Mobilizing Insights in National Defence and Security (MINDS), the Department of National Defence's engagement program, for their financial support for this project. Thank you also to the Centre for International Policy Studies (CIPS) at the University of Ottawa, the Faculty of Public Affairs at Carleton University, and the Canadian Association for Security and Intelligence Studies (CASIS) for hosting a series of webinars in early 2021 where contributors presented their work. Additionally, we want to thank our incredible team of research assistants: Jake Norris, who was with us from start to finish, Peter Shyba, and Anne-Marie Chevalier. We also wish to thank everyone at University of Calgary Press for their help in making this book a reality, from grant application to publication, in less than eighteen months, especially Brian Scrivener and Ryan Perks. Stephen Ullstrom also prepared the index.

Finally, a profound thank-you goes out to Stephanie Carvin, Michael Nesbitt, Jessica Davis, and Craig Forcese for your help in shaping this project and your steadfast support throughout this process.

PART I:
Threats

They Got It All under Control: QAnon, Conspiracy Theories, and the New Threats to Canadian National Security

Marc-André Argentino and Amarnath Amarasingam

Introduction

On 4 December 2016, Edgar Maddison Welch drove from North Carolina to the Comet Ping Pong pizza restaurant in Washington, DC. He had with him an AR-15 rifle and a .38 revolver, and he wanted the owners of the restaurant to show him their basement, believing that children were being sexually abused and trafficked through the restaurant. On the drive there, he recorded a video for his daughters. In it, he says, "I can't let you grow up in a world that's so corrupt by evil, without at least standing up for you and for other children just like you" (Miller 2021). Years later, on Christmas Day 2020, Anthony Quinn Warner detonated a bomb in Nashville, killing himself and injuring eight people. In the days before the attack, Warner mailed packages to several individuals containing nine typed pages and some flash drives. These writings evince a deep interest in 9/11 conspiracy theories, theories that the moon landing was a hoax, as well as a belief that reptilians and lizard people secretly control the world (Hall and Wisniewski 2021). These isolated cases, and others like them, began to worry many researchers and law enforcement officials that conspiracy theories were no longer just circulating in dark corners of the Internet, but were starting to mobilize people to commit violence.

On 6 January 2021, protestors violently breached the US Capitol with the intent of disrupting the certification of the 2020 presidential election. As a result of the insurrection, five individuals, including US Capitol Police officer Brian Sicknick, were killed. Another hundred people were injured. According to analysis by the National Consortium for the Study of Terrorism and Responses to Terrorism (START), thirty-one QAnon followers, as of 1 March 2021, were charged for participating in the Capitol insurrection (Jensen and Kane 2021). However, this was not the first instance of violence of this kind. On 29 August 2020, ideologically motivated violent extremists, QAnon supporters, and anti-lockdown protesters attempted to storm Germany's parliamentary building, occupying the steps leading up to the Reichstag (Felden et al. 2021; Bennhold 2020).

The Capitol Hill insurrection and the storming of the Reichstag is evidence not only of the increasingly global reach of QAnon, but also of how conspiracy theories and disinformation about the pandemic have rapidly evolved into threats to democratic institutions, extremist violence, threats against elected officials, and attacks against critical infrastructure.

This chapter will closely examine the impact of the global pandemic on conspiracy theories and how this may prove to be an ongoing security concern. As we note in the short literature review below, much of the research so far has focused on the broader social impact of the pandemic—on social trust, on vaccine hesitancy, and misinformation. Less attention has been paid to how the pandemic and measures taken by the government to limit its spread have contributed to the unprecedented rise in conspiracy theories and the merging and blending of different conspiracies. There is probably no better example of this than the QAnon movement, which grew in popularity partly because it rode the wave of COVID-19-related conspiracies after March 2020.

In this chapter, we first provide a short introduction to some of the recent research on COVID-19 and conspiracy theories before delving into the QAnon movement, how the pandemic helped its rise in popularity and impact, and how this cocktail of beliefs and grievances has pushed some individuals to violent activity.

COVID-19 Conspiracies and Their Social Impact

Past research makes clear that pandemics and other moments of social crisis are often accompanied by conspiracy theories (Van Prooijen and Douglas 2017). As Imhoff and Lamberty (2020, 1110) note, for almost all major events over the last several decades, the "official version of why these came about were confronted with various conspiracy allegations that proposed an explanation involving plots hatched in secret by powerful agents instead."

The COVID-19 pandemic was no different. From the start, theories were floated about whether the launch of 5G technology in China produced the virus, whether the virus was actually a bioweapon, and whether it was a political ploy to bring about a new global order (Argentino and Amarasingam 2020). Several important studies soon followed, gauging not only the public health impact of COVID-19 conspiracies but also the broader social impact this kind of misinformation is likely to have on democratic institutions in a post-COVID-19 world.

Daniel Romer and Kathleen Hall Jamieson (2020) conducted a national survey of 1,050 adults in the United States in the second half of March 2020 and a follow-up survey with 840 of the same individuals in July 2020. They found that conspiratorial thinking has a significant impact on whether individuals took preventive measures related to the virus and whether they are open to taking the vaccine. Significantly, they found that "conspiracy beliefs early in the pandemic continued to be related to subsequent behavior and intentions four months later" (6). Tomasz Oleksy and colleagues similarly looked at whether the presence of conspiratorial beliefs impacted whether people engaged in preventative measures recommended by public health officials. Based on two studies conducted in Poland with a sample of 2,726 participants, they found that belief in COVID-19 conspiracies was correlated to acceptance of xenophobic policies. They also discovered that conspiracy theories arguing that governments were using COVID-19 for nefarious purposes were positively correlated with the dismissal of public health recommendations (Oleksy et al. 2020).

Other studies explicitly focused on social media platforms and their role in spreading COVID-19-related misinformation. Daniel Allington and colleagues (2020) conducted three surveys related to social media use, conspiracy beliefs, and health-protective behaviours related to COVID-19 among residents of the United Kingdom. Like the previous studies mentioned here, they found a positive association between COVID-19 conspiracy beliefs, the "use of social media as a source of information about COVID-19," and people's willingness to engage in protective behaviours recommended by public health officials (6). Interestingly, they found that people who received most of their COVID-19 news from traditional broadcast media were more likely to adopt protective measures.

The larger sociological literature on conspiracy theories also notes how important they can be with respect to the notion of theodicy, or the question of why evil exists in the world if God is good, all-knowing, and all-powerful. Conspiracy theories permit the development of symbolic resources that enable humans to define and address the problem of evil. As Michael Barkun (2013, 4) notes, "not only are events nonrandom, but the clear identification of evil gives the conspiracist a definable enemy against which to struggle, endowing life with purpose." The essence of many COVID-related conspiracy theories lies in their attempts to delineate and explain evil (the pandemic and its multiple negative impacts).

In his influential work on conspiracy theories, Barkun argues that a conspiracist world view implies a universe governed by design rather than randomness. Barkun highlights three characteristics of conspiracy theories:

1. nothing happens by accident: the world is governed by intentionality, there are no accidents or coincidences, and whatever happens is by design.

2. nothing is as it seems: evil forces are constantly trying to deceive the world, and so what may appear as benign is actually a cosmic threat.

3. everything is connected: building on the first two characteristics, it follows that seemingly disconnected events and occurrences across human history form a seamless pattern that can be unearthed through diligent research. (2013, 3–4)

The core of most COVID-related conspiracy theories is linked to an intentionality behind the origin, spread, and duration of the pandemic (e.g., the virus was human-made, an elite group of individuals orchestrated the virus, or the virus is being used to control the population through quarantine and lockdown), and to the secrecy behind the plans to achieve an evil goal. Thus, the conspiracy theorist is not simply engaging in mindless sleuthing; they are a warrior in an ongoing battle between good and evil. Those who believe in COVID-19 conspiracy theories hold to a world view whereby humans can and do direct the course of history according to their own will and intentions.

Thousands of studies look at the causes and consequences of conspiratorial thinking, and our discussion here only scratches the surface. However, for this chapter, it is sufficient to set the stage for our examination of how COVID-19 conspiracies could impact Canadian national security. We do this by looking closely at the QAnon movement as a case study. First, we examine how it rose to prominence during the COVID-19 lockdown period, and second, we look at how it has contributed to several instances of violence and civil unrest.

The QAnon Movement

QAnon is a decentralized ideology rooted in an unfounded conspiracy theory that a globally active "Deep State" cabal of satanic pedophile elites is responsible for all the evil in the world. Adherents of QAnon also believe that this same cabal sought to bring down President Trump, whom they saw as the world's only hope in defeating it. The name "QAnon" refers to its followers' belief that "Q" is a military intelligence operation geared toward supporting President Trump in his efforts to root out and eliminate the "Deep State" (GNET 2020).[1] The QAnon conspiracy emerged in October 2017, on 4chan's[2] /pol/ (politically incorrect) page in a thread called "Calm Before the Storm," when an anonymous user signing off as "Q" stated that "Hillary Clinton will be arrested between 7:45 AM–8:30 AM EST on Monday—the morning on 30 October, 2017." Q claims to have special government access, which is a strategy employed in the past by 4chan users and is part of a wider "anon genre" of individuals claiming to be government officials with top secret information they need to share with the public.[3]

QAnon has become a master narrative capable of explaining in simple terms various complex events. The result is a world view characterized by a sharp distinction between the realms of good and evil that is non-falsifiable. No matter how much evidence journalists, academics, and civil society offer to counter the claims promoted by the movement, belief in QAnon as the source of truth is a matter of faith—specifically faith in Trump and "Q". Though it started as a series of conspiracy theories and false predictions, over the past three years, QAnon has evolved into a religio-political ideology.

Why do people believe in conspiracy theories like QAnon? It is because they offer a way to make sense of a world in crisis. Where others see chaos, violence, and suffering, QAnon adherents see patterns and intentionality behind the pandemic, child abuse, political strife, war, etc. By rejecting coincidence and connecting the dots others do not—by "doing your own research," as the saying goes—an individual adherent can build an answer that provides a coherent explanation for the pandemic that attributes malicious intent to an enemy toward whom they can channel their efforts.

The "do your own research" ethos and the crowdsourcing of answers to otherwise inexplicable questions makes QAnon adherents resilient to official messaging from governments, medical experts, scientific studies, journalists, etc. Many of these individuals do not trust traditional sources of information, such as science, the media, or academics—who are either deluded or part of the conspiracy—and so they have no choice but to circumvent traditional sources of expertise and attempt to uncover the truth themselves. This exercise is deeply meaningful for many; they feel they have been vested with a purpose and are part of a global movement to awaken a sleeping world.

A popular explanation for why conspiracy theories are attractive is what scholars call "proportionality bias," defined as the tendency to assume that major events must have major causes (Leman and Cinnirella 2007). The pandemic, arising suddenly and having global consequences, seems to invite a kind of proportionality bias: something so major that brought the world to a halt could not possibly be caused by a random series of events thousands of miles away. This produces what Timothy Melley (2000) has termed "agency panic"—a sense of anxiety arising from not being in control of events that impact you or your loved ones. COVID-19 conspiracy theories and QAnon identify various culprits behind the pandemic while also offering adherents the possibility of reversing these events and preventing similar ones in the future. For QAnon followers who believe that COVID-19 is a hoax perpetrated by sinister conspirators, exposing these conspirators will mean waking the world up to the truth. Under this world view, their actions are righteous. Targeting individuals, institutions, or infrastructure responsible for the pandemic, along with pedophiles and those seeking to destroy the world, means that their actions are not problematic; they are revolutionary.

How COVID-19 Impacted QAnon: Evidence from Online Spaces

The 6 January 2021 insurrection at the US Capitol is a stark example of how offline violence can occur when online conspiracy theories are left to foment unchecked during a crisis. Although January 6 is the culmination of years of misinformation and disinformation, the leading cause of the spike in conspiracy theories, especially for the QAnon movement, was the pandemic and government policies to stem the spread of the virus. By mid-2019, the QAnon movement struggled to sustain itself, especially after the 15 March 2019 Christchurch attack in New Zealand, the 3 August 2019 shooting in El Paso, Texas, and the 4 August 2019 shooting in Dayton, Ohio. Because many of these attackers had posted manifestos and other content on 8chan, the page was taken down on 5 August 2019 (Robertson 2019; Mezzofiore and O'Sullivan 2019). At the time, 8chan was the only place where "Q" posted. A key concept from QAnon is "no outside coms," which implies that "Q" will only post on 8chan and nowhere else—a deliberate strategy to prevent copycats. After its service providers and domain host took down 8chan, there were no posts from "Q" until 8chan re-emerged as 8kun four months later (Glaser 2019).

The news of a new virus spreading in Wuhan, China, in January 2020 caught the attention of certain QAnon influencers, who began to amplify various conspiracy theories about the disease. It started with these influencers—who also peddle alternative health information and sell cure-all products to their followers—promoting and selling a product known as Miracle Mineral Solution as a way of warding off COVID-19 (Sommer 2020). As the pandemic began to spread around the world, so

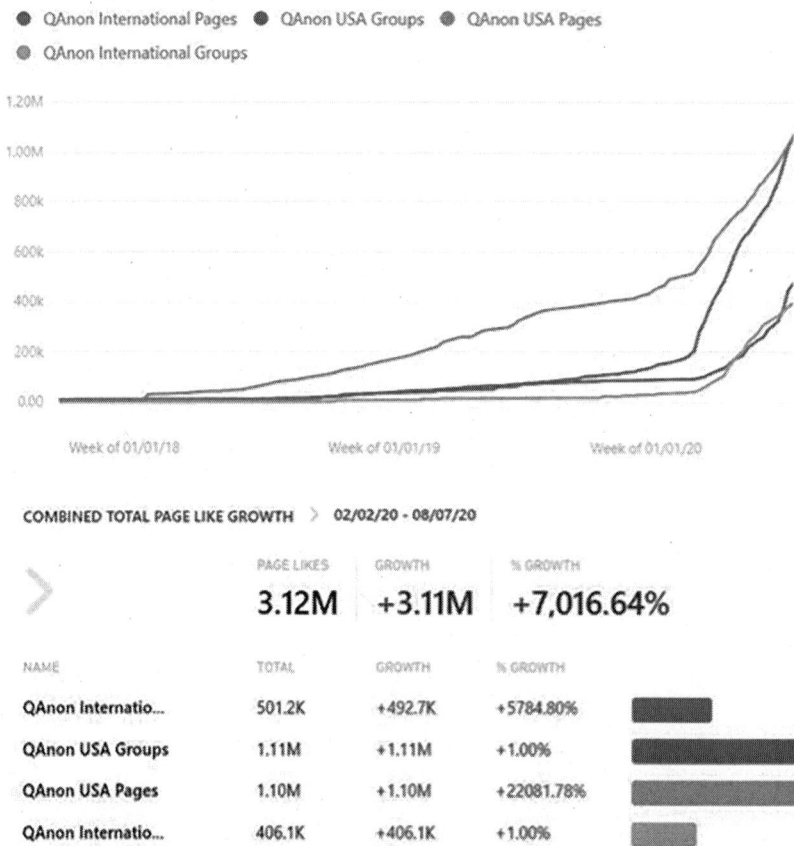

Legend:
- QAnon International Pages
- QAnon USA Groups
- QAnon USA Pages
- QAnon International Groups

COMBINED TOTAL PAGE LIKE GROWTH > 02/02/20 - 08/07/20

	PAGE LIKES	GROWTH	% GROWTH
	3.12M	**+3.11M**	**+7,016.64%**

NAME	TOTAL	GROWTH	% GROWTH	
QAnon Internatio...	501.2K	+492.7K	+5784.80%	
QAnon USA Groups	1.11M	+1.11M	+1.00%	
QAnon USA Pages	1.10M	+1.10M	+22081.78%	
QAnon Internatio...	406.1K	+406.1K	+1.00%	

FIGURE 1.1: QAnon group and page membership as of 8 August 2020

did conspiracy theories about the virus. QAnon theories about the virus, as well as QAnon ideology more broadly, followed closely behind. This time, though, they were not relegated to the fringe image boards of 8kun, but rather were being pushed on mainstream platforms like Twitter, Facebook, and Instagram.

The turning point for QAnon's mainstreaming was March 2020, when the United States, along with many other nations, closed its borders to control the spread of COVID-19. Taking a close look at the data related to QAnon Facebook pages, it is clear how much QAnon grew during this period.[4] The authors collected Facebook data from 406 QAnon and QAnon-aligned Facebook groups and pages. The graphs shown in figure 1.1 demonstrate that QAnon groups before March 2020 had approximately 220,600 members, whereas QAnon pages had 558,800 likes. By 7 August 2020, QAnon groups had approximately 1,516,100 members and QAnon pages had 1,610,200 likes.

Not only did group membership increase, but levels of engagement within these groups and pages grew drastically after March 2020. There are similar patterns of behaviour with respect to the number of posts, whereby posting increased following the March 2020 border closures in the United States and the dramatic impact of COVID-19 in Spain and Italy in March and April. Posts between March 2020 and August 2020 accounted for 65 per cent of all QAnon posts ever made on Facebook.[5] With respect to overall activity, posts on international group pages were almost as high as the US-based groups following the impact of COVID-19 and the prolonged lockdowns (see figure 1.2). This increase immediately followed the growing anti-lockdown movements in Europe.

It is important to highlight that, based on a qualitative assessment of the groups and pages collected, not all groups reflect a "canonical" treatment of QAnon. Within the aggregate of these QAnon ecosystems, ideological elements of QAnon have mixed with other movements and conspiracy theories linked to the pandemic. In Canada and globally, QAnon has latched on to anti-mask, anti-vaccine, anti-lockdown movements, as well as groups who believe that COVID-19 is a hoax. What all of these ideas have in common is that they are inherently anti-establishment and anti-government. Since QAnon served as an umbrella conspiracy theory, it grew in popularity as other conspiracies also came to prominence. QAnon was, for example, involved in spreading viral disinformation campaigns about the pandemic and where it came from, as well as fake cures for the virus (Brown 2020; ADL 2020; Frenkel, Decker, and Alba 2020).

Additionally, the mainstreaming of QAnon in the American political arena during the 2020 US election cycle was significant. Reporter Alex Kaplan noted that 2020 was the year "QAnon became all of our problem," evidenced by the fact that 97 US congressional candidates publicly showed support for QAnon (Kaplan 2020a, 2020b). Lastly, 2020 was the year that

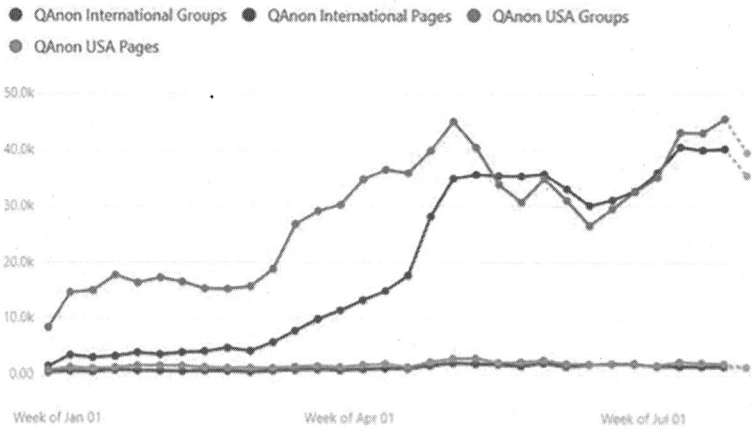

	50.0k
	40.0k
	30.0k
	20.0k
	10.0k
	0.00

Week of Jan 01   Week of Apr 01   Week of Jul 01

ALL POSTS > **COMBINED TOTAL POSTS** > 01/01/20 - 08/07/20

	TOTAL POSTS	AVG. WEEKLY POSTS
	1.65M	**12,882**

NAME	TOTAL	%	
QAnon Internatio...	640.7K	38.86%	
QAnon Internatio...	37.8K	2.29%	
QAnon USA Groups	915.4K	55.51%	
QAnon USA Pages	55.0K	3.34%	

FIGURE 1.2: QAnon group and page posts as of 8 August 2020

former President Donald Trump finally gave QAnon supporters what they always wanted: respect. Since the start of the pandemic, Trump recognized the QAnon community in a way its followers could have only fantasized about when the movement started over three years ago. Trump is perceived as a messianic figure among QAnon adherents. He plays a central role in QAnon's prophetic belief that he will lead its followers to victory over the Deep State and usher in a promised golden age of peace and prosperity. Therefore, when Trump acknowledged QAnon by repeatedly boosting or "quote tweeting" QAnon-related material, the movement's followers perceived this as Trump sending them coded messages in response to significant events. Not only did this reinforce belief for QAnon adherents, but reporters, even those who were not on the QAnon or extremism beat, created a Streisand effect, bringing QAnon further into the mainstream by reporting about how Trump was boosting QAnon during his presidency.

Conspiracy Theories and National Security in Canada

There have been several attacks over the last two years in Canada, seemingly spurred on by conspiratorial thinking (Amarasingam 2019). With the onset of the COVID-19 pandemic, conspiracies related to the virus became quite prevalent and started to push some individuals toward criminal activity (Argentino and Amarasingam 2020). On 2 July 2020, for instance, Corey Hurren drove his truck into the gates of Rideau Hall, where he believed Prime Minister Justin Trudeau would be staying, armed with several loaded firearms and multiple rounds of ammunition. Hurren penned a two-page letter before the incident in which he expressed despair at how his life was turned upside down by the virus and the lockdown and how Canada was "now a communist dictatorship." Event 201 is also briefly mentioned by Hurren, suggesting that he was consuming conspiratorial content. Event 201, a real pandemic tabletop event conducted in October 2019 and funded by the World Economic Forum and the Bill and Melinda Gates Foundation, is now one of many examples used by conspiracists to claim that COVID-19 was planned in advance.

Hurren's case highlights many of the second- and third-order effects of the pandemic that many who research political violence feared: an individual loses their business, financial consequences follow, and conspiracies come into the picture to provide clear explanations. Hurren recently noted in an interview with a psychiatrist that he believed he would be shot and killed as soon as he drove up to Rideau Hall, and he wanted his death "to be his message of discontent with the government's response to COVID-19 and gun control" (Humphreys 2021). According to reports, the consumption of COVID-19 conspiracy theories arguing that global elites planned the pandemic "indirectly aggravated" Hurren to attack because it meant that "all the misery it unleashed in his life didn't have to happen" (Humphreys 2021).

QAnon adherents in Canada are heavily invested in COVID-19-related conspiracy theories, such as the idea that 5G causes COVID-19, that the pandemic is a hoax used by the government to control the Canadian population, and that preventive measures are an example of government overreach. QAnon believers have also moved their narratives offline in the form of political action centred on the anti-mask, anti-lockdown, and anti-vaccine movements. Moreover, between July and August 2020 in Quebec, conspiracy theories about the pandemic played a role in on- and offline violent behaviour targeting journalists and elected officials (Monpetit 2020).

On 28 July 2020, police arrested a twenty-six-year-old man from Saint-Placide, Quebec, for allegedly making online threats against a journalist. His Facebook page had links to conspiracy videos about the pandemic and content from QAnon supporters. On 30 July 2020, police charged a twenty-seven-year-old man from Gatineau, Quebec, with intimidation, obstructing an officer, and three counts of uttering threats against Premier François Legault, Public Health Director Horacio Arruda, and Prime Minister Justin Trudeau. His Facebook page featured links to far-right content, videos by Radio-Québec, and various other conspiracy videos about the pandemic. This incident was related to one of Quebec's most prominent QAnon advocates and COVID-19 conspiracists, Alexis Cossette-Trudel. A forty-seven-year-old Montreal man with past ties to Quebec's Far Right, Cossette-Trudel is one of the leading figures of the anti-mask movement, broadcasting conspiratorial web journals rejecting the gravity of the pandemic (Remski 2021).

Radio-Québec is a collection of hour-long videos by Cossette-Trudel. Facebook removed Cossette-Trudel's personal page, which had about forty thousand followers at the time. The media channel gained a large following by translating into French QAnon's groundless claims about a secret cabal of child-sex traffickers that control world events. Since March 2020, Cossette-Trudel's videos have focused almost exclusively on COVID-19 and the pandemic. Like many QAnon followers, he believes the dangers of the disease are exaggerated as part of a plot to undermine Trump. He has become a leading figure in the movement to protest Quebec's public health rules, which include the wearing of masks in stores and on public transit. Cossette-Trudel has spoken at several anti-mask demonstrations alongside Stéphane Blais from the Fondation pour la défense des droits et libertés du peuple. He has demonstrated a capacity to mobilize QAnon believers and anti-maskers in Quebec, and his Radio-Québec videos played a role in exporting QAnon to France, Belgium, Spain, and Italy, where his radio show has also been translated into Spanish and Italian.

There are also a few other, comparatively less serious, incidents related to QAnon and COVID-19 conspiracies. On 4 August 2020, a man in his sixties from Sainte-Brigitte-de-Laval, Quebec, was arrested for allegedly making online threats against both Legault and Arruda. The arrest came shortly after a Facebook account that circulates QAnon conspiracies published Arruda's home address. On August 7, a forty-five-year-old man from Drummondville was charged with intimidation and two counts of uttering threats, reportedly against Arruda. Along with conspiracies about the pandemic, his Facebook page also featured racist and antisemitic content.

Conspiracy theorists also targeted critical infrastructure in the United Kingdom and Canada due to conspiracy theories about 5G causing COVID-19. Over Easter 2020, there were twenty attacks on cell towers in England, Wales, and Scotland (Kelion 2020). A month later, seven cell towers were set ablaze in the Greater Montreal area. Jessica Kallas, a twenty-five-year-old Laval resident, and Justin-Philippe Pauley, twenty-eight, of Ste-Adèle, have since gone on trial for these crimes (Thomas 2020). According to reports about the court proceedings, Pauley and Kallas believed that their lives depended on the destruction of 5G cell towers (Lacroix 2020; Nguyen 2021).

Though mobilization by QAnon adherents and conspiracy theorists in Canada is on a small scale, all of these efforts have occurred during the COVID-19 pandemic. The QAnon and conspiracy theory community in Canada is strong, with top influencers living in Canada and large and active communities online. The transnational relationship between QAnon in Canada and QAnon in the European Union and Australia also presents a transnational threat different from QAnon in the United States. While QAnon as a movement accelerated with the COVID-19 pandemic, the long-term consequences are still unknown.

Conclusion

Historically, the Canadian government has rarely viewed conspiracy theories and misinformation as national security concerns. But times are changing. As a May 2019 FBI bulletin noted, it is probable that "anti-government, identity based, and fringe political conspiracy theories very likely motivate some domestic extremists, wholly or in part, to commit criminal and sometimes violent activity" (FBI 2019). The same report went on to note that conspiracy theories "very likely encourage the targeting of specific people, places, and organizations, thereby increasing the likelihood of violence against these targets" (FBI 2019). As our discussion above makes clear, ideas that used to live and die in the dark corners of the Internet are now making their way into the mainstream, pushing people to commit violent acts and impacting their overall commitment to democratic society.

The 6 January 2021 Capitol insurrection, as well as multiple acts of violence over the past twelve months, demonstrate that the spread of disinformation and conspiracy theories are a threat to national security and public safety more broadly (Amarasingam and Argentino 2020). Policymakers should take a more proactive approach to foster Canadians' critical thinking and digital literacy and to help individuals cope with the second- and third-order impacts of the pandemic and lockdown. COVID-19 may, in hindsight, be a practice run for disasters to come—and the government should take an inventory of these hard-won lessons.

NOTES

1   There has been a fair amount of speculation about who "Q" is since the inception of the movement. There is no conclusive evidence as to who Q was, though there is ample evidence to suggest that the account was controlled by different individuals over the years. In an investigation for *NBC News*, Zadrozny and Collins (2018) found that the theory can be traced back to three people who sparked some of the first conversations about QAnon: 4chan /pol/ moderators, Pamphlet Anon (Coleman Rogers), BaruchtheScribe (Paul Furber), and minor YouTube celebrity Tracy Diaz. Some have inferred that the early Q account was controlled by these individuals; however, no one has yet to prove this conclusively. Presently, Q is believed to be either Jim or Ron Watkins, according to multiple media reports. In March 2021, "Q: Into the Storm," a six-part HBO docuseries by filmmaker Cullen Hoback, argued that Q is Ron Watkins,

the son of 8chan founder Jim Watkins. Though this is the most common narrative, there is so far no conclusive evidence that this is the case. What can be confirmed is that Jim and Ron Watkins facilitated the continued existence of Q up until the last post on 8 December 2020.

2   4Chan is an anonymous image board broken up into threads in which users can discuss and debate different topics. Moderation was minimal, and, as such, vile content—including child pornography—flourished on the site in its early days.

3   Before Q, several 4chan posters asserted they had special government access, including FBIAnon and HLIAnon in 2016, and CIAAnon and WHInsiderAnon in 2017. QAnon devotees, many of whom may be familiar with this "anon genre," are familiar with Q's apparent need for anonymity and presumably take it as a sign of credibility.

4   The data was collected using CrowdTangle, a social media analysis tool owned by Facebook. It provides an aggregate count of group membership. For example, if a user would join fifty of the QAnon groups or pages identified by the authors, this user would be counted fifty times. This provides a measurement of the mainstreaming of the QAnon movement on Facebook, rather than a real count of unique members.

5   Posts on Facebook were collected between 27 October 2017 and 8 August 2020.

REFERENCES

ADL (Anti-Defamation League). 2020. " 'The Great Reset' Conspiracy Flourishes Amid Continued Pandemic." ADL.org, 29 December, 2020. https://www.adl.org/blog/the-great-reset-conspiracy-flourishes-amid-continued-pandemic.

Allington, Daniel, Bobby Duffy, Simon Wessely, Nayana Dhavan, and James Rubin. 2020. "Health-Protective Behavior, Social Media Usage and Conspiracy Belief during the COVID-19 Public Health Emergency." *Psychological Medicine,* 9 June 2020. https://doi.org/10.1017/S003329172000224X.

Amarasingam, Amarnath. 2019. "The Impact of Conspiracy Theories and How to Counter Them: Reviewing the Literature on Conspiracy Theories and Radicalization to Violence." In *Jihadist Terror: New Threats, New Responses*, edited by Anthony Richards, Devorah Margolin, and Nicolo Scremin, 27–40. New York: Bloomsbury.

Amarasingam, Amarnath, and Marc-André Argentino. 2020. "The QAnon Conspiracy Theory: A Security Threat in the Making?" *CTC Sentinel* 13 (7). https://ctc.usma.edu/the-qanon-conspiracy-theory-a-security-threat-in-the-making/.

Argentino, Marc-André, and Amarnath Amarasingam. 2020. "The COVID Conspiracy Files." *Global Network on Extremism and Technology*, 8 April 2020. https://gnet-research.org/2020/04/08/the-covid-conspiracy-files/.

Barkun, Michael. 2013. *A Culture of Conspiracy: Apocalyptic Visions in Contemporary America*. 2nd ed. Berkeley: University of California Press.

Bennhold, Katrin. 2020. "Far-Right Germans Try to Storm Reichstag as Virus Protests Escalate." *New York Times*, 31 August, 2020. https://www.nytimes.com/2020/08/31/world/europe/reichstag-germany-neonazi-coronavirus.html.

Brown, Matthew. 2020. "A Bill Gates-Backed Pandemic Simulation in October Did Not Predict COVID-19." *USA Today*, 26 March, 2020. https://www.usatoday.com/story/news/factcheck/2020/03/26/fact-check-bill-gates-backed-pandemic-exercise-didnt-predict-covid-19/5081854002/.

FBI (Federal Bureau of Investigation). 2019. "Anti-government, Identity Based, and Fringe Political Conspiracy Theories Very Likely Motivate Some Domestic Extremists to Commit Criminal, Sometimes Violent Activity." *Just Security*, 30 May 2019. https://www.justsecurity.org/wp-content/uploads/2019/08/420379775-fbi-conspiracy-theories-domestic-extremism.pdf.

Felden, Esther, Jordan Wildon, Anne Hohn, and Lewis Sanders IV. 2021. "As Donald Trump Exits, QAnon Takes Hold in Germany." *Deutsche Welle*, 19 January 2021. https://www.dw.com/en/as-donald-trump-exits-qanon-takes-hold-in-germany/a-56277928.

Frenkel, Sheera, Ben Decker, and Davey Alba. 2020. "How the 'Plandemic' Movie and Its Falsehoods Spread Widely Online." *New York Times*, 20 May 2020. https://www.nytimes.com/2020/05/20/technology/plandemic-movie-youtube-facebook-coronavirus.html.

Glaser, April. 2019. "Where 8Channers Went after 8Chan." *Slate*, 11 November 2019. https://slate.com/technology/2019/11/8chan-8kun-white-supremacists-telegram-discord-facebook.html.

GNET (Global Network on Extremism and Technology). 2020. "What is QAnon?" *Global Network on Extremism and Technology*, 15 October 2020. https://gnet-research.org/2020/10/15/what-is-qanon/.

Hall, Ben, and Kevin Wisniewski. 2021. "Nashville Bomber's Bizarre Writings Reveal Belief in Aliens and Lizard People." *NewsChannel 5 Nashville*, 4 January 2021. https://www.newschannel5.com/news/newschannel-5-investigates/nashville-bombers-bizarre-writings-reveal-belief-in-aliens-and-lizard-people.

Humphreys, Adrian. 2021. "Corey Hurren on Rideau Hall Attack: 'I Figured as Soon as I Got on the Property, I Would Get Shot Down.' " *National Post*, 3 March 2021. https://nationalpost.com/news/canada/corey-hurren-on-rideau-hall-attack-i-figured-as-soon-as-i-got-on-the-property-i-would-get-shot-down.

Imhoff, Roland, and Pia Lamberty. 2020. "A Bioweapon or a Hoax? The Link between Distinct Conspiracy Beliefs about the Coronavirus Disease Outbreak and Pandemic Behavior." *Social Psychological and Personality Science* 11 (8): 1110–18.

Jensen, Michael, and Sheehan Kane. 2021. "QAnon Offenders in the United States." *START*, March 2021. https://start.umd.edu/publication/qanon-offenders-united-states.

Kaplan, Alex. 2020a. "Here Are the QAnon Supporters Running for Congress in 2020." *Media Matters*, 7 January 2020. https://www.mediamatters.org/qanon-conspiracy-theory/here-are-qanon-supporters-running-congress-2020.

———. 2020b. "In 2020, QAnon Became All of Our Problem." *Media Matters*, 31 December 2020. https://www.mediamatters.org/qanon-conspiracy-theory/2020-qanon-became-all-our-problem.

Kelion, Leo. 2020. "Coronavirus: 20 Suspected Phone Mast Attacks over Easter." *BBC News*, 14 April 2020. https://www.bbc.com/news/technology-52281315.

Lacroix, Antoine. 2020. "Convinced He Was Going to Die If He Didn't Set the Towers on Fire." *TVA Nouvelles*, 1 October 2020. https://www.tvanouvelles.ca/2020/10/01/convaincu-quil-allait-mourir-sil-ne-mettait-pas-le-feu-aux-tours.

Leman, P. J., and Marco Cinnirella. 2007. "A Major Event Has a Major Cause: Evidence for the Role of Heuristics in Reasoning about Conspiracy Theories." *Social Psychological Review* 9 (2): 18–28.

Melley, Timothy. 2000. *Empire of Conspiracy: The Culture of Paranoia in Postwar America*. Ithaca, NY: Cornell University Press.

Mezzofiore, Gianluca, and Donie O'Sullivan. 2019. "El Paso Mass Shooting Is at Least the Third Atrocity Linked to 8Chan This Year." *CNN*, 5 August 2019. https://www.cnn.com/2019/08/04/business/el-paso-shooting-8chan-biz/index.html.

Miller, Michael E. 2021. "Pizzagate's Violent Legacy." *Washington Post*, 16 February 2021. https://www.washingtonpost.com/dc-md-va/2021/02/16/pizzagate-qanon-capitol-attack/?arc404=true.

Monpetit, Jonathan. 2020. "Quebec Extremists Radicalized by COVID-19 Conspiracy Theories Could Turn to Violence, Experts Warn." *CBC News*, 17 September 2020. https://www.cbc.ca/news/canada/montreal/qanon-quebec-anti-mask-conspiracy-theory-violence-1.5726891.

Nguyen, Michael. 2021. "Guilty of Helping to Burn Cell Towers." *TVA Nouvelles*, 5 February 2021. https://www.tvanouvelles.ca/2021/02/05/coupable-davoir-aide-a-bruler-des-tours-cellulaires-1.

Oleksy, Tomasz, Anna Wnuk, Dominika Maison, and Agnieszka Lys. 2021. "Content Matters: Different Predictors and Social Consequences of General and Government-Related Conspiracy Theories on COVID-19." *Personality and Individual Differences* 168:1–7.

Remski, Matthew. 2021. "When QAnon Came to Canada." *Walrus*, 9 March 2021. https://thewalrus.ca/when-qanon-came-to-canada/.

Robertson, Adi. 2019. "8Chan Goes Dark after Hardware Provider Discontinues Service." *Verge*, 5 August 2019. https://www.theverge.com/2019/8/5/20754943/8chan-epik-offline-voxility-service-cutoff-hate-speech-ban.

Romer, Daniel, and Kathleen Hall Jamieson. 2020. "Conspiracy Theories as Barriers to Controlling the Spread of COVID-19 in the U.S." *Social Science and Medicine* 263:1–8.

Sommer, Will. 2020. "QAnoners' Magic Cure for Coronavirus: Just Drink Bleach." *Daily Beast*, 28 January 2020. https://www.thedailybeast.com/qanon-conspiracy-theorists-magic-cure-for-coronavirus-is-drinking-lethal-bleach.

Thomas, Katelyn. 2020. "Two Arrested after Two More Quebec Cell Towers Go Up in Flames." *CTV News*, 7 May 2020. https://montreal.ctvnews.ca/two-arrested-after-two-more-quebec-cell-towers-go-up-in-flames-1.4928666.

Van Prooijen, J. W., and K. M. Douglas. 2017. "Conspiracy Theories as Part of History: The Role of Societal Crisis Situations. *Memory Studies* 10:323–33.

Zadrozny, Brandy, and Ben Collins. 2018. "How Three Conspiracy Theorists Took Q and Sparked QAnon." *NBC News*, 14 April 2018. https://www.nbcnews.com/tech/tech-news/how-three-conspiracy-theorists-took-q-sparked-qanon-n900531.

Exploiting Chaos: How Malicious Non-state Actors Leverage COVID-19 to Their Advantage in Cyberspace

Casey E. Babb and Alex S. Wilner

Introduction

Since the beginning of 2020, while societies and economies around the world have struggled to cope with the realities of the COVID-19 pandemic, cyberspace has given governments, businesses, and general end-users the ability to work, play, and connect in new and innovative ways. With everything from workspaces and classrooms to family gatherings and exercise routines forced online, the Internet has enabled people across the globe to carry on and maintain a sense of normalcy during very abnormal times.

However, at the same time, while the world has been focused on the health, economic, political, and social ramifications of the pandemic, terrorist organizations, fringe groups, and extremist communities around the world have become emboldened, finding opportunity to exploit the situation, incite hate, (re)mobilize, and promote their ideologies online in novel ways. These groups—which we loosely classify as malicious non-state actors for the purposes of this chapter—have been primarily focused on exploiting and contributing to the diffusion of information during the pandemic for their own strategic gain. These actors are not primarily interested in for-profit criminal activities, but rather seek to weaponize the information environment toward other objectives. From synagogues and

Jewish organizations worldwide being "Zoom bombed" with antisemitic messages (Schiffer 2020), to the Islamic State and al-Qaeda suggesting online that martyrs are immune to the virus (Hunter 2020) or that the coronavirus is a divine punishment targeting non-believers (Hanna 2020), to white supremacist groups using platforms such as Telegram and Gab to spread propaganda (Perrigo 2020), COVID-19 has added a new dimension to malicious online activities. Indeed, the European Union's counterterrorism chief, the US Department of Homeland Security, the US National Counterterrorism Center, and the Federal Bureau of Investigation (FBI), among others, have all issued statements warning of the potential ways militant and extremist groups are leveraging the pandemic to their advantage (Baker 2020; Bertrand 2020; FBI 2020).

Surprisingly, aside from a handful of senior-level government speeches highlighting these trends, comparatively little has been said about these challenges in Canada, despite the government having become increasingly concerned with individuals and groups who espouse extremist views, spread propaganda, and promote violence online (CSIS 2019; Vigneault 2021; Public Safety Canada 2019). The current situation compels us to explore a central question: How are malicious non-state actors using cyber space to exploit the pandemic for their own strategic gain, and what might these trends mean for Canada's national security over the coming years? Informed primarily by international trends, the intent of this chapter is threefold. First, it will serve as a primer on how various types of dangerous non-state actors are manipulating the information environment and exploiting increased user connectivity for strategic gain. Specifically, we have homed in on three distinct yet overlapping online trends that have proven to be particularly detrimental to national security: delegitimation, recruitment, and incitement. Second, we provide a concise snapshot of what these trends may mean for Canada, and how some of these online activities have or could take shape domestically. Third, we hope our analysis will support the Government of Canada in the years to come as it assesses the national security implications and fallout from the pandemic and develops appropriate policy responses and mitigation strategies for addressing nefarious online activities.

Hostile Cyber Activities: Types and Trends

On 15 February 2020, Tedros Adhanom Ghebreyesus, Director General of the World Health Organization, noted that the world was not only fighting an epidemic—it was "fighting an infodemic" (Ghebreyesus 2020). Indeed, since the onset of COVID-19, the Internet and social media have facilitated the global circulation and proliferation of an unprecedented amount of problematic information. "Crisis informatics"—which is the interdisciplinary academic study of how people rely on technology to cope with and respond to uncertainties—suggests that to a degree, this is to be expected (Starbird 2020). When information is sparse or conflicting, it is natural that people will look to fill the information gap, ease their anxieties, get answers, and participate in a sort of "collective sensemaking" (Stephens et al. 2020). However, the extent to which we are witnessing disinformation, misinformation, and individuals intentionally capitalizing on the information void is unique, both in terms of volume and in the ways in which this online discourse has been injurious to national security. In part, this is a result of worldwide social distancing measures and a surge in user engagement with online technologies. This has led to a proliferation of online groups and communities dedicated to COVID-related conspiracy theories, anti-science discourse, and fighting government regulations during the pandemic. In some cases, the distinction between anti-lockdown measures and broader anti-government rhetoric has been blurred, with deadly consequences. The storming of the United States Capitol on 6 January 2021—seemingly instigated, abetted, and encouraged by former President Donald Trump—is a case in point: dis- and misinformation mixed with real and perceived individual and group grievances led to physical altercations, violence, and mayhem.[1]

That said, for the purposes of this chapter, we have identified a number of distinct yet complementary and overlapping types of information circulating online during the pandemic, which academics, health-care professionals, and policy-makers should monitor and study further as the pandemic drags on and, perhaps more importantly, once it ends. Doing so may enable the government to better understand the long-term residual effects of these activities while also providing online users and consumers with greater knowledge with which to identify and combat inaccurate and potentially dangerous information during future large-scale crises and disasters. In this context, what follows is a discussion of three different forms of pandemic-related (or pandemic-induced) extremist information and activity, categorized as delegitimation, recruitment, and incitement.

Delegitimation

Throughout the last year, governments and authorities around the world have faced extraordinary pressure. Not only have they had to deal with containing the virus, they have also had to defend their public health measures and the subsequent economic repercussions those measures may have created. In some instances, governments have failed to (expeditiously) recognize the seriousness of the virus, while others have struggled to cope with the fallout. Either way, authorities everywhere have faced unprecedented scrutiny. As a result, various types of malicious non-state actors have used social media and messaging apps to capitalize on the situation and further delegitimize governments. In some cases, they have provided goods and services where the state has failed, while in other instances they have provided support for people and communities affected by strict public health measures (Hegazi 2020; Heffes and Somer 2020). Strategically, this type of activity serves at least two primary purposes. First, it delegitimizes and undermines trust in governments and authorities in affected areas, sowing distrust, chaos, and division. Second, it legitimizes whichever group has stepped up to provide support while also reinforcing their extremist narratives and recruitment strategies (Binetti et al. 2020; Daymon 2020).

Illustrations of this kind of activity abound; consider these disparate examples. Al-Shabaab, al-Qaeda's branch in Somalia, used various platforms to blame the African Union Mission in Somalia and the "international crusaders" for bringing the virus to Africa (Joscelyn 2020). Likewise, Nigeria's Boko Haram has suggested through audio recordings disseminated online that "infidels" such as Muhammadu Buhari, the President of Nigeria, Idris Deby, the former President of Chad, and Muhammed Issoufu, the President of Niger, are responsible for the virus, which is God's punishment against non-believers and secular Muslims (Campbell 2020). In Afghanistan, the Taliban have taken a different approach, launching a public-health-awareness campaign, publicly signalling via Twitter their willingness to co-operate with international health organizations, and using other online platforms such as WhatsApp to share images of government health-care workers assisting patients (Kapur and Saxena 2020). The Islamic State of Iraq and Syria (ISIS or Daesh, in its Arabic acronym) has also tapped into social media and online publications to discredit governments, arguing that these governments have intentionally withheld information on the virus from citizens, while presenting themselves as a better alternative to imposed public health measures (Phelan et al. 2020). Similarly, in Mexico, international criminal groups and syndicates, such as the Gulf Cartel, have distributed aid boxes in territories they control or seek to control bearing labels with the names and logos of the different groups; these efforts are then promoted on social media (Binetti et al. 2020; Cordoba 2020). Similarly, videos showing Alejandrina Giselle Guzman Salazar, daughter of drug lord Joaquin "El Chapo" Guzman, providing aid packages to those in need were widely circulated on Facebook (Jorgic 2020).

Far-right groups in Italy, Germany, the Netherlands, Austria, Spain, Belgium, France, and elsewhere have undertaken similar strategies, using social media to publicize their alternative economic support efforts while espousing anti-government rhetoric, which in many cases is also being supported by far-right nationalist parties to which they have links (Youngs 2020). In the United States and Canada, far-right extremist groups like the Proud Boys, the Three Percenters, and the Oath Keepers, as well as other loosely organized or affiliated organizations, have used social media and other fringe platforms like Telegram and Gab to fuel a range of anti-government conspiracy theories. On the Telegram messenger app, experts have also identified "accelerationists"—those who seek to erode liberal democracy in order to develop white ethnostates—and "ecofascists"—who extol genocidal solutions to environmental problems. Both groups continually and openly discuss recruitment strategies, white supremacy, and anti-government ideologies (Wilson 2020). That said, conspiratorial messaging, hate speech, and extremist rhetoric is not exclusive to the far right. During the pandemic, far-left movements—who use the same social media, encrypted networks, and messaging apps to spread their messages—have also capitalized on increased Internet usage and pandemic-related hardships and anxieties to aggressively push populist, anti-government, and anti-elite narratives. Often, this messaging is antisemitic, conspiratorial in nature, and rooted in pre-existing beliefs that predate the pandemic. These include suggestions that Jews are part of a white majority establishment set on exploiting people of colour, or that Jews (and Israel) were involved in creating or spreading the virus and profiting from the vaccines (Schwartz 2020; Rowe 2020).

While the majority of damaging and disruptive online discourse related to the pandemic is conspiratorial in nature, its underlying anti-government messaging not only suggests that government responses to the pandemic are malevolent, but also that these fringe groups know the "real truth" about the pandemic. As Neil MacFarquhar (2020) has written, the pandemic has become a "battle cry" for US extremists: "various violent incidents have been linked to white supremacist or anti-government perpetrators enraged over aspects of the pandemic," including public health measures ranging from mask wearing and curfews to stay-at-home orders, state-wide lockdowns, and vaccine mandates and passports. Evidently, undermining trust and confidence in governments has been a key strategy of various groups who purport to be able to provide an alternative option.

Recruitment

Many of these same groups also use the pandemic as an opportunity to recruit new followers to their cause, movement, and organization, recruits who perceive these groups and their ideologies as "more capable or more honest than . . . governments" (Bloom 2020). Echoing this theme, the Soufan Center argued in April 2020 that "the fallout from the coronavirus pandemic is likely to provide a boost to extremists from across the ideological spectrum. COVID-19 is a rare event that offers a range of terrorist and extremist groups with an opening to bolster or promote their ideologies and narratives," expanding their base as a result (Soufan Center 2020).

For instance, the ISIS-affiliated Al-Qitaal Media Center shared a message in its online magazine suggesting that the virus is a divine punishment and that only true believers are immune (Binetti 2020). Likewise, ISIS has implied online that the virus is God's punishment for anyone who does not adhere to the group's interpretation of Islam, suggesting that individuals who join ISIS will develop a form of immunity (Qandil 2020). In Indonesia, Malaysia, and the Philippines, reports suggest there has been an uptick in ISIS propaganda and online recruitment efforts during the pandemic, with one expert explaining that "the group is actively re-cruiting and indoctrinating supporters through online platforms such as Facebook" (Lee et al. 2020). Al-Qaeda has also claimed the virus is an ex-pression of God's wrath, and a message to non-believers to turn (or return) to Islam (Qandil 2020).

Far-right extremists are likewise trying to capitalize on the pandemic for recruitment purposes. Groups including the Hundred-Handers and the Nordic Resistance Movement in Europe have been spreading con-spiracy theories, hate speech, and xenophobic propaganda to attract new supporters (Dodd 2020). In fact, authorities in the United Kingdom have suggested that right-wing extremist groups, even more so than religiously inspired terrorist organizations, "have been much more pro-active during the lockdown to try and reach young people" (Smith 2020). In July 2020, the United Nations Security Council's Counter-Terrorism Committee Executive Directorate, whose member states include the United States, the United Kingdom, Ireland, France, Norway, and Estonia, among others, wrote in a "Trends Alert" that "extreme right-wing terrorist groups and in-dividuals have sought to co-opt the pandemic, using conspiracy theories to attempt to radicalize, recruit and inspire plots and attacks" (CTED 2020). In Canada, researchers have also noticed a significant spike in engagement with far-right extremist material online, with weekly searches for "violent, far-right keywords" increasing by nearly 20 per cent following lockdowns across a number of major Canadian cities (Britneff 2020). Researchers at the UK-based Institute for Strategic Dialogue concur, finding nearly seven thousand right-wing extremist channels, pages, and individual accounts linked to Canadians across seven social media platforms, designed to mobilize, recruit new members, broadcast disinformation, and harass op-ponents, among other activities. Cumulatively, this content reached over eleven million users worldwide (Davey, Hart, and Guerin 2020).

In sum, the pandemic's toll since early 2020—reflected in such things as economic turmoil, job losses and unemployment, physical and social isolation, psychological, individual and communal hardship, political un-certainty and instability, and increased online activity and engagement—has created an ideal recruitment opportunity for many different types of malicious non-state actors. Taking advantage of our collective situation, various groups across the globe are broadcasting their message to an expanding online community, hoping to identify and attract potential followers, broaden their appeal, and recruit new members along the way.

Inciting Violence and Intimidation

Finally, in addition to online efforts to delegitimize governments and recruit new members, many of these same groups have also used cyberspace during the pandemic to incite violence and intimidate opponents. For example, ISIS has publicly urged supporters to carry out attacks on "over-burdened health care systems in various Western countries" (CEP 2020), while right-wing extremist groups in the United States and Europe have used social media to encourage biological attacks using the virus itself, with specific emphasis on the targeting of medical centres and minority communities (Avis 2020). Early reports also suggest that much of the violence that occurred during the January 2021 Capitol riots in Washington, DC, was openly and deliberately planned on far-right conspiratorial websites and forums such as Parler, Gab, TheDonald, and MeWe. Analysis conducted by Advanced Democracy found that over 80 per cent of the top posts on TheDonald the day of the riots featured calls for violence (Wamsley 2021). Likewise, the same researchers found that nearly fifteen hundred posts during the week leading up to the riots were from QAnon-related accounts. QAnon is a pre-pandemic, international, and largely far-right conspiracy theory that suggests that a cabal of Democratic-leaning, Satan-worshipping pedophiles are mobilized against President Trump (see Argentino and Amarasingam, this volume). Many of these posts had violent connotations and promoted acts of aggression. Similar videos shared via TikTok generated hundreds of thousands of views (Wamsley 2021). Anna Schecter has suggested that "right-wing extremists" were "using channels on the encrypted communication app Telegram to call for violence against government officials on January 20 [2021]," the day of President Biden's inauguration, "with some extremists sharing knowledge of how to make, conceal and use homemade guns and bombs" (Schecter 2021).

Research and reports suggest similar online discourse is also espoused in Canada, with a number of cases illustrating the dangerous, sometimes deadly linkages between violent language online and physical harm and attacks offline. For example, in Toronto in March 2020, Derek

Soberal, a founder of the Occupy Canada activist group, filmed himself on Facebook speaking about his political views before stabbing himself multiple times and setting himself on fire near a gas station. Evidence suggests his self-immolation was the result of his becoming engrossed by COVID-19 conspiracy theories (Bell 2020). In another episode, in July 2020, Corey Hurren, a reservist in the Canadian Armed Forces, breached the grounds of Rideau Hall with a loaded firearm; his intention was to arrest and/or harm Prime Minister Justin Trudeau. Hurren had apparently become fixated with QAnon conspiracy theories circulating online and had expressed an inability to cope with the government's lockdown measures (Brewster 2020; Tunney 2021). Hurren, who pled guilty to seven charges, was sentenced to six years in prison in March 2021 (Canadian Press 2021). In addition, in December 2020, a Toronto man who regularly posted antisemitic and racist conspiracy theories related to the pandemic was arrested in what the Toronto Police Service described as their "biggest single-day drug and firearm seizure" (Collen 2021). In his apartment, the suspect, Daniel Dubajic, had nearly fifteen thousand rounds of ammunition, sixty-five firearms, and millions of dollars' worth of narcotics. Also, in January 2020, a Quebec man linked to social media accounts that referred to COVID-19 as a "scamdemic" urged Canadians to "start shooting the police," and he spoke about storming Parliament to "clean up house." He was arrested with eighteen firearms in his possession (Bell 2021). There have also been other incidents in Western Canada with an apparent nexus to online conspiratorial and fabricated information: a Calgary man used Facebook to threaten purposefully spreading the virus to Indigenous communities (Fletcher 2020), and a Vancouver man attacked a ninety-two-year-old Asian Canadian (suffering from dementia) while shouting anti-Asian slurs related to COVID-19 (Young 2020).

These and other incidents point to the potential for online hate speech and conspiracy theories to motivate extremists to conduct or participate in acts of violence, a trend that long predates the pandemic. The difference today, however, is the way the pandemic itself, along with societal responses to COVID-19, have seemingly amplified these concerns. Indeed, the sheer volume of extremist content available online and the number of platforms used to spread it grow daily.

Potential Impacts on Canada's National Security

Over the last number of years, the Government of Canada has undertaken a range of efforts designed to address and curb dangerous online activities. These include supporting initiatives like Tech Against Terrorism—a consortium designed to create a digital repository to notify companies when new terrorist content is detected—as well as the Youth Summit on Countering Violent Extremism Online. More recently, and specifically in response to COVID-19, the federal government also allocated $3.5 million in funding to "amplify the current efforts of eight organizations supporting citizens to think critically about the health information they find online," with an emphasis on identifying mis- and disinformation as well as racist and misleading information related to the pandemic (Canadian Heritage 2020). We also know that Canada's security and intelligence community is aware of and continuously tracking these emerging and evolving threats and the risks they pose. An April 2020 briefing note, for instance, prepared by the Canadian Security Intelligence Service (CSIS) and obtained by Global News noted that "ideologically motivated violent extremists and others are using the COVID-19 pandemic as an opportunity to promote disinformation and alternative narratives regarding both the cause of the pandemic and potential societal outcomes" (Bell 2020). Furthermore, CSIS Director David Vigneault said in February 2021 that "COVID-19 has created a situation ripe for exploitation by threat actors seeking to cause harm or advance their own interests. With many Canadians working from home, threat actors are presented with even more opportunities to conduct malicious online activities" (Vigneault 2021). Likewise, the Canadian Centre for Cyber Security recently wrote that "cyber threat actors are taking advantage of people's heightened levels of concern and legitimate fear around COVID-19, trying to spread misinformation and scam people out of their money or private data" (CCCS 2020).

And yet the actual national security implications of these online activities during the pandemic are still not well understood. This is no fault of Canada's security and intelligence community; rather, it simply reflects the fact that the threat environment (including the pandemic itself) is evolving and unfolding in such a way that it risks outpacing the government's ability to assess, act, and preempt emerging concerns. What is more, COVID-related conspiracy theories and the online (and physical) activities that stem from them are far from having run their course. These and other as yet unforeseen security challenges will continue to emerge in the coming months and years. Also, while Canada's security and intelligence community does have a vital role to play in investigating and supporting broader government and law enforcement efforts to counter security threats stemming from the various challenges explored in this chapter, these same agencies cannot (and should not) counter the expression of public or individual opinion, however disagreeable these opinions may be to the vast majority of Canadians. As other contributors to this volume have noted, Canada's response to the social, political, and ideological challenges spurred by COVID-19 requires activities that go well beyond those reserved for the security and intelligence community, including providing counter-narratives, supporting marginalized communities, establishing deradicalization programs, and otherwise facilitating activities that address the underlining factors that contribute to individual discontent and the growth of extremist mindsets, including systemic racism, economic inequality, and polarizing electoral processes.

In terms of Canada's national security—and in light of the government's prioritization of curbing the spread of the disease and launching large-scale inoculation campaigns across the country—terrorist organizations, right- and left-wing extremist movements, and criminal syndicates will not only continue pursuing the online strategies identified in this chapter, but will also likely continue developing, improving, and adjusting their activities in order to capitalize on the post-COVID environment. In other words, as the pandemic evolves, so will the online narratives peddled by various threat actors. Regardless of the situation, malicious groups will find ways to pivot, adapt, and exploit people's insecurities, the unknown, human suffering, and other epistemic, existential, and social factors that contribute to individuals' susceptibility to destructive and inaccurate information. That said, Canada's security and intelligence community should pay particular attention to online activities engineered to undermine the Government of Canada, to recruit new members to terrorist organizations and extremist groups, and to incite or motivate acts of violence. These online trends are proliferating worldwide, and Canada is no exception.

The Internet will remain a favoured domain for dangerous non-state actors and individuals to carry out their work and achieve their objectives. From our perspective, these are still early days in terms of dealing with the pandemic and addressing its collateral damage, including its effect on malicious online activity. There have already been numerous arrests across Canada of individuals who have made online threats against journalists, politicians, and public health officials (Montpetit 2020), and the environment remains rife for increased extremist activity and real-world physical attacks. Furthermore, exogenous factors, including a fragile Canadian (and global) economy, continued lockdown measures across the country, a seemingly permanent shift to the amount of time we all spend online, and a new and untested US administration, point to a range of potential trigger points that could lead to heightened levels of malicious online activity. In our view, the key themes covered in this chapter—delegitimation, recruitment, and incitement—represent the three most common and deleterious trends related to extremist use of the Internet to have been exacerbated by the COVID-19 crisis. Ongoing and more comprehensive research and analysis will be required to fully understand and respond to the ways in which the Internet has been weaponized during the pandemic.

Funding

The larger research project from which this chapter stems was awarded two grants (August 2021), one from the Canadian Network for Research on Terrorism, Security and Society Small Research Projects program (# 50658-10054), and one from the Department of National Defence's Mobilizing Insights in Defence and Security (MINDS) program's COVID-19 Challenge award.

NOTE

1   Generally speaking, the term "disinformation" is used to describe intentional—
often strategically designed—attempts to shape the information environment and
to mislead and confuse individuals. Similar to, but distinct from, disinformation
is "misinformation," which tends to describe untrue or misleading information
disseminated without the intent to deliberately mislead people or maliciously shape the
information environment.

REFERENCES

Avis, William. 2020. "*The COVID-19 Pandemic and Response on Violent Extremist
Recruitment and Radicalization.*" K4D Helpdesk Report 808. Brighton, UK:
Institute of Development Studies. https://reliefweb.int/sites/reliefweb.int/files/
resources/808_COVID19%20_and_Violent_Extremism.pdf.

Baker, Luke. 2020. "Militants, Fringe Groups Exploiting COVID-19, Warns EU Anti-
terrorism Chief." *Reuters*, 30 April 2020. https://www.reuters.com/article/
us-health-coronavirus-eu-security/militants-fringe-groups-exploiting-covid-19-
warns-eu-anti-terrorism-chief-idUSKBN22C2HG.

Bell, Stuart. 2020. "Neo-Nazis, Extremists Capitalizing on COVID-19, Declassified
CSIS Documents Say." *Global News*, 7 December 2020. https://globalnews.ca/
news/7501783/neo-nazis-extremists-capitalizing-coronaviruscovid-19-csis/.

———. 2021. "RCMP Arrest Quebec Man Linked to Social Media Accounts that Call
COVID-19 a Scam, Talk of Taking Arms to Parliament." *Global News*, 26 January
2021. https://globalnews.ca/news/7600018/rcmp-quebec-man-linked-to-social-
media-account/.

Bertrand, Natasha. 2020. "DHS Warns of Increase in Violent Extremism Amid
Coronavirus Lockdowns." *Politico*, 23 April 2020. https://www.politico.com/
news/2020/04/23/dhs-increase-in-coronavirus-inspired-violence-205221.

Binetti, Soraya, Fabrizio De Rose, Mariana Diaz Garcia, and Francesco Marelli. 2020.
*Stop the Virus of Disinformation: The Risk of Malicious Use of Social Media during
COVID-19 and the Technology Options to Fight It.* Torino, IT: United Nations
Interregional Crime and Justice Research Institute. http://www.unicri.it/sites/
default/files/2020-11/SM%20misuse.pdf.

Bloom, Mia. 2020. "How Terrorist Groups Will Try to Capitalize on the Coronavirus
Crisis." *Just Security*, 3 April 2020. https://www.justsecurity.org/69508/how-
terrorist-groups-will-try-to-capitalize-on-the-coronavirus-crisis/.

Brewster, Murray. 2020. "Military Reviewing What Its Intelligence Branch Knew about
Rideau Hall Attacker." *CBC News*, 21 August 2020. https://www.cbc.ca/news/
politics/rideau-hall-attackranger-1.5694022.

Britneff, Beatrice. 2020. "Searches for Extremist Content Spiked after Canada's Coronavirus Lockdown: Report." *Global News*, 12 June 2020. https://globalnews.ca/news/7054410/coronavirus-extremist-content-searches-canada/.

Campbell, John. 2020. "Boko Haram's Shekau Labels Anti-COVID-19 Measures an Attack on Islam in Nigeria." Council on Foreign Relations, 17 April 2020. https://www.cfr.org/blog/boko-harams-shekau-labels-anti-covid-19-measures-attack-islam-nigeria.

Canadian Heritage. 2020. "Online Disinformation." Government of Canada, last modified 17 August 2020. https://www.canada.ca/en/canadian-heritage/services/online-disinformation.html#special.

Canadian Press. 2021. "Military Reservist Who Rammed Rideau Hall Gate with Truck Sentenced to Six Years." *CTV News*, 10 March 2021. https://www.ctvnews.ca/canada/military-reservist-who-rammed-rideau-hall-gate-with-truck-sentenced-to-six-years-1.5340945.

CEP (Counter Extremism Project). 2020. "Online Extremists Exploit Coronavirus Pandemic to Incite Violence and Encourage Terrorism." *Counter Extremism Project*, 3 April 2020. https://www.counterextremism.com/blog/online-extremists-exploit-coronavirus-pandemic-incite-violence-encourage-terrorism.

Collen, Dan. 2020. "Antisemitic Anti-masker Arrested with 65 Illegal Guns, $18 Million in Street Drugs." Canadian Anti-Hate Network, 18 January 2021. https://www.antihate.ca/antisemitic_anti_masker_arrested_65_illegal_guns_18_million_street_drugs.

Cordoba, Jose de. 2020. "Mexico's Cartels Distribute Coronavirus Aid to Win Popular Support." *Wall Street Journal*, 14 May 2020. https://www.wsj.com/articles/mexicos-cartels-distribute-coronavirus-aid-to-win-popular-support-11589480979.

CSIS (Canadian Security Intelligence Service). 2019. "CSIS 2018 Public Report." Government of Canada, last modified 21 June 2019. https://www.canada.ca/en/security-intelligence-service/news/2019/06/release-of-csis-2018-public-report.html.

———. 2020. "Staying Cyber-Healthy during COVID-19 Isolation." Government of Canada, last modified 9 April 2020. https://cyber.gc.ca/en/news/staying-cyber-healthy-during-covid-19-isolation.

CTED (Counter-Terrorism Committee Executive Directorate). 2020. "Member States Concerned by the Growing and Increasingly Transnational Threat of Extreme Right-Wing Terrorism." CTED, April 2020. https://www.un.org/securitycouncil/ctc/sites/www.un.org.securitycouncil.ctc/files/files/documents/2021/Jan/cted_trends_alert_extreme_right-wing_terrorism.pdf.

Davey, Jacob, Mackenzie Hart, and Cecile Guerin. 2020. *An Online Environmental Scan of Right-Wing Extremism in Canada: Interim Report*. London: Institute for Strategic Dialogue. https://www.isdglobal.org/wp-content/uploads/2020/06/An-Online-Environmental-Scan-of-Right-wing-Extremism-in-Canada-ISD.pdf.

Daymon, Chelsea. 2020. "The Coronavirus and Islamic State Supporters Online." Global Network on Extremism and Technology, 13 March 2020. https://gnet-research. org/2020/03/13/the-coronavirus-and-islamic-state-supporters-online/.

Dodd, Vikram. 2020. "Fears of Rise in UK Terrorist Recruits as Anti-radicalisation Referrals Collapse." *Guardian*, 22 April 2020. https://www.theguardian. com/uknews/2020/apr/22/fears-of-rise-in-uk-terrorism-recruits-after-anti-radicalisation-referrals-collapse-coronavirus.

FBI (Federal Bureau of Investigation). 2020. "Cyber Actors Take Advantage of COVID-19 Pandemic to Exploit Increased Use of Virtual Environments." FBI Alert Number I-040120-PSA, 1 April 2020. https://www.ic3.gov/media/2020/200401.aspx.

Fletcher, Robson. 2020. "Calgary Police Charge Man over Threat to Spread COVID-19 to Indigenous People." *CBC News*, 1 April 2020. https://www.cbc.ca/news/canada/calgary/calgary-police-covid-19-threats-charge-investigation-1.5517980.

Ghebreyesus, Tedros Adhanom. 2020. "Remarks by the Director-General of the World Health Organization at the Munich Security Conference." World Health Organization, 15 February 2020. https://www.who.int/director-general/speeches/detail/munich-security-conference.

Hanna, Andrew. 2020. "What Islamists Are Doing and Saying on COVID-19 Crisis." Wilson Center, 14 May 2020. https://www.wilsoncenter.org/article/what-islamists-are-doing-and-saying-covid-19-crisis.

Heffes, Ezequiel, and Jonathan Somer. 2020. "Inviting Non-state Armed Groups to the Table." Briefing Note, Center for the Study of Armed Groups, December 2020. https://cdn.odi.org/media/documents/odi-ec-nonstatearmedgrioups-briefingnote-dec20-proof01a.pdf.

Hegazi, Farah. 2020. "Climate Change, Disease and the Legitimacy of Armed Non-state Actors." Stockholm International Peace Research Institute, 1 July 2020. https://www.sipri.org/commentary/essay/2020/climate-change-disease-and-legitimacy-armed-non-state-actors.

Hunter, Brad. 2020. "Terror Will Make You Immune to COVID-19: ISIS to Fanatics." *Toronto Sun*, 24 March 2020. https://torontosun.com/news/world/isis-tells-fanatics-that-terror-will-make-them-immune-to-covid-19.

Jorgic, Drazen. 2020. "El Chapo's Daughter, Mexican Cartels Hand Out Coronavirus Aid." *Reuters*, 16 April 2020. https://www.reuters.com/article/us-health-coronavirus-mexico-cartels/el-chapos-daughter-mexican-cartels-hand-out-coronavirus-aid-idUSKBN21Y3J7.

Joscelyn, Thomas. 2020. "How Jihadists Are Reacting to the Coronavirus Pandemic." Foundation for Defense of Democracies, 6 April 2020. https://www.fdd.org/analysis/2020/04/06/how-jihadists-are-reacting-to-the-coronavirus-pandemic/.

Kapur, Roshni, and Chayanika Saxena. 2020. "The Taliban Makes the Most of Covid-19 Crisis in Afghanistan." Lowy Institute, 27 April 2020. https://www.lowyinstitute.org/the-interpreter/taliban-makes-most-covid-19-crisis-afghanistan.

Lee, Noah, Tia Asmara, Ronna Nirmala, Mark Navales, and Shailaja Neelakantan. 2020. "Southeast Asian Analysts: IS Steps Up Recruitment in Indonesia, Malaysia, Philippines." *BenarNews*, 23 September 2020. https://www.benarnews.org/english/news/indonesian/SEA_ISIS-Threat-09232020163502.html.

MacFarquhar, Neil. 2020. "The Coronavirus Becomes a Battle Cry for U.S. Extremists." *New York Times*, 3 May 2020. https://www.nytimes.com/2020/05/03/us/coronavirus-extremists.html.

Montpetit, Jonathan. 2020. "Quebec Extremists Radicalized by COVID-19 Conspiracy Theories Could Turn to Violence, Experts Warn." *CBC News*, 17 September 2020. https://www.cbc.ca/news/canada/montreal/qanon-quebec-anti-mask-conspiracy-theory-violence-1.5726891.

Perrigo, Billy. 2020. "White Supremacist Groups Are Recruiting with Help From Coronavirus—and a Popular Messaging App." *Time*, 8 April 2020. https://time.com/5817665/coronavirus-conspiracy-theories-white-supremacist-groups/.

Phelan, Alexandra, Nuri Veronika, Helen Stenger, and Irine Gayatri. 2020. "COVID-19 and Violent Extremist Groups: Adapting to an Evolving Crisis." Monash University, 28 April 2020. https://lens.monash.edu/@politics-society/2020/04/28/1380103/covid-19-and-non-state-armed-groups-adapting-to-an-evolving-crisis.

Public Safety Canada. 2019. *2018 Public Report on the Terrorist Threat to Canada: Building a Safe and Resilient Canada*. Ottawa: Department of Public Safety and Emergency Preparedness, April 2019. https://www.publicsafety.gc.ca/cnt/rsrcs/pblctns/pblc-rprt-trrrsm-thrt-cnd-2018/pblc-rprt-trrrsm-thrt-cnd-2018-en.pdf.

Qandil, Mohamed Mokhtar. 2020. "Terrorism and Coronavirus: Hyperbole, Idealism, and Ignorance." Washington Institute, 28 April 2020. https://www.washingtoninstitute.org/policy-analysis/terrorism-and-coronavirus-hyperbole-idealism-and-ignorance.

Rowe, Daniel J. 2020. "Anti-Semitic and Anti-Asian Incidents on the Rise during COVID-19: Reports." *CTV News*, 4 May 2020. https://montreal.ctvnews.ca/anti-semitic-and-anti-asian-incidents-on-the-rise-during-covid-19-reports-1.4924306.

Schecter, Anna. 2021. "Extremists Move to Secret Online Channels to Plan for Inauguration Day in D.C." *NBC News*, 12 January 2021. https://www.nbcnews.com/politics/congress/extremists-move-secret-line-channels-plan-inauguration-day-d-c-n1253876.

Schiffer, Zoe. 2020. "White Supremacists Are Targeting Jewish Groups on Zoom." *Verge*, 15 April 2020. https://www.theverge.com/2020/4/15/21221421/white-supremacist-zoombombers-target-jewish-community-zoom.

Schwartz, Felicia. 2020. "Coronavirus Sparks Rise in Anti-Semitic Sentiment, Researchers Say." *Wall Street Journal*, 20 April 2020. https://www.wsj.com/articles/coronavirus-sparks-rise-in-anti-semitic-incidents-researchers-say-11587405792.

Smith, Victoria. 2020. "Far-Right 'Exploiting Coronavirus Crisis to Try to Recruit People.'" *Leading Britain's Conversation*, 5 October 2020. https://www.lbc.co.uk/news/far-right-exploiting-coronavirus-crisis-to-try-to-recruit-people/.

Soufan Center. 2020. "IntelBrief: The Coronavirus Will Increase Extremism Across the Ideological Spectrum." Soufan Center, 13 April 2020. https://thesoufancenter.org/intelbrief-the-coronavirus-will-increase-extremism-across-the-ideological-spectrum/.

Starbird, Kate. 2020. "How a Crisis Researcher Makes Sense of Covid-19 Misinformation." *OneZero*, 9 March 2020. https://onezero.medium.com/reflecting-on-the-covid-19-infodemic-as-a-crisis-informatics-researcher-ce0656fa4d0a.

Stephens, Keri K., Jody L. S. Jahn, Stephanie Fox, Piyawan Charoensap-Kelly, Rahul Mitra, Jeannette Sutton, Eric D. Waters, Bo Xie, and Rebecca J. Meisenbach. 2020. "Collective Sensemaking Around COVID-19: Experiences, Concerns, and Agendas for our Rapidly Changing Organizational Lives." *Management Communication Quarterly* 34, no. 3 (June 2020): 426–57. https://doi.org/10.1177%2F0893318920934890.

Tunney, Catharine. 2021. "Corey Hurren Pleads Guilty to 8 Charges Tied to Rideau Hall Incident." *CBC News*, 5 February 2021. https://www.cbc.ca/news/politics/corey-hurren-rideau-hall-plea-1.5902362.

Vigneault, David. 2021. "Remarks by Director David Vigneault to the Centre for International Governance Innovation." CSIS, 9 February 2021. https://www.canada.ca/en/security-intelligence-service/news/2021/02/remarks-by-director-david-vigneault-to-the-centre-for-international-governance-innovation.html.

Wamsley, Laurel. 2021. "On Far-Right Websites, Plans to Storm Capitol Were Made in Plain Sight." *NPR*, 7 January 2021. https://www.npr.org/sections/insurrection-at-the-capitol/2021/01/07/954671745/on-far-right-websites-plans-to-storm-capitol-were-made-in-plain-sight.

Wilson, Jason. 2020. "Disinformation and Blame: How America's Far Right Is Capitalizing on Coronavirus." *Guardian*, 19 March 2020. https://www.theguardian.com/world/2020/mar/19/america-far-right-coronavirusoutbreak-trump-alex-jones.

Young, Ian. 2020. "Coronavirus: Suspected Racist Attacker of 92-Year-Old Asian Man Identified by Vancouver Police after 'Overwhelming' Public Response." *South China Morning Post*, 24 April 2020. https://www.scmp.com/news/world/united-states-canada/article/3081328/coronavirus-vancouver-police-identify-suspect.

Youngs, Richard. 2020. "Coronavirus and Europe's New Political Fissures." *Carnegie Europe*, June 2020. https://carnegieendowment.org/files/Youngs_Coronavirus_and_fissures.pdf.

Supply Chains during the COVID-19 Pandemic

*Stephanie Carvin, Edie Brenning, Djomeni Raphael Desire,
Walid Elgazzar, Habab Elkhalifa, Annie Huang, Ilia Nizenko,
Richard Oum, Rafael Pozuelo-Perron, Raman Singh, Erin van
Weerdhuizen, Randall Whiteside, and Anisha Yogalingam*[1]

Introduction

Recent years have brought attention to the relationship between the economy and national security. Canada experienced an era of protectionism in the 1960s and '70s before turning to free trade from the 1980s to the 2000s. However, concerns over the security implications of state-owned enterprises, foreign investment, and joint ventures have increasingly raised questions over the appropriate role of Western governments in protecting elements of the economy with strategic or national importance. In this context, the security of supply chains was already under discussion before the COVID-19 pandemic reached Western countries in early 2020 (CSE 2018; Farrell and Newman 2019; Williams, Lueg, and LeMay 2008).

The sudden shortage of supplies experienced in Canada during the pandemic, especially in the first few months, reveals shortfalls in how the country manages its supply chains, both domestically and internationally. Experiencing a surge in demand for certain products but cut off from many of its sources abroad, Canada struggled to maintain food security and protect vital workers in the health sector. Importantly, these issues represent more than an inconvenience—they show that supply chains are vital lifelines upon which Canada's well-being and national security increasingly depend.

This chapter explores these issues using two case studies to understand the pandemic's impact on supply chains—one where adaptation challenges proved difficult (manufacturing personal protective equipment) and another where the sector proved to be more resilient (food and agriculture). The chapter then evaluates Canada's policy response to supply chain disruptions and makes preliminary policy recommendations. It concludes by noting that in an era of adversarial geo-economic strategies, both the government and private sector must do more to prepare supply chains for additional long-term global disruptions.

Supply Chain

Generally, "supply chain" refers to the production flow of a good or service, starting from raw components and ending with the delivery of the final product to the consumer. To maintain this production flow, a company will create a network to move the components from suppliers to the end-user (adapted from IBM n.d.). The advantage of the supply chain is that when done efficiently, it helps both manufacturers and retailers reduce excess inventory, which in turn reduces costs associated with production, shipping, insuring, and storing goods and services (Perkins and Wailgum 2017).

As the nature of the supply chain is globalized, critical infrastructure systems are vulnerable to shocks from global events such as natural disasters, accidents, national instability, and, of course, epidemics and pandemics. A disruption in a single country may seriously impact a well-integrated, "just-in-time" approach to supply chain management worldwide. Governments recognize the security risks to such global vulnerabilities and incentivize local companies to make their supply chains more resilient.

We define resiliency in this chapter as a capacity for successful adaptation in the face of disturbance, stress, or adversity. One way to achieve this is to create redundancies (being able to obtain key components from more than one source or stockpiling others). Some democracies, such as Denmark, Japan, and the United States, encourage their domestic firms to return to producing goods in their home countries (Nuttall 2020). In other cases, states are placing limits on certain activities, such as preventing takeovers by foreign companies in areas deemed strategic. For example, in April 2020, the Government of Canada announced that it was now subjecting "certain foreign investments into Canada to enhanced scrutiny under the *Investment Canada Act*" (ISED 2020). These investments include those into Canadian business related to "public health or involved in the supply of critical goods and services to Canadians or to the Government" due to national security risks. However, efforts to prevent further takeovers of Canadian companies should be understood as an emergency stopgap measure to prevent further weakening of sectors in disarray, rather than a genuine effort to promote resilience in Canadian supply chains and manufacturing.

Regardless of the steps taken before COVID-19, analysis of the supply chains in the following case studies reveals that Canadian supply chains struggled to adapt once the pandemic hit for five key reasons: a lack of manufacturing and production capacity; short time frames; non-diversified sources for materials and consumers; vulnerabilities to global disruptions; and a lack of redundant systems in place. Nevertheless, the pandemic did not impact all sectors evenly Indeed, while Canada struggled to obtain personal protective equipment, the agriculture and food sector managed to adapt faster and more comprehensively. The following two sections outline the experience of both sectors and provide a brief comparison to help inform future policy decisions.

PPE: Health and Manufacturing Sectors

The outbreak of the COVID-19 pandemic in Canada caused an extraordinary surge in demand for personal protective equipment (PPE) that domestic and international suppliers could not match. As a result, many Canadian health-care providers, front-line workers, and vulnerable populations lacked sufficient quantities of PPE as the pandemic took hold. This section explores why.

Manufacturing Capacity

At the onset of the pandemic, no factories produced N95 masks in Canada (Tumilty 2020). As a result, foreign restrictions and competition impacted Canada's access to the supply of this needed resource (Silcoff 2020).

Moreover, pre-COVID-19, Canada's international supply chain for PPE relied primarily on a few manufacturers based in the United States and China and did not have the mechanisms in place to counter disruptions (Dyer 2020; Linton and Vakil 2020). Canada could only procure 0.2 per cent of its required PPE from domestic sources, placing tremendous pressure on the country's health-care sector (Blatchford 2020).

To address the domestic shortage, both federal and provincial governments turned to emergency measures, investing in domestic companies to retool and develop Canadian PPE manufacturing capacity to meet demand. For example, investments from the federal and Ontario governments helped open a 3M production line to manufacture new N95 masks in Brockville, Ontario, which reportedly will supply 100 million masks annually over five years (Canadian Press 2020). Similarly, Medicom, a Quebec-based mask producer that previously had no manufacturing capacity in Canada, received funds from the federal government to produce 20 million masks in Canada (Blatchford 2020). As a result of the above investments, in September 2020, Navdeep Bains—the Minister of Innovation, Science and Economic Development—remarked that Canada is now buying almost half its PPE from domestic manufacturers (Blatchford 2020).

Another challenge was certification: just because a factory switches from producing cars or shirts does not mean it can produce medical-grade PPE. Certifications ensure that PPE meets specific standards and ensures that it does not allow blood and other liquids through the fabric. As such, certifications are not easily given, particularly in non-certified plants (Oved 2020). However, on 18 March 2020, the government announced that it was expediting authorizations at no cost to manufacturers (PHAC 2020). However, while these efforts brought more PPE manufacturers online, access to materials needed to make PPE remained a problem.

Lack of Diversity for Supply and Source Material

Pre-COVID-19, Canada's international supply chains for PPE prioritized cost over potential supply disruptions. This choice resulted in a concentration of suppliers that could not meet the country's needs after the onset of the pandemic. Canada's heavy reliance on single-sourcing methods in a small number of factories, primarily based out of China and the United States, was arranged to save costs. The disruptions experienced in

China-based supply chains in the early weeks of the pandemic demonstrate the downside of prioritizing cost over reducing risk. Procurement and supply fulfillment took on a "Wild West" nature, whereby confirmed orders of PPE were redirected to higher bidders (Flanagan 2020).

Importantly, however, it was not just masks that were affected, but also the materials used to produce them. With the shortage of N95 masks, states turned to importing polypropylene meltblown non-woven fabric (commonly referred to as meltblown fabric), a polypropylene resin product. Indeed, the shortage of this product was arguably the biggest constraint in the procurement process for masks.

Canada was forced to outsource meltblown fabric for two reasons. First, Canada's production capacity of polypropylene is not high; this was not necessarily due to a lack of local resources, but rather to a market-driven cost-cutting decision resulting in an increasingly asymmetrical trade in polypropylene. Second, the production of meltblown fabric is an exacting and complicated process. A single machine needed for the manufacturing process takes five to six months to produce and another month to assemble (Feng and Cheng 2020; Oved 2020). Considering these constraints, most companies choose to import polypropylene and polypropylene-related products from foreign countries. Unfortunately, the Chinese government banned the exports of meltblown fabric in early February (Subramanian 2020). Thus, countries like Canada were left without masks or the materials to make them. This supply shortage suggests that a close trading relationship may serve short-term economic interests, but it hinders the manufacturing sector's ability to be self-reliant in an emergency.

China was not alone: at least sixty-seven other countries placed restrictions on the export of PPE and materials needed for PPE production in the first weeks of the pandemic (Reynolds 2020). This included the European Union, which followed Taiwan's lead and banned all exports of PPE in March 2020, impacting hospitals in Toronto and southwestern Ontario that relied on one 3M plant in the United Kingdom for masks (which, despite Brexit, was still subject to EU rules at the time). This move raised concerns that by the end of March 2020, some areas of Canada would be down to two weeks' worth of PPE (Oved 2020).

Canada narrowly avoided another major disruption when the Trump administration reversed a halt order placed on the export of

3M-manufactured PPE to Canada and Latin America under the *Defense Production Act* (BBC 2020). While 3M appears to have argued against the order, media reports indicate that the Canadian government resorted to threatening US supply chains by cutting off Canadian exports in the event the country is cut off from American PPE (MacCharles 2021). Had these steps not worked, Canada would have had very few mechanisms left to meet the demand for PPE.

Short Time Frame

Canada's dependence on international suppliers operating with short lead times on order fulfillment meant that when countries enacted policies to halt exports and stockpile supplies, Canada could not respond to supply disruptions. Somewhat ironically, several disruptions were caused by attempts to ensure quality. For example, complaints from some Western countries about the poor quality of PPE from China resulted in the Chinese government clamping down on exports, requiring manufacturers to obtain certification through a national registry and documentation proving it meets the importing country's standards (Reynolds 2020).

Finally, even when internationally based PPE and manufacturing supplies were available, transportation to bring these goods into Canada was also disrupted. In the early days of the pandemic, the cost of air cargo rates doubled and, in some cases, tripled. This increase was due to plummeting travel demand, and the fact that passenger planes often carry freight as well as passenger luggage (Reynolds 2020). High prices continued throughout 2020 due to both an increase in e-commerce and, in the later part of the year, shipments of vaccines throughout the world (Nebehay 2020).

Lack of Redundancy

Finally, it is worth noting that once international options were no longer available, Canada did not have alternative options or redundancies in place that could have helped to manage the transition from importing to manufacturing its own PPE. On paper, the most important alternative is the Canadian National Emergency Strategic Stockpile (NESS), a government-managed PPE stockpile dispersed across numerous warehouses and depots in Canada (Dyer 2020; Laing and Westervelt 2020; Leo 2020). Importantly, NESS is not considered part of the regular PPE supply chain; rather, it is part of an emergency stockpile intended to temporarily provide critical sectors and key customers with PPE in case of a disruption at the manufacturing or distribution levels. While the NESS was activated in early 2020 to counter the supply shortage and demand surge caused by the COVID-19 pandemic, it was immediately apparent that it could not fully meet the PPE demands of the health-care sector and vulnerable populations.

There are numerous reasons why this failure took place. First, NESS was clearly unprepared to cope with an event like COVID-19. The stockpile, created in 1952 in a Cold War context, was designed for natural disasters and violent extremist attacks, not backing up provincial health-care systems in the event of a major and sustained pandemic (Tumilty 2020). Moreover, the NESS has a regular staff of only eighteen people, and an annual budget of about $3 million, although both the Harper and Trudeau governments reportedly routinely failed to spend that much (Dyer 2020).

Finally, in recent years, the Public Health Agency of Canada (PHAC) decided to shrink the NESS from eleven warehouses in nine cities to eight warehouses in six cities. As part of this this downsizing, PHAC threw away 2 million N95 masks and 440,000 medical gloves that had been expired for years (Leo 2020; Tumilty 2020). This suggests that officials had not only stored expired equipment for sustained periods—they also lacked any plan to cycle supplies out of the stockpile prior to expiration (Leo 2020). This was likely complicated by the lack of a comprehensive inventory management system capable of monitoring incoming and outgoing supplies, meaning that exact stock levels and needs were at times unknown (Laing and Westervelt 2020; Leo 2020).

Agriculture and Food Sector

The COVID-19 pandemic exposed both the fragility and resiliency of Canada's food supply chain. The pandemic changed consumer purchasing behaviours, which in turn created challenges in agriculture production, food processing, and distribution. In addition, Canadian producers and businesses had to adapt to the Government of Canada's protective measures, which caused significant disruptions in the accessibility and affordability of food products. In this way, both domestic and international factors contributed to disruptions in the food supply chain, although the majority of the disruptions were domestic in nature.

Manufacturing/Production

When provincial governments imposed mandatory closures on businesses, the demand for some products quickly diminished (Israelson 2020). For example, what would usually be a steady demand for potatoes suddenly dropped as restaurants no longer regularly served french fries (Israelson 2020). Instead, as consumers were largely at home, there was increased demand for comfort foods such as peanut butter (Israelson 2020). Additionally, with growing concerns about outbreaks in meat packaging and processing plants, some consumers began to purchase meat directly from local farmers (Tucker 2020). To manage the shift in demand, the Canadian Food Inspection Agency made a number of temporary changes to the regulations surrounding the labelling and packaging of food, making it easier for items originally destined for restaurants, hotels, and other entertainment venues to be sold at retail (Hobbs 2020). In addition, some farmers quickly adjusted to what consumers wanted: fresh local produce and meat rather than their usual products, which they may have lost confidence in due to the pandemic (Hobbs 2020; Tucker 2020).

Some international factors contributed to a change in supply as well. For instance, border restrictions between the United States and Canada directly affected the availability of temporary foreign workers during the 2020 growing season. The restrictions put in place by both countries at the onset of the pandemic created confusion among these workers about whether they were permitted into the country (MacGregor 2020). The noticeable decrease in human labour affected Canadian harvesting. The government ultimately permitted temporary foreign workers entry into Canada and put in place measures to expedite the screening process (Statistics Canada 2020). Those measures included waiving some recruitment requirements, prioritizing key positions, and increasing the employment duration from one to two years for workers in the low-wage stream as part of a three-year pilot (Statistics Canada 2020). These proved to be a successful remedy to labour shortages among Canadian farms (Sheldon 2020).

Lack of Diversity

There is a lack of diversity in Canada's food chain in at least two respects. First, Canada is heavily dependent on both exports and imports from the United States. In 2016, that country accounted for 50 per cent of all Canadian agriculture and agri-food exports, as well as approximately 60 per cent of the value of Canadian food imports (Agriculture and Agri-Food Canada 2020; Hobbs 2020). The United States is a net importer of Canadian beef and cattle, while Canada imports seasonal food, such as fresh produce, from the United States and Mexico. For this reason, border closures posed a serious risk to the food supply chain, particularly in the first weeks of the pandemic. By the end of March 2020, the Canadian Food Inspection Agency (CFIA) activated its business continuity plan, prioritizing activities related to food safety to facilitate trade across the closed border. These activities include food safety investigations and recalls, animal disease investigations, inspection services, export certification, import inspection services, emergency management, and laboratory diagnostics in support of the above (CFIA 2020; Hobbs 2020).

The second issue is the small number of large food manufacturers within Canada. A concentration of production left few alternatives when there were outbreaks of COVID-19 in these production facilities, which made it challenging to meet the demand for perishable items and frozen foods (Aday and Aday 2020; Holland 2020). Holland (2020) specifically points to the concentration of meat processing plants as an example of this issue. She notes that two plants in Alberta are responsible for over 70 per cent of Canada's beef processing capacity. Writing in June 2020, she observed that

> Cargill's High River facility closed on 20 April for two weeks, reopening with reduced production levels, and the JBS plant in Brooks has cut its production by half. Potential shortages are anticipated to be only short-term for consumers but this decrease in beef supply has already led major buyers, like McDonald's Canada, to begin importing beef to meet their needs. (4–5)

Short Time Frame

Concentration in the agriculture and food sectors within Canada is a concern not only for food trade and production, but also for distribution. As Hobbs (2020) notes, the food retailing sector in Canada "is dominated by large, concentrated supermarket chains with significant buying power and an emphasis on cost efficiencies." Those chains rely on "just-in-time" approaches to delivery, which have increased efficiencies but resulted in short-term problems during the pandemic. For example, transport logistics were also disrupted by the pandemic, as companies could not deliver certain food items on time or in large quantities, hampering companies' ability to ensure food accessibility for their consumers. Given the geography of Canada and its dispersed population, food supply chains tend to be long and heavily dependent on well-functioning, long-distance road and rail transportation networks (Hobbs 2020). For the most part, however, Hobbs assesses that these supply chains were able to adjust rapidly "to the demand signals from consumer markets with increased product flows," and as such, the short-run problems of shortages eased.

Domestic disruptions in production also lead to disruptions in the international market. Typically, trucks travelling to the United States are full of Canadian-manufactured goods, such as automotive and meat products (Reuters 2020). However, Canada's largest beef, cattle, and automotive plants temporarily closed to prevent COVID-19 outbreaks, and, as a result, drivers drove empty trucks to the United States to import fresh produce (Castaldo 2020; Hill 2020; Neustaeter 2020).

Lack of Redundancy

Ultimately, the agriculture and food sector was able to adapt to the challenges posed by the pandemic faster than the manufacturing sector. Unfortunately, this does not mean that Canada is protected from future disruption or pandemics. Nor does it mean that Canada's agriculture and food sector has the necessary redundancy built into its systems to withstand other disruptions. When dealing with perishable foods over short time frames, there are vulnerabilities in this heavily concentrated sector that may yet manifest in future emergencies or crises.

Although food resiliency is not truly redundancy, it is worth noting that Canadians who are food insecure cannot be resilient. Unfortunately, food banks were severely affected by the pandemic due to an increase in demand and the above-noted challenges with food distribution and supply. In response, the Canadian government released a $100-million emergency fund to support food banks, transport food to distribution centres, and provide basic necessities to food-insecure households (Agriculture and Agri-Food Canada 2021). While this is an effective strategy to sustain food bank operations, not all communities have the capacity to take full advantage of these funds (Leblanc-Laurendeau 2020). Specifically, some people have expressed concern that many communities are not part of "strong local and regional food systems," nor do they have the logistical support required to supply food among their citizens (FEHNCY 2020).

Analysis and Sector-Specific Recommendations

Although major disruptions impacted both the manufacturing and the food and agriculture sectors during the COVID-19 pandemic, they did not impact them evenly. The agriculture and food sector was affected, but not to the same extent as the manufacturing sector. What explains this difference? Some reasons are readily apparent. For example, while each supply chain was disrupted, we also saw a sudden surge in the demand for PPE. Additionally, farmers and grocery chains familiar with the environment and with Canadian consumers had the knowledge and capacity to adapt to the new market within weeks. PPE suppliers and manufacturers, however, found themselves in a geopolitical competition; products were sold and sent to unknown highest bidders at a time when global transportation logistics were in disarray.

There are no doubt other explanations, such as the level of government involvement in each sector. The federal government regularly intervenes in and regulates supply chains within the agriculture and food sector, and it is familiar with its operations. This familiarity likely assisted the government in making changes to rules and regulations, such as those surrounding foreign workers and product packaging. In contrast, the evidence presented in this chapter suggests that, before the pandemic, the government was unfamiliar with the manufacturing sector as it relates to PPE, despite the SARS pandemic that hit Canada seventeen years earlier. In this sense, it could neither make quick changes nor understand the impact of certain decisions (such as those related to quality management) concerning access to PPE and related materials. If there is a success in the PPE story, it is that Canadian officials were able to lean on their international counterparts to ensure some level of supply—but we can hardly attribute this to government knowledge of, or familiarity with, the manufacturing sector.

All of this suggests that the government needs a better understanding of the manufacturing landscape in industries where disruptions—no matter how remote the possibility—could seriously impact the health and well-being of Canadians and the Canadian economy. It should work with industries to develop an awareness of the production capacity of companies that can produce critical products within our borders and their limitations (Dai, Bai, and Anderson 2020). It should also work with stakeholders to map risk in the form of dependencies and interdependencies. Businesses should be encouraged by government authorities and regulators to look beyond local and domestic factors toward their entire supply chains (Sodhi and Tang 2009) and cross-sector relationships like transportation (Golan, Jernegan, and Linkov 2020). Finally, Canada would benefit from developing international standards for PPE and other medical equipment (Ciuriak 2020). Such standards would not only assist in the rapid procurement of goods and materials in an emergency, but they could also help improve the production of PPE and medical devices worldwide.

Despite its relative success, the federal and provincial governments should take steps to enhance the security of the agriculture and food sector as well. Governments should work with industry to improve storage options that could keep a supply of food items that do not expire quickly and are likely to be in demand during a crisis (Aday and Aday 2020). They should also diversify Canada's export market (Farm Credit Canada 2019; Knutt 2020). In addition, Canada should maintain pressure on its trading partners to ensure they uphold trade agreements and that borders remain open, even in a crisis (Holland 2020). Finally, governments must better understand which areas are experiencing food insecurity generally and are consequently most likely to be hardest hit by another major disruption. The attempt to build such knowledge should start with an improvement in the way Canada collects data on food insecurity. Currently, provinces and territories are not required to collect statistics on food insecurity, leading to inconsistent data upon which to make decisions (Pollard and Booth 2019; PROOF Food Insecurity Policy Research n.d.).

The Wider Context and Policy Recommendations

While the previous section provided some recommendations for each sector, this section outlines key lessons and issues that the federal government should consider to secure Canada's supply chains in a post-pandemic but still uncertain future.

Recognizing the Limits of Co-operation

As noted in the introduction to this chapter, even before COVID-19, Western countries have been rethinking supply chains and encouraging their domestic companies to move manufacturing back home from overseas. There has also been discussion about Western countries working together to create an alliance of democracies that can provide an alternative to countries like China when it comes to securing supply chains, particularly in relation to emerging technology (The Economist 2020; Reuters 2020). In this sense, Canada may be able to seize opportunities to work with its allies on securing and diversifying its supply chains in key areas.

Unfortunately, Canada's experience during the COVID-19 pandemic suggests that its ability to depend on its allies in the crunch is decidedly mixed. In the agriculture and food sector, Canada engaged in co-operation with its partners in terms of bringing in temporary foreign workers. Additionally, in the early weeks of the pandemic, Canada signed an agreement with twenty-two other countries, representing 63 per cent of global exports and 55 per cent of global imports of agriculture and agri-food products, to ensure that international co-operation and trade continued (Global Affairs Canada 2020; World Trade Organization 2020). Although there were problems, there appears to be a certain level of willingness to work through food and agriculture issues at the international level.

The same cannot be said for PPE. This chapter makes clear that Canada's closest allies—the United States and the European Union—were willing to turn their backs on Canada and restrict PPE exports. There is no evidence that Canada would not have done the same were its position reversed. However, the restrictions imposed do raise questions about the strengths of Canada's international treaties and agreements. Indeed, it would not serve Canada's interests to see a surge of nationalist or isolationist economic policies in the post-COVID-19 world. However, Canada's experience suggests that when it comes to supply chains, policy-makers need to rethink some of the assumptions about trade and global co-operation the country has relied on for the last four decades. For example, appreciating that international agreements may not hold up in a global crisis should inspire more long-term thinking about emergency preparedness, stopgap measures, and redundancy in security and supply chain strategies.

Planning for More Long-Term Global Disruptions

Although government departments and agencies have business continuity plans, it is clear that they never anticipated worldwide disruptions lasting for two years. Nor did these plans consider supply chains. These assumptions are not entirely unreasonable—few (if any) countries appear to have had adequate policies in place for a pandemic like COVID-19. For now, it is more important to consider whether governments and private industry need to be more creative in their business continuity and emergency planning. Predictions that pandemics may become more common in the future (BBC 2021; Tollefson 2020) suggest that both governments and businesses should be considering plans for long-term disruptions. Indeed, beyond pandemics, given the anticipated changes in weather patterns due to climate change, an increase in geopolitical rivalries, and vulnerabilities coming from dependencies and interdependencies in our increasingly online and interconnected societies, Canada and its supply chains will face greater levels of uncertainty in the future. All of this speaks to a need for both the public and private sectors to take a much more coordinated and ambitious approach to conducting "all-hazard" risk assessments that can estimate the level and likelihood of events that may cause disruptions in the future as a result of natural hazards, accidents, and deliberate malicious acts.

Appreciating the Potential and Limits of Technology

Part of the effort to create more resilient and agile supply chains will involve investments in technology. Advances in artificial intelligence and robotics mean that the factories of the future will feature higher levels of automation, resulting in the need for less employees working in close contact. These changes should result in a more hygienic production of goods, as is needed during a pandemic.

In the future, artificial intelligence and machine learning will also help companies adjust their supply chains, improving their overall agility and ability to respond to disruption (Momani 2020). For example, companies may be able to sense and understand changes in market demand earlier. It is also likely that the pandemic will bring about changes in the way Canadians order and receive online goods. The food supply chain may change with the creation of highly autonomous food warehouses that deliver groceries and other goods directly to customers. Additionally, some studies estimate that automation could increase productivity by 25 per cent by automating tasks like loading/unloading, placing, and packaging goods (Iqbal, Khan, and Khalid 2017). Finally, more automation would have helped to manage Canada's outdated and woefully inadequate NESS—and, if implemented, could help prepare the NESS for future emergencies and crises. Indeed, the application of technology to the NESS may help better align it with Canada's emergency-management framework.

At the same time, planners in government and business need to appreciate the limits of technology. Had such developments been in place in early 2020, it is unlikely that Canada's situation would have been considerably better. Canada experienced challenges due to closed borders and limits on supplies—something automation and artificial intelligence may help to predict but not necessarily remedy in a hurry. Further, while technology may improve the agility of Canadian businesses, it likely cannot fix a situation in which sixty-eight countries impose export restrictions on needed goods at the same time.

Economic National Security Strategy

As noted at the beginning of this chapter, the Canadian government has sought to extricate itself from business for decades, believing that the market should resolve key supply, demand, manufacturing, and production questions. However, in the last decade, thanks to concerns arising from foreign investment and from acquisitions by foreign state-owned enterprises, there is growing awareness of how economic decisions affect Canada's national security interests (CSIS 2021). Any such discussion of Canada's national security posture or emergency planning post-pandemic must consider supply chain management. The best way to accomplish this is to develop an economic national security strategy, one that identifies those elements of the economy that are most relevant to national security and establishes what level of state involvement in the economy government and businesses will accept.

Conclusion

Generally, the literature on supply chains emphasizes the need for companies to fully map and diversify their supply chains and create redundancy to manage economic and financial risks. This risk management approach should consider these issues in terms of both economic and national security and emergency management. Ideally, a resilient system should be able to maintain essential functions despite the double shocks of a pandemic and the severe disruption to supply chains in the short term, and to adapt and transform in the long term (Kruk et al. 2015). Policymakers need to create a platform for inter-sectoral dialogue, encourage the transparent sharing of information about manufacturing capabilities and bottlenecks, and stress test the system to identify vulnerabilities, foster innovation, and provide incentives for investment. These moves are necessary to build and support resilient supply chains that will help secure Canada's vital supplies in an increasingly unpredictable world.

NOTE

1   This chapter is based on research conducted during the fall 2020 term by students in the Critical Infrastructure Protection: Issues and Strategies class in the Infrastructure Protection and International Security Program at Carleton University. It was compiled and edited by Stephanie Carvin with the assistance of Jessica Davis.

REFERENCES

Aday, Serpil, and Mehmet Seckin Aday. 2020. "Impact of COVID-19 on the Food Supply Chain." *Food Quality and Safety* 4 (4): 167–80. https://doi.org/10.1093/fqsafe/fyaa024.

Agriculture and Agri-Food Canada. 2017. "An Overview of the Canadian Agriculture and Agri-Food System 2017." Government of Canada, last modified 25 February 2020. https://www.agr.gc.ca/eng/canadas-agriculture-sectors/an-overview-of-the-canadian-agriculture-and-agri-food-system-2017/?id=1510326669269.

———. 2021. "Emergency Food Security Fund." Government of Canada, last modified 4 February 2021. https://www.agr.gc.ca/eng/agricultural-programsand-services/emergency-food-security-fund/?id=1585855025072.

BBC. 2020. "Coronavirus: U.S. 'Wants 3M to End Mask Exports to Canada and Latin America.'" *BBC News*, 3 April 2020. https://www.bbc.com/news/world-us-canada-52161032.

———. 2021. "Stopping the Next One: What Could the Next Pandemic Be?" *BBC News*, 11 January 2021. https://www.bbc.com/future/article/20210111-what-could-the-next-pandemic-be.

Blatchford, Andy. 2020. "Bains: Domestic Industry Now Supplying Half of Canada's PPE Needs." *Politico*, 9 November 2020. https://www.politico.com/news/2020/09/30/navdeep-bains-canada-ppe-424029.

Canadian Press. 2020. "Trudeau, Ford Unveil Deal to Produce N95 Masks at Brockville, Ont., 3M plant." *CTV News*, 21 August 2020. https://www.ctvnews.ca/politics/trudeau-ford-unveil-deal-to-produce-n95-masks-at-brockville-ont-3m-plant-1.5073486.

Castaldo, Joe. 2020. "Big Four Car Companies Closing All North American Factories Due to Coronavirus." *Globe and Mail*, 18 March 2020. https://www.theglobeandmail.com/business/article-ford-general-motors-closing-all-north-american-factories-due-to/.

CFIA (Canadian Food Inspection Agency). 2020. "The CFIA Is Prioritizing Critical Activities during COVID-19 Pandemic." Government of Canada, last modified 9 June 2020. https://www.inspection.gc.ca/covid-19/cfia-information-for-industry/critical-activities-during-covid-19-pandemic/eng/1587076768319/1587076768647.

Ciuriak, Dan. 2020. "The Policy Response to the Coronavirus Pandemic: Recommendations for Canada." *Centre for International Governance Innovation*, 3 April 2020. https://www.cigionline.org/articles/policy-response-coronavirus-pandemic-recommendations-canada.

CSE (Canadian Centre for Cyber Security). 2018. *National Cyber Threat Assessment.* Ottawa: Canadian Centre for Cyber Security. https://cyber.gc.ca/sites/default/files/publications/national-cyber-threat-assessment-2018-e_1.pdf.

CSIS (Canadian Security Intelligence Service). 2021. "Remarks by Director David Vigneault to the Centre for International Governance Innovation." Government of Canada, last modified 9 February 2021. https://www.canada.ca/en/security-intelligence-service/news/2021/02/remarks-by-director-david-vigneault-to-the-centre-for-international-governance-innovation.html.

Dai, Tinglong, Ge Bai, and Gerard F. Anderson. 2020. "PPE Supply Chain Needs Data Transparency and Stress Testing." *Journal of General Internal Medicine* 35 (9): 2748–9. https://doi.org/10.1007/s11606-020-05987-9.

Dyer, Evan. 2020. "The Great PPE Panic: How the Pandemic Caught Canada with Its Stockpiles Down." *CBC News*, 11 July 2020. https://www.cbc.ca/news/politics/ppe-pandemic-covid-coronavirus-masks-1.5645120.

The Economist. 2020. "Democracies Must Team Up to Take on China In the Technosphere." 19 November 2020. https://www.economist.com/briefing/2020/11/19/democracies-must-team-up-to-take-on-china-in-the-technosphere.

Farm Credit Canada. 2019. *Diversifying Canada's Agriculture Exports: Opportunities and Challenges in Wheat, Canola, Soy and Pulses.* Regina: Farm Credit Canada, 2019. https://www.fcc-fac.ca/fcc/resources/trade-rankings-report-2019-e.pdf.

Farrell, Henry, and Abraham L. Newman. 2019. "Weaponized Interdependence: How Global Economic Networks Shape Coercion." *International Security* 44 (1): 42–79. https://doi.org/10.1162/ISEC_a_00351.

FEHNCY (Food, Environment, Health and Nutrition of First Nations Children and Youth). 2020. "Commentary/Open Letter: Immediate Action Is Needed to Support Food Security and Housing in First Nations, Inuit and Métis Communities." *Le Devoir*, 7 April 2020. https://www.ledevoir.com/documents/pdf/2020-04-09_lettre-autochtones-covid-19.pdf.

Feng, Emily, and Amy Cheng. 2020. "COVID-19 Has Caused a Shortage of Face Masks. But They're Surprisingly Hard to Make." *NPR*, 16 March 2020. https://www.npr.org/sections/goatsandsoda/2020/03/16/814929294/covid-19-has-caused-a-shortage-of-face-masks-but-theyre-surprisingly-hard-to-mak.

Flanagan, Ryan. 2020. "With Some Provinces Reopening, Where Does Canada's PPE Supply Chain Stand?" *CTV News*, 3 May 2020. https://www.ctvnews.ca/health/coronavirus/with-some-provinces-reopening-where-does-canada-s-ppe-supply-chain-stand-1.4922887.

Global Affairs Canada. 2020. "Statement on Joint WTO Efforts to Ensure Open and Predictable Trade for Food and Agricultural Products Amid COVID-19." Government of Canada, last modified 22 April 2020. https://www.canada.ca/en/global-affairs/news/2020/04/statement-on-joint-wto-efforts-to-ensure-open-and-predictable-trade-for-food-and-agricultural-products-amid-covid-19.html.

Golan, Maureen S., Laura H. Jernegan, and Igor Linkov. 2020. "Trends and Applications of Resilience Analytics in Supply Chain Modeling: Systematic Literature Review in the Context of the COVID-19 Pandemic." *Environment Systems and Decisions* 40:222–43. https://doi.org/10.1007/s10669-020-09777-w.

Hill, Brian. 2020. " 'I'm Not willing to Go': Canadian Truckers Worry about Entering U.S. Due to Coronavirus." *Global News*, 20 June 2020. https://globalnews.ca/news/7194604/im-not-willing-to-go-canadian-truckers-worry-about-entering-u-s-due-to-coronavirus/.

Hobbs, Jill E. 2020. "Food Supply Chains during the COVID-19 Pandemic." *Canadian Journal of Agricultural Economics* 68 (2): 171–6. https://doi.org/10.1111/cjag.12237.

Holland, Kerri L. 2020. "Canada's Food Security during the COVID-19 Pandemic." *SPP Research Paper* 13, no. 13 (June 2020). http://dx.doi.org/10.11575/sppp.v13i0.70350.

IBM. n.d. "What Is Supply Chain Management? Accessed 22 February 2021. https://www.ibm.com/topics/supply-chain-management.

Iqbal, Jamshed, Zeashan H. Khan, and Azfar Khalid. 2017. "Prospects of Robotics in Food Industry." *Food Science and Technology (Campinas)* 37 (2): 159–65. https://doi.org/10.1590/1678-457X.14616.

ISED (Innovation, Science and Economic Development Canada). 2020. "Policy Statement on Foreign Investment Review and COVID-19." Government of Canada, last modified 19 April 2020. https://www.ic.gc.ca/eic/site/ica-lic.nsf/eng/lk81224.html.

Israelson, David. 2020. "Canada's Agri-Food Sector Adapts to Pandemic Challenges to Keep Exporting Goods." *Globe and Mail*, 10 August 2020. https://www.theglobeandmail.com/featured-reports/article-canadas-agri-food-sector-adapts-to-pandemic-challenges-to-keep/.

Knutt, Cory. 2020. "Opportunities and Challenges to Diversify Canada's Food Exports: FCC Report." *SwiftCurrent Online*, 18 November 2020. https://www.swiftcurrentonline.com/ag-news/opportunities-and-challenges-to-diversify-canada-s-food-exports-fcc-report.

Kruk, Margaret E., Michael Myers, S. Tornorlah Varpilah, and Bernice T. Dahn. 2015. "What Is a Resilient Health System? Lessons from Ebola." *Lancet* 385 (9980): 1910–12. https://doi.org/10.1016/S0140-6736(15)60755-3.

Laing, Scott, and Ellen Westervelt. 2020. "Canada's National Emergency Stockpile System: Time for a New Long-Term Strategy." *CMAJ* 192 (28): E810–11. https://doi.org/10.1503/cmaj.200946.

Leblanc-Laurendeau, Olivier. 2020. "COVID-19, Food Insecurity and Related Issues. *Hill Notes*, 17 April 2020. https://hillnotes.ca/2020/04/17/covid-19-food-insecurity-and-related-issues/.

Leo, Geoff. 2020. "Health Minister Reviewing Management of Canada's Emergency Stockpile." *CBC News*, April 15 2020. www.cbc.ca/news/canada/saskatchewan/heath-minister-emergency-stockpile-1.5530081.

Linton, Thomas, and Bindiya Vakil. 2020. "Coronavirus Is Proving We Need More Resilient Supply Chains." *Harvard Business Review*, 5 March 2020. https://hbr.org/2020/03/coronavirus-is-proving-that-we-need-more-resilient-supply-chains.

MacCharles, Tonda. 2021. "Documents Reveal the Trudeau Government Warned Donald Trump Not to Cut Off Canada's Supply of Critical COVID-19 Masks—

or Else." *Toronto Star*, 10 March 2021. https://www.thestar.com/politics/
federal/2021/03/10/documents-reveal-the-trudeau-government-warned-
donald-trump-not-to-cut-off-canadas-supply-of-critical-covid-19-masks-
or-else.html?utm_source=Facebook&utm_medium=SocialMedia&utm_
campaign=Federalpolitics&utm_content=trudeau-warned-trump.

MacGregor, Bill. 2020. "FAQS: Covid and Temporary Foreign Workers (TFWS) in
Canada." *Gowling WLG*, 1 September, 2020. https://gowlingwlg.com/en/insights-
resources/articles/2020/covid-and-temporary-foreign-workers-in-canada/.

Momani, Bessma. 2020. "Building Resiliency in Supply Chains Post-COVID-19." *Centre
for International Governance Innovation*, 24 August 2020. https://www.cigionline.
org/articles/building-resiliency-supply-chains-post-covid-19.

Nebehay, Stephanie. 2020. "Air Freight Prices 'Outrageous' as COVID-19 Shots Rolled Out,
Says WHO Expert." *Reuters*, 8 December 2020. https://www.reuters.com/article/
health-coronavirus-who-vaccines/air-freight-prices-outrageous-as-covid-19-shots-
rolled-out-says-who-expert-idUKL8N2IO4QX?edition-redirect=uk.

Neustaeter, Brooklyn. 2020. "These Are the Meat Plants in Canada Affected by the
Coronavirus Outbreak." *CTV News*, 29 April 2020. https://www.ctvnews.ca/health/
coronavirus/these-are-the-meat-plants-in-canada-affectedby-thecoronavirus-
outbreak-1.4916957.

Nuttall, Jeremy. 2020. "Can Canada Move Its Manufacturing Back from China? It's
Complicated." *Toronto Star*, 30 April 2020. https://www.thestar.com/news/
canada/2020/04/30/can-canada-move-its-manufacturing-back-from-china-its-
complicated.html.

Oved, Marco Chown. 2020. "Converting Canada's Industry to Produce Medical Supplies
Won't Be Easy." *Toronto Star*, 26 March 2020. https://www.thestar.com/news/
canada/2020/03/26/converting-canadas-industry-to-produce-medical-supplies-
wont-be-easy.html.

Perkins Bart, and Thomas Wailgum. 2017. "What Is Supply Chain Management (SCM)?
Mastering Logistics End to End." *CIO*, 27 August 2017. https://www.cio.com/
article/2439493/what-is-supply-chain-management-scm-mastering-logistics-end-
to-end.html.

PHAC (Public Health Agency of Canada). 2020. "Notice: Expedited Review of Health
Product Submissions and Applications to Address COVID-19." Government of
Canada, 18 March 2020. https://www.canada.ca/en/health-canada/services/drugs-
health-products/drug-products/announcements/notice-expediated-review-health-
products-covid-19.html.

Pollard, Christina M., and Sue Booth. 2019. "Food Insecurity and Hunger in Rich
countries—It Is Time for Action against Inequality." *International Journal of
Environmental Research and Public Health* 16 (10): 1804. https://doi.org/10.3390/
ijerph16101804.

PROOF Food Insecurity Policy Research. n.d. "Monitoring Food Insecurity in
Canada." PROOF, accessed 17 June 2021.https://proof.utoronto.ca/wp-content/
uploads/2016/06/monitoring-factsheet.pdf.

Reuters. 2020. "U.K. Seeks Alliance to Avoid Reliance on Chinese Tech: The Times." *Reuters*, 28 May 2020. https://www.reuters.com/article/us-britain-tech-coalition-idUSKBN2343JW.

Reynolds, Christopher. 2020. "Canada Looks to Secure PPE, but 68 Countries Have Restricted Exports." *Global News*, 2 April 2020. https://globalnews.ca/news/6769162/canada-medical-supplies-coronavirus/.

Sheldon, Mia. 2020. " 'We Need All Hands On Deck': Canadian Farmers Struggle with Labour Shortfall Due to COVID-19." *CBC News*, 20 April 2020. https://www.cbc.ca/news/canada/farm-labour-foreign-workers-covid-19-1.5535727.

Silcoff, Sean. 2020. "Medicom to Begin Manufacturing N95 Masks in Canada as Foreign Countries Curb Exports." *Globe and Mail*, 5 April 2020. https://www.theglobeandmail.com/business/article-quebec-mask-maker-amd-medicom-launching-canadian-manufacturing/.

Sodhi, ManMohan, and Christopher S. Tang. 2009. "Managing Supply Chain Disruptions via Time-Based Risk Management." In *Managing Supply Chain Risk and Vulnerability*, edited by Jennifer Blackhurst and Teresa Wu, 29–40. London: Springer.

Statistics Canada. 2020. "COVID-19 Disruptions and Agriculture: Temporary Foreign Workers." Government of Canada, 17 April 2020. https://www150.statcan.gc.ca/n1/pub/45-28-0001/2020001/article/00002-eng.htm.

Subramanian, Samanth. 2020. "How the Face Mask Became the World's Most Coveted Commodity." *Guardian*, 28 April 2020. https://www.theguardian.com/world/2020/apr/28/face-masks-coveted-commodity-coronavirus-pandemic.

Tollefson, Jeff. 2020. "Why Deforestation and Extinctions Make Pandemics More Likely." *Nature*, 7 August 2020. https://www.nature.com/articles/d41586-020-02341-1.

Tucker, R. 2020. "COVID-19 Will Change Grocery Shopping Forever." *Pivot Magazine* (Chartered Professional Accountants Canada), 24 June 2020. https://www.cpacanada.ca/en/news/pivot-magazine/2020-06-24-post-covid-19-grocery-shopping.

Tumilty, Ryan. 2020. "Liberals Spending Millions on Home-Grown Industry to Shore Up Canada's PPE Supply." *National Post*, 28 August 2020. https://nationalpost.com/news/politics/liberals-spending-millions-on-home-grown-industry-to-shore-up-canadas-ppe-supply.

Williams, Zachary, Jason E. Lueg, and Stephen A. LeMay. 2008. "Supply Chain Security: An Overview and Research Agenda." *International Journal of Logistics Management* 19 (2): 254–81. https://doi.org/10.1108/09574090810895988.

World Trade Organization. 2020. "Responding to the COVID-19 Pandemic with Open and Predictable Trade in Agricultural and Food Products." World Trade Organization General Council, Committee on Agriculture, 22 April 2020. https://trade.ec.europa.eu/doclib/docs/2020/april/tradoc_158718.pdf

Getting the Politics of Protecting Critical Infrastructure Right

Bessma Momani and Jean-François Bélanger

Introduction

Canada has generally not been the target of cyber attacks, but these types of threats must become a concern in the post-COVID-19 digitized world. The digitalization of critical infrastructures should eliminate any sense of complacency the country once had. Critical infrastructures include energy and utilities, financial systems, food systems, transportation, government, information and communication technology, health systems, water, emergency services, and critical manufacturing (Public Safety Canada 2014); these are all vital components of our daily lives. Our move to a digitalized world has been rapidly accelerated by COVID-19, pushing Canada's national security and intelligence community to be even more vigilant about foreign and domestic cyber attacks. We note in this chapter that critical infrastructure can be particularly exposed to cyber attacks and therefore needs added policy attention. Some of these risks are further complicated by the fact that Canada's critical infrastructure has shifted from public to private ownership and control, thereby adding multiple operators, varied corporations with their own shareholder interests, and a vast number of asset owners. As the federal government often shares the public responsibility for keeping Canadians safe, getting the politics of critical infrastructure protection right falls in its remit.

A Case for Better Protection of Critical Infrastructure

Like many other aspects of our economy and society, critical infrastructure is increasingly hyperconnected and now vulnerable to malicious cyber attacks. While the universal challenge for many organizations is to secure their information technology systems, the added and most important concern from a critical infrastructure perspective is to ensure that the operational technology systems that effectively control their equipment become smart and remote-enabled. Moreover, these operational technology systems are now reliant on software and hardware that are more accessible and therefore penetrable by hackers (WEF 2020). Relying on hyperconnected operational technology systems is problematic when some critical infrastructure does not have manual backups. In a global survey of approximately a thousand businesses, academics, and government experts in 2020, cyber attacks on critical infrastructures ranked fifth on the list of global risks (WEF 2020). Moreover, in a survey of nearly two thousand global utilities' technicians and administrators, more than half expected a cyber attack on their systems within the year, a quarter reported having been attacked, likely by a state actor, and nearly a third noted that cyber attacks on their operational technology often goes undetected (Siemens and Ponemon Institute 2019). In other words, the increased connectedness of critical infrastructure to the Internet of Things and other digitized infrastructure will complicate things further (Khari et al. 2016). Critical infrastructure has become the soft underbelly of cyber attacks, with disproportionate impacts on citizens' lives.

The Canadian Centre for Cyber Security (often known as the Cyber Centre; see Robinson, this volume), in its 2020 National Cyber Threat Assessment, made a direct risk assessment of Canada's critical infrastructure (CI) and found that "foreign state-sponsored cyber programs are probing our critical infrastructure for vulnerabilities" (CCCS 2020a). The same assessment noted that CI operators may be willing to pay millions in ransom to resume operations—a not-so-subtle warning that CI systems are indeed being attacked. The Cyber Centre report goes further and notes that state-sponsored actors are "very likely attempting to develop cyber capabilities to disrupt Canadian critical infrastructure, such as the supply of electricity, to further their goals" (CCCS 2020a, 5). While the threat is constant, the Cyber Centre notes that the likelihood of state-sponsored cyber attacks against critical infrastructure is low as long as "international hostilities" are kept at bay (CCCS 2020a, 5). This is a crucial point. When international conflict flares or escalates, as has been the case recently between Canada and China over the arrest of a senior Huawei executive, the threat of an attack is then elevated. While state actors may not necessarily want to target Canada, they are acquiring the capability and know-how in case they need it in the future for political leverage. In light of increased global tensions, especially between the United States and China, and the rise of populist-nationalist regimes that have eroded international co-operation and multilateralism, one cannot discount the fact that such an uneasy context could spur a cyber attack on Canadian CI from vengeful state or state-sponsored actors (CCCS 2020a).

Cyber attacks by malicious states or non-state actors on critical infrastructure could be catastrophic, potentially impacting millions. For example, Russian-sponsored cyber attacks attempted to penetrate American electrical systems in 2019 and have been tied to power outages in Ukraine in 2015 and 2016. Iranian operatives were reportedly able to infiltrate the computer system of a dam in New York in 2013. Perhaps the most famous cyber attack on CI is Stuxnet, a joint US-Israel effort that successfully inserted malware in Iranian nuclear infrastructures, damaging many centrifuges (Zetter 2014). The energy sector is not the only target, of course. North Korea, for example, attacked the SWIFT banking system, leading to millions of stolen dollars (Buchanan 2020). In late 2020, many news outlets reported that the United States suspected Russia had gained access to several US federal agencies' systems, which included access to a power grid. Russia was able to do so by operating a back door placed in a software widely used in the federal US government (Sanger, Perlroth, and Schmidt 2021).

It is important to keep in mind that cyber attacks can have widely diffused consequences. Stuxnet's impact, for example, included Iranian critical infrastructure, but its spread infected other global systems as well. Even companies like Chevron in the United States found the same worm in their system (Kushner 2013). Stuxnet is not the only computer worm that spread beyond its intended target. NotPetya, the malware developed by Russia in the cyber attack against Ukraine, spread all over Europe, forcing

Denmark's largest export company, Maersk, to briefly shutdown its entire operation. In the end, the virus's path was wide, causing about $10 billion dollars (McQuade 2019). As nation-states increasingly use cyber weapons, we should therefore expect more spillover and collateral damage. As such, the thinking behind the defence of critical infrastructure cannot rest solely on expecting a direct attack from technologically capable adversaries or rivals.

While the most capable threat to CI comes from state actors, there is increasing concerns that cyber criminals are also interested and willing to attack CI for ransom. Sadly, a US Defense Information Systems Agency assessment noted that when they conducted war games to test the resiliency of their systems, only 4 per cent of operators had realized there was an attack, with just 1 in 150 reporting the attempted attack; more often than not, the phishing attempts were successful (Congressional Record 2000). This led Congressman Rob Andrews, Democrat of New Jersey, to conclude that

> a properly prepared and well-coordinated attack by fewer than 30 computer virtuosos, strategically located around the world, with a budget of less than $10 million, could bring the United States to its knees. Such a strategic attack mounted by a cyber-terrorist group, either sub-state or non-state actors, that is to say either terrorist groups that are not part of any state or terrorist groups that are sponsored by a rogue state, would shut down everything from electric power grids to air traffic control centers. (Congressional Record 2000)

Canada and the United States are increasingly adept at tracing the origins of an attack after the fact. The Cybersecurity and Infrastructure Security Agency (CISA) and the US Department of Defense (DoD), for example, are confident that they are able to trace back any cyber attack to its source if asked to do so by the relevant state actors and agencies.[1]

The question remains, however: What to do once the attacker is identified? Would Canada mount a counterattack against state or non-state actors? Even if the damages were significant, how to disentangle the web of actors involved? China, North Korea, and Russia, for example, use various proxies in the form of state-funded hacking groups (Stevens 2021). While state agencies can likely pinpoint the origin of an attack, the chain of certainty breaks down afterwards as to whether it was an independent action from the group or commanded by state officials. When there is a high chance of plausible deniability, as is often the case with cyber attacks, states are less likely to want to counterattack.

As technological advancements in cyber capabilities progress and are increasingly available to non-state actors, vulnerabilities in Canada's CI increase (Majot and Yampolskiy 2015). This is further complicated by the move toward emerging technologies like quantum computing. While existing encryption methods can at times resist traditional cyber attacks, the future of quantum computing, which follows the rules of quantum physics, is making computers and cyber attacks more robust (Chen et al. 2016; Alagic et al. 2019). Quantum computers are faster and more sophisticated, speeding up the process of decoding security measures such as security keys. As some states develop their quantum capabilities sooner than others, this technology will represent a powerful advantage. Our critical infrastructure, and invariably our public safety and sense of national security, will be threatened by the "supercomputers" capable of quantum cyber attacks by either state adversaries or malicious actors (Herman and Friedson 2018). For example, if China or Russia develop quantum computers able to dismantle cybersecurity measures, Canada's CI system will be exposed. Patching these vulnerabilities through new and sophisticated cryptography will take considerable resources, expertise, and political commitment. Moreover, much of Canada's CI ecosystem is further exposed because its designs are retrofitted for connectivity and can be outdated (Ellinas et al. 2015, 5–6). In other words, these old systems are increasingly exposed in the era of quantum computing. While the risks are high, it is also essential to be mindful of an important and yet neglected concern that CI assets are often owned and supervised by multiple stakeholders with varied regulatory responsibility and governing authority (Slayton and Clark-Ginsberg 2018).

While citizens require access to critical infrastructure, the increasing complexity of these systems requires improved government coordination. Ensuring technical resilience to a potential cyber attack requires a multi-stakeholder approach synchronizing multiple levels of government, policy-makers from difference agencies, scientific and academic experts, and the private sector. Indeed, Canadians' well-being, as well as the Canadian government's effectiveness and cyber defences, are locked in relationships of interdependence.

The pandemic provides the necessary disruption to attract policy-makers' attention and to challenge conventional thinking about threats to critical infrastructure. We have already seen that the pandemic has exposed how the health sector is subject to cyber attacks, thereby noting the gaps in the security of vital systems and information. Canadians expect governments to be well-coordinated when responding to potential cyber attacks and well-prepared to prevent exposure to critical infrastructure systems' technical vulnerabilities (CIRA 2018). Canadians presume that they will have reliable and uninterrupted service and that governments will maintain the integrity of CI systems. If a CI sector is disrupted, the negative economic, political, and socio-psychological impact on Canadians would be broad and impact millions (see Dynes, Goets, and Freeman 2008, 15–16, for an American study of this issue). Officials need to bridge the potential gaps in preparedness to withstand a cyber attack on Canadian CI by working better with diverse communities of technical, policy, and industry professionals. This includes identifying vulnerabilities and developing intervention opportunities to pre-empt malicious actors who would use cyber attacks to harm people living in Canada.

Getting the Politics of Protecting Critical Infrastructure Right

Canada's history of governing critical infrastructure is unique and unlike our southern neighbour, where many tend to look at the federal government with skepticism. As Boyle and Speed (2018) note, Canada's constitutional framework has empowered the federal government to be more active in coordinating a response to emergencies and external attacks. This is an advantage Canada has over other federal systems. In this context, Canada's national security and intelligence community has an important role to play in ensuring the resilience of its interconnected critical infrastructure.

Public Safety Canada is tasked by the National Cross Sector Forum's 2018–2020 Action Plan for Critical Infrastructure and by the *Emergency*

Management Act to take the lead. Public Safety has the necessary legislative authority and is in the process of reviewing CI resilience, as per the 2018–2020 Action Plan. However, it is hobbled by the fact that the National Strategy for Critical Infrastructure was published in 2010 and is, therefore, outdated. One way to secure Canadian infrastructure would be to take stock of the rapid advances in technology and techniques developed in the last ten years and to revise the strategy accordingly.

Protecting critical infrastructure is also riskier because of the challenges of policy coordination among multiple government agencies, gaps in varying levels of authority and responsibility, and the information asymmetry among various stakeholders. As former Assistant Deputy Minister Andrew Graham, writing on Canadian critical infrastructure, put it, "research to date would indicate that the federal government, while trying to provide a form of general leadership and sharing platforms, lacks most of the policy and operational clout to impose solutions, even when they are known. It therefore tries to provide leadership in partnership with many actors, a nascent effort" (Graham 2012, 2). In other words, there are limits to what a solely technical solution can provide, as stakeholders often face imperfect information, cognitive biases, and attribution and detection failures. This is further complicated when stakeholders such as CI operators experience two-level problems, whereby organizational preferences to stay quiet can be incompatible with the need to alert authorities (Bellé, Cantarelli, and Belardinelli 2018; Head and Alford 2015).

In addition to the threat of cyber attacks by state adversaries and malicious non-state actors, the complex network of stakeholders and decision-makers with varied levels of responsibility and authority also creates vulnerabilities in Canada's CI ecosystem (Bernstein 2009). This is compounded by the diffuse nature of responsibility and authority over many systems, as there is no centralization of control over a wide number of stakeholders, from private industry owners/operators to provincial and federal governments and regulatory bodies. This division of authority and the multiple layers of responsibility challenge Canada's emergency preparedness to prevent and respond to cyberattacks (Boyle and Speed 2018).

Critical infrastructure insecurity also opens the door to cascading failures. These governance challenges can further undermine Canada's ability to prevent and respond to cyber attacks. This is where the national security and intelligence community needs to ensure that gaps in governance do not expose systems to foreign attacks. While citizens require access to critical infrastructure to live secure and prosperous lives, the increasing complexity of these systems means that stakeholders cannot respond to threats without proper coordination. Moreover, threats are distributed asymmetrically: some groups and communities are more vulnerable to critical infrastructure failures than others. Only governments can best protect the most vulnerable from these failures.

COVID-19 and Critical Infrastructure

The COVID-19 pandemic, and the digital transformation it has accelerated, means that policy-makers must contend with a new landscape in which non-state actors, both violent and peaceful, have access to technology that can disrupt social, political, and economic life. Moreover, the pandemic makes it necessary for the Canadian government to further assess the impact of exogenous shocks on critical infrastructure, the opportunities this type of event creates to attack CI, and the proper tactics to maintain security. Large-scale disasters are often exploited for cyber attacks, for example, and COVID-19 is a case in point. Recent meta-analyses have demonstrated a significant increase of cybercrimes and more advanced attacks since the start of the pandemic (Aladenusi 2020; Williams et al. 2020). Attacks on banking infrastructure have multiplied, for example, since the UK government announced relief funding for its citizens (Lallie et al. 2020, 6). The health-care system in Canada, as in other nations, has been the target of ransomware attacks during the pandemic (CCCS 2020b). Given the seriousness of the situation and what it would mean for patients to delay their treatments and the potential reputational damage hospitals would accrue, many hospitals opt to pay the ransom (Hijji and Alam 2020, 7160; Lallie et al. 2020, 13).

As cyber capabilities advance and as the connectedness of critical infrastructure opens new vulnerabilities, threats increase. Some of these risks are further complicated by the fact that Canada's critical infrastructure has shifted from public ownership and control to more private control, adding multiple operators, varied corporations with their own shareholder interests, and a vast number of asset owners. Private-sector operators, for example, may agree to pay small ransomware requests to get their data returned or to access their systems if, from their perspective, the cost-benefit calculation makes complying with the demands less costly. Moreover, there is an impulse in the normative shift toward building resiliency by encouraging operators to self-govern. Governments are increasingly investing in raising awareness and self-reporting but are less interested in playing a heavy hand in terms of enforcement. As Boyle (2019) explains, since Public Safety Canada started its Regional Resilience Assessment Program, CI operators are asked to voluntary self-assess their operations using a US-designed critical infrastructure resilience tool (CIRT). This CIRT helps operators measure their own security, preparedness, and mitigation strategies, and then compare these to other operators, who could see how they measure up without disclosing potentially embarrassing vulnerabilities (also see Quigley, Bisset, and Mills 2017, 66–70).

The COVID-19 pandemic has also highlighted other difficulties in securing and governing CI. Specifically, it has made salient the issue of low-tech methods putting infrastructure at risk. The pandemic has forced a massive and rapid shift of work and operations online for most private and public entities. Companies, like Zoom, that were previously relatively unknown outside of the business world are now household names. Concurrently, this has led to an increase in the use of social-engineering techniques to access critical infrastructure through the most vulnerable access point: individuals operating from home. These are techniques where the user, rather than the system, is the primary target (Carrapico and Farrand 2020, 1111–12). Almost 80 per cent of known cyber attacks during the pandemic have involved social-engineering techniques, which include phishing and other email scams (Hijji and Alam 2020, 7153). The most secure system is only as secure as the computer literacy and digital hygiene of its operators. In other words, the more access points that cyber attackers have to inflict damage on CI operators, the more the CI is at risk. Platforms like Zoom and Microsoft Teams, for example, have been targeted in part due to the lack of users' vigilance (Matthews 2020). Other factors are at play as well. Online video conferencing such as Zoom, for example, have a lot of their traffic directed through Chinese servers. This has raised Western government and corporate fears that using Zoom might expose their data and information to the Chinese government or corporate espionage.

Conclusion

The federal government is in charge of, and accountable for, keeping Canada's critical infrastructure safe. In this context, there is a need for better coordination across departments and agencies within the national security and intelligence community, and between the public and private sectors. A lack thereof has proven time and again to be the vulnerable point in many attacks on critical infrastructure.

The COVID-19 pandemic has rung the alarm bell: we are, willingly or not, moving online (Murugesan 2020). We are already at the next frontier; it is now a question of how the Canadian government, and others, will react. Another recommendation is, therefore, to leverage the pandemic to reorganize how national security and intelligence departments and agencies engage with the private sector. Canadians as a whole have a tendency to think of cybersecurity in remote terms, something that is applicable elsewhere but not here. Yet too many Canadians have been the victim of Canada Emergency Response Benefit (CERB) fraud, for example, or have had their information stolen from their banks. Cyber attacks are no longer a faraway or speculative threat: they are now affecting us in the present (Quigley, Bisset, and Mills 2017, 187). The current trend toward greater privatization, on the one hand, and the distrust of government action, on the other, must be bridged. Moreover, moving toward a more coordinated and centralized cyber-response capability may be even more necessary moving forward, given the reluctance of the private sector to adequately invest in risk management (59–60). Lastly, we recommend the mandatory use of tabletop exercises on attacks against CI to better inform operators and governments of gaps in preparedness. While these are voluntary for now, a greater uptake and involvement of CI operators would help keep Canadians safe.

NOTE

1   This was discussed by officials from both agencies during the 2020 Homeland Defense Academic Symposium, held by the North American Aerospace Defense Command and US Northern Command from 1 to 3 December 2020.

REFERENCES

Aladenusi, Tope. 2020. "COVID-19's Impact on Cybersecurity." *Deloitte*, March 2020. https://www2.deloitte.com/ng/en/pages/risk/articles/covid-19-impact-cybersecurity.html.

Alagic, Gorjan, Jacob M. Alperin-Sheriff, Daniel Apon, David Cooper, Quynh H. Dang, Carl A. Miller, Dustin Moody, Rene C. Peralta, Ray A. Perlner, Angela Y. Robinson, Daniel Smith-Tone, and Vi-Kai Liu. 2019. "Status Report on the First Round of the NIST Post-Quantum Cryptography Standardization Process." *National Institute of Standards and Technology*, report no. 8240 (January). https://doi.org/10.6028/NIST. IR.8240.

Bellé, Nicola, Paola Cantarelli, and Paolo Belardinelli. 2018. "Prospect Theory Goes Public." *Public Administration Review* 78, no. 6 (June): 828–40. https://doi. org/10.1111/puar.12960.

Bernstein, Daniel J. 2009. "Introduction to Post-Quantum Crytography." In *Post Quantum Cryptography*, edited by Daniel J. Bernstein, Johannes Buchmann, and Erik Dahmen, 1–14. Berlin: Springer.

Boyle, Philip J. 2019. "Building a Safe and Resilient Canada: Resilience and the Mechanopolitics of Critical Infrastructure." *Resilience* 7, no. 1 (October): 59–82. https://doi.org/10.1080/21693293.2018.1531476.

Boyle, Philip J., and Shannon T. Speed. 2018. "From Protection to Coordinated Preparedness: A Genealogy of Critical Infrastructure in Canada." *Security Dialogue* 49 (3): 217–31. https://doi.org/10.1177/0967010617748541.

Buchanan, Ben. 2020 "How North Korea Hackers Rob Banks Around the World." *Wired*, 28 February 2020. https://www.wired.com/story/how-north-korea-robs-banks-around-world/.

Carrapico, Helena, and Benjamin Farrand. 2020. "Discursive Continuity and Change in the Time of Covid-19: The Case of EU Cybersecurity Policy." *Journal of European Integration* 42 (8): 1111–26. https://doi.org/10.1080/07036337.2020.1853122.

CCCS (Canadian Centre for Cyber Security). 2020a. "National Cyber Threat Assessment." Government of Canada, last modified 16 November 2020. https://cyber.gc.ca/sites/default/files/publications/ncta-2020-e-web.pdf.

———. 2020b. "Renewed Cyber Threats to Canadian Health Organizations." Government of Canada, 30 October 2020. https://cyber.gc.ca/en/alerts/renewed-cyber-threats-canadian-health-organizations.

Chen, Lily, Stephen Jordan, Yi-Kai Liu, Dustin Moody, Rene Peralta, Ray Perlner, and Daniel Smith-Tone. 2016. "Report on Post-Quantum Cryptography." *National Institute of Standards and Technology*, report 8105 (April). http://dx.doi. org/10.6028/NIST.IR.8105.

CIRA (Canadian Internet Registry Authority). 2018. "Canadian Cybersecurity Survey." Canadian Internet Registry Authority, Spring 2018. https://www.cira.ca/resources/cybersecurity/report/2018-canadian-cybersecurity-survey-spring-edition.

Congressional Record. 2000. "Cyber Terrorism, a Real Threat to Society." *Congressional Record* 146, no. 28 (14 March): H974–9. https://www.govinfo.gov/content/pkg/CREC-2000-03-14/html/CREC-2000-03-14-pt1-PgH974.htm.

Dynes, Scott, Eric Goetz, Eric, and Michael Freeman. 2008. "Cyber Security: Are Economic Incentives Adequate?" In *Critical Infrastructure Protection*, edited by E. Goetz and E. Shenoi, 15–28. New York: Springer.

Ellinas, Georgios, Christos Panayiotou, Elias Kyriakides, and Marios Polycarpou. 2015. "Critical Infrastructure Systems: Basic Principles of Monitoring, Control, and Security." In *Intelligent Monitoring, Control, and Security of Critical Infrastructure Systems*, edited by E. Kyriakides and Marios Polycarpou, 1–30. Berlin: Springer.

Graham, Andrew. 2012. "Canada's Critical Infrastructure: When Is Safe Enough Safe Enough?" *Macdonald-Laurier Institute*, 7 December 2011. https://www.macdonaldlaurier.ca/files/pdf/Canadas-Critical-Infrastructure-When-is-safe-enough-safe-enough-December-2011.pdf.

Head, Brian W., and John Alford. 2015. "Wicked Problems: Implications for Public Policy and Management." *Administration and Society* 47, no. 6 (March): 711–39. https://doi.org/10.1177/0095399713481601.

Herman, Arthur, and Idalia Friedson. 2018. *Quantum Computing: How to Address the National Security Risk*. Washington, DC: Hudson Institute. https://s3.amazonaws.com/media.hudson.org/files/publications/Quantum18FINAL4.pdf

Hijji, Mohammad, and Gulzar Alam. 2021. "A Multivocal Literature Review on Growing Social Engineering Based Cyber-Attacks/Threats during the COVID-19 Pandemic: Challenges and Prospective Solutions." *IEEE Access* 9:7152–69. DOI: 10.1109/ACCESS.2020.3048839.

Khari, Manju, Manoj Kumar, Sonakshi Vij, Priyank Pandey, and Vaishali. 2016. "Internet of Things: Proposed Security Aspects for Digitizing the World." 3rd International Conference on Computing for Sustainable Global Development, 31 October 2016. https://ieeexplore.ieee.org/document/7724648.

Kushner, David. 2013. "The Real Story of Stuxnet." *IEEE Spectrum*, 26 February 2013. https://spectrum.ieee.org/telecom/security/the-real-story-of-stuxnet.

Lallie, Harjinder Singh, Lynsay A. Shepard, Jason R. C. Nurse, Arnau Erola, Gregory Epiphanio, Carsten Maple, and Xavier Bellekens. 2020. "Cyber Security in the Age of COVID-19: A Timeline and Analysis of Cyber-Crime and Cyber-Attacks during the Pandemic." *arViv* (June): 1–20. https://arxiv.org/abs/2006.11929.

Majot, Andy, and Roman Yampolskiy. 2015. "Global Catastrophic Risk and Security Implications of Quantum Computers." *Future: The Journal of Policy, Planning, and Futures Studies*, no. 72 (December): 17–26. https://doi.org/10.1016/j.futures.2015.02.006.

Matthews, Lee. 2020. "500,000 Hacked Zoom Accounts Given Away for Free on the Dark Web." *Forbes*, 13 April 2020. https://www.forbes.com/sites/leematthews/2020/04/13/500000-hacked-zoom-accounts-given-away-for-free-on-the-dark-web/?sh=29b9e89c58c5.

McQuade, Mike. 2008. "The Untold Story of NotPetya, the Most Devasting Cyberattack in History." *Wired*, 22 August 2008. https://www.wired.com/story/notpetya-cyberattack-ukraine-russia-code-crashed-the-world/.

Murugesan, San. 2020. "IT Risk and Resilience—Cybersecurity Response to COVID-19." *IT Professional* 22 (3): 12–18. DOI: 10.1109/MITP.2020.2988330.

Public Safety Canada. 2014. "Critical 5: Forging a Common Understanding for Critical Infrastructure." Government of Canada, March 2014. https://www.publicsafety.gc.ca/cnt/rsrcs/pblctns/2016-frgng-cmmn-ndrstndng-crtcalnfrstrctr/2016-frgng-cmmn-ndrstndng-crtcalnfrstrctr-en.pdf.

Quigley, Kevin, Ben Bisset, and Bryan Mills. 2017. *Too Critical to Fail: How Canada Manages Threats to Critical Infrastructure*. Montreal: McGill-Queen's University Press.

Sanger, David E., Nicole Perlroth, and Eric Schmidtt. 2020. "Scope of Russian Hacking Becomes Clear: Multiple U.S. Agencies Were Hit." *New York Times*, 14 December 2020. https://www.nytimes.com/2020/12/14/us/politics/russia-hack-nsa-homeland-security-pentagon.html.

Siemens and Ponemon Institute. 2019. "Caught in the Crosshairs: Are Utilities Keeping Up with the Industrial Cyber Threat?" *Siemens and Ponemon Institute*, 4 October 2019. https://assets.new.siemens.com/siemens/assets/api/uuid:35089d45-e1c2-4b8b-b4e9-7ce8cae81eaa/version:1572434569/siemens-cybersecurity.pdf.

Slayton, Rebecca, and Aaron Clark-Ginsberg. 2018. "Beyond Regulatory Capture: Coproducing Expertise for Critical Infrastructure Protection." *Regulation and Governance* 12 (1): 115–30. https://doi.org/10.1111/rego.12168.

Stevens, Corbin. 2021. "Cyber Doctrines and the Risk of Nuclear Crisis Instability Part 2: Russian and Chinese Use of Proxy." *Council on Foreign Relation*, 25 January 2021. https://www.cfr.org/blog/cyber-doctrines-and-risk-nuclear-crisis-instability-part-2-russian-and-chinese-use-proxies.

WEF (World Economic Forum). 2020. *The Global Risks Report 2020*. Insight Report, 15th ed. Geneva: World Economic Forum. http://www3.weforum.org/docs/WEF_Global_Risk_Report_2020.pdf.

Williams, Meilee Christina, Rahul Chaturvedi, and Krishnan Chakravarthy. 2020. "Cybersecurity Risks in a Pandemic." *Journal of Medical Internet Research* 22 (9): 1–4. https://doi.org/10.2196/23692.

Zetter, Kim. 2014. "An Unprecedented Look at Stuxnet, the World's First Digital Weapon." *Wired*, 11 March 2014. https://www.wired.com/2014/11/countdown-to-zero-day-stuxnet/.

PART II:
Responses

A Health Intelligence Priority for Canada? Costs, Benefits, and Considerations

Jessica Davis and Alexander Corbeil

Introduction

International responses to the COVID-19 pandemic have been mixed. Some states have responded effectively and proactively, while others have lagged in their policy responses, with devastating consequences. A few of these responses have incorporated surveillance techniques usually associated with national or international security in an effort to stop the spread of this deadly disease. In Canada, to date, national security tools and practices have not been used to track the spread of COVID-19 or respond to the pandemic. While there have been some calls for expanding the scope of Canada's intelligence activities to include health intelligence, the question remains whether Canadian intelligence institutions should treat health events as intelligence priorities. Greater integration and information sharing between Canada's traditional security and intelligence community and its health intelligence community could yield earlier warning, and by extension better policy responses.

At the same time, there are very real concerns about a possible expansion of the Canadian intelligence community's mandate and practices to include more of a focus on health intelligence, including proportionality, the right use of tools and technologies, and privacy. Further issues with expanding that mandate include the limited resources Canada currently has to respond to and engage with security threats. While a wholescale adoption of health intelligence as a national security and intelligence priority might be premature, better integration and information sharing are certainly warranted. In this chapter, we canvas these arguments and ultimately propose that Canada's existing health intelligence capabilities could be better resourced and supported, both domestically and internationally.

Intelligence in Canada

Michael Warner defines intelligence as "secret, state activity to understand or influence foreign entities" (2002). In the intelligence literature, this broad definition is often broken down into component parts, such that intelligence is defined by specific intelligence actions, such as collection, analysis, and dissemination. The practice of intelligence is best, although imperfectly, understood through reference to the intelligence cycle. Under this model, intelligence is conceptualized in five phases: planning and coordination; collection; processing; production and analysis; and dissemination and feedback (Johnson in Gill, Marrin, and Phythian 2008). Underpinning the intelligence process are four constants: activity—gathering and exploitation of information; subjects—the targets of intelligence gathering; product—converting unprocessed data into an informative intelligence product; and function—to understand relevance, seek truth, and provide useful information to decision-makers (Herman 2001).

This definition applies in Canada, where intelligence is often employed against threats to the security of Canada and in support of Canadian interests (*Canadian Security Intelligence Service Act*, RSC, 1985, c C-23). Canadian intelligence agencies provide different kinds of intelligence to the Government of Canada, including strategic intelligence, warning intelligence, and security intelligence. For instance, several departments and agencies produce strategic intelligence products, including the Financial Transactions and Reports Analysis Centre of Canada (FINTRAC 2018), the Privy Council Office's Intelligence Assessment Secretariat (Barnes 2020), and CSIS (SIRC 1997), while other departments and agencies produce intelligence tailored for their specific operations. Canadian intelligence also includes foreign, criminal, and defence intelligence (PCO 2021, 21).

In this chapter, the authors conceive of threats to the security of Canada as primarily emanating from individuals, states, and non-state actors. Events such as pandemics and natural disasters can compound the threats posed by these actors. While some may conceive of events as threats in and of themselves, it is important to remember that threat is, in most commonly understood definitions, a combination of intent, capability, and opportunity (Riehle 2013). Events have no intent; their capacity to be disruptive or cause destruction is a function of the type of event. As such, these events can certainly shape and impact threats and national security, but in and of themselves are not threats. However, some governments have an incentive to both underplay the extent and impact of events within their jurisdiction, such as pandemics, and oversell the effectiveness of their responses, as we have seen with the COVID-19 pandemic (N. P. Walsh 2020). This is not to say that events like pandemics and natural disasters should necessarily be excluded from intelligence collection, but rather that there are limits on what intelligence and threat assessment can offer. Focusing on the (in)actions of governments in relation to an event, whether it be a pandemic or natural disaster, may hold the most promise. In addition, risk assessment, done by the appropriate agencies with specialized knowledge, has much to offer Canadian preparedness.

As the COVID-19 pandemic progressed, traditional Canadian intelligence activities expanded to include enhanced cybersecurity and outreach to the private sector to protect intellectual property, such as vaccine development (CSE 2020). While there is a clear role for intelligence agencies to play, the question remains whether health events such as pandemics should be intelligence priorities and whether Canada's intelligence resources should be divided among traditional threats and health events. Ultimately, Canada should review its existing early warning processes and pandemic alert systems to see where our response can be improved. Once a full assessment of these tools is complete (and utilized), there may be scope for expanding the intelligence community's mandate to include a limited health intelligence priority. However, we should not view health intelligence as a panacea to solve problems generated by current gaps in early warning systems, lack of response, or under-resourced programs in other departments. The following discussion on this topic also has implications for Canada's approach to other global events, such as climate change and related instability and forced migration.

Global Health Environment

The global health environment is rapidly changing, as evidenced by the current COVID-19 pandemic. We have now entered the "Pandemic Era" (*Lancet Planetary Health* 2021). A convergence of factors has created the conditions for an increase in the frequency of future global pandemics, to which Canada will not be immune. Four interrelated global trends are at the centre of this change: climate change, income growth, urbanization, and globalization (Wu et al. 2017). Increasing the likelihood of the emergence and re-emergence of new zoonoses[1] is climate change, which negatively impacts ecosystem processes and functioning, making disease more likely. Income growth is associated with an increase in the consumption of animal protein in developing countries, resulting in the expanded transfer of land to livestock production. Increased interaction between humans and animals enhances the likelihood that diseases will spread from one species to another. Urbanization—the greater clustering and interaction of people in dense urban environments—increases the speed at which disease spreads. Globalization ensures that such diseases are not contained within national boundaries but instead proliferate from one internationally connected urban centre to another. Together, these trends have increased the probability of the emergence and global spread of zoonoses. These trends have made outbreaks of new zoonoses difficult to control, even with significant increases in international co-operation, including through the World Health Organization (WHO).

It may be tempting to focus on China as the source of many of these global health security challenges, given the current COVID-19 pandemic and other historical influenza pandemics originating in that country. However, the convergence of climate change, income growth, urbanization, and globalization presents similar risks in other countries. India, Indonesia, and Nigeria are a few examples of countries with similar predisposing socio-ecological risk factors. As stated by Wu et al., these countries all have "large and growing human and livestock populations, high levels of interaction between species, and large-scale ecological change"

(2017, 25). Unlike China, these and other countries are increasingly at risk of zoonosis transmission while simultaneously facing public health conditions that increase vulnerability to disease (Wu et al. 2017).

India, Indonesia, and Nigeria, among other countries, are also experiencing the negative ecological impacts of climate change. The warming of the climate is a principal driver of the loss of species diversity, reducing the resiliency of ecosystems and the flora and fauna contained within. Stressed ecosystems that encounter expanding livestock production can lead to the development of new zoonoses, as shown by epidemiologists studying the roots of disease in South Asia (Lustgarten 2020). Urbanization and globalization then provide the conduits through which such emergent diseases become global pandemics.

Health Intelligence

Health intelligence, a specific brand of intelligence focused on health surveillance (Mykhalovskiy and Weir 2006), generally falls into the category of early warning or warning intelligence, which is meant to provide the government with decision advantage and create options for policy action. In the United States, the National Center for Medical Intelligence (NCMI) is partially responsible for early pandemic warning. Located in Fort Detrick, Maryland, the NCMI is home to around a hundred epidemiologists, virologists, chemical engineers, toxicologists, biologists, and military medical experts trained in intelligence tradecraft (Riechmann 2020). It uses all-source methods, from communication intercepts to satellite imagery, social media, and classified intelligence, to gather information on public health issues for its primary consumer, the US military. This includes information relevant to overseas troop deployments and health threats to the homeland. In addition to efforts to identify emergent and re-emergent zoonoses, the NCMI also assesses whether foreign governments are forthcoming and truthful about public health crises and the effectiveness of their responses (Dilanian 2020). In November 2019, the NCMI released its first warning that a contagion was sweeping through China's Wuhan region, concluding that it could become a cataclysmic event, according to a source familiar with the assessment (Margolin and Meek 2020). NCMI reporting continued into December, culminating in a detailed analysis in the President's Daily Brief in January 2020 (Margolin and Meek 2020). Furthermore, on 25 February 2020, the NCMI shared its conclusion that COVID-19 would become a pandemic within thirty days; a conclusion that came fifteen days before the WHO declared COVID-19 a global pandemic (Riechmann 2020). It is unknown whether the Trump administration received the NCMI's conclusion that COVID-19 would become a pandemic, though we know a briefing provided to the Joint Chiefs of Staff included such an assessment (Riechmann 2020). The United States likely shared this information with the Canadian military's medical intelligence unit through the Quadripartite Medical Intelligence Committee,[2] which began issuing warnings about COVID-19 in January 2020 (Brewster 2021).

Unlike the United States, which has an established intelligence agency dedicated to emerging public health issues, Israel turned its intelligence apparatus to the COVID-19 pandemic once it had taken hold globally. In March 2020, Israel declared a national state of emergency, which included a decision to leverage the capabilities of its intelligence community. Three national intelligence agencies were instructed to help with the national response to COVID-19: the Military Intelligence Directorate, the Israeli Security Agency (Shin Bet), and the Mossad (Kahana 2020). Unit-8200 and the Research Division of the Military Intelligence Directorate engaged in data collection and research for civilian medical needs within Israel. This included upgrading antiquated Health Ministry computer systems, establishing the Information and Knowledge Centre to study the effectiveness and dynamics of other governments' responses to the crisis, and liaising with international intelligence partners. Together, Unit-8200 and Unit-269 of the Israeli Defence Forces also assisted in monitoring COVID-19 testing. Until a recent Supreme Court ruling, the Shin Bet took responsibility for digital tracking (Kahana 2020). Using both a national ID and cell phone number, it tracked every individual exposed to COVID-19, transferring this information to the Ministry of Health. For its part, the Mossad supported the Israeli Ministry of Health in securing medical equipment by leveraging its international contacts. This included 1.5 million surgical masks, tens of thousands of N-95 masks, testing kits, protective clothes, medications, and expertise for the domestic manufacturing of ventilators (Kahana 2020).

While it is unknown whether the Trump administration received the NCMI's assessment that COVID-19 would become a pandemic, we also know that the administration continually received an abundance of information and projections underlining the severity of the pandemic and the danger posed to Americans, as highlighted by the inclusion of the NCMI's January analysis in the President's Daily Brief (Mangan and Breuninger 2020). However, for political gain, former President Donald Trump, most of his staff, and surrogates continually downplayed the gravity of the situation, mischaracterized the effectiveness of his government's response, and provided mixed and at times contradictory public health guidance (Summers 2020). Given the politicization of the COVID-19 response and incompetence of the Trump administration in its attempt to address the pandemic (Reuters 2021)—dynamics that were beyond the influence of the US intelligence community—it is difficult to assess whether early warning would have been beneficial to the US COVID-19 response had the country had more effective leadership.

Unlike the Trump administration, the Israeli government used its intelligence community to great, although at times controversial, effect. In Israel, the intelligence community leveraged its traditional activities and tools to combat the pandemic. These tools included data mining and analysis, technological monitoring, covert operations to obtain medical supplies, and recommendations for national decision-making (Shapira 2020). One Israeli intelligence commentator and former practitioner sees the response of the Israeli intelligence community as an extension of Israeli national intelligence culture. This culture can be described as a culture of practice, friction, initiative, and adaptation that favours reflection after the fact, including questions about whether the intelligence community should play a role in medical issues (Shapira 2020). From the evidence provided through public reporting and academic analysis, it seems that the Israeli intelligence community's most significant contributions came at the beginning of the pandemic. At that time, Israel did not have a clear understanding of the disease and its global spread or whether the effectiveness of specific health measures employed by other states required updates to its domestic health infrastructure, and it needed to procure crucial medical supplies (Kahana 2020). Israel used this information to manage its response to the pandemic and adjust existing intelligence tools

(Huggard and Sachs 2020) to track coronavirus disease spread (with limited success).

Intelligence Priorities in Canada

In Canada, the collection priorities of security and intelligence services are set at the highest levels of government and direct the types of intelligence that the government needs, which in turn dictates the capabilities and products of the intelligence community (NSICOP 2019, 34). They are established at two-year intervals by a cabinet committee through a Memorandum to Cabinet (MC). The priorities are broad, unranked, and meant to direct the intelligence community's focus "to the issues of greatest importance to the Government of Canada, but do not provide specific activities or entities of interest" (PCO 2021, 2).[3] These priorities remain classified. Even the broader subjects of these priorities are classified, so it is unknown if health intelligence is currently a priority for the Government of Canada or a standing intelligence requirement for one (or more) of the members of the security and intelligence community.

Despite this lack of information, some academics have called for Canada to adopt a "health intelligence mission" (Wark 2020). Wark suggests that "communications intercepts, satellite imagery, diplomatic reporting, open-source information and even traditional spying (HUMINT)" should be deployed to create health intelligence reporting. Wark further argues that assessment of this intelligence reporting could be done through Canada's existing assessment capability at CSIS, the Privy Council Office, the Department of National Defence, and Global Affairs Canada. The main argument supporting the idea of an enhanced health intelligence mission for Canadian security and intelligence agencies suggests that early warning of the pandemic would have created decision-making advantages for Canada. Moreover, it would have allowed the Canadian government to proactively address the pandemic through a series of policies geared toward stopping the spread of COVID-19.

There are several issues with this argument that require exploration of the counterfactual. First, early warning does not necessarily equal early action. Government officials could well have received better early warning of the emergence of the pandemic; the question remains what they would have done with that information. Indeed, this was the case with the NCMI in the United States; they had intelligence earlier than the WHO, but the US government did not respond to the pandemic in an effective manner.

In Canada, with more warning, government officials could have perhaps ordered more personal protective equipment (PPE) or provided the intelligence to health officials to better understand how the virus works, or perhaps had more time to design better policies to combat the spread of COVID-19, but this is not a given. The US and Israeli examples highlight that the intelligence community can play important early warning and response roles during global health events like pandemics. However, as shown by the US example, political leaders must be willing to listen to and act upon information provided by intelligence institutions as part of an effective response. The politicization or plain ignoring of intelligence highlighting the severity of a global health event and other states' responses diminishes the effectiveness of this early warning role.

To facilitate a successful early response to a global health event, the Canadian government would have to receive those warnings and act on them. Additionally, the intelligence would have to provide sufficient detail to allow for better interventions, and the federal government would have to be successful in implementing better policies federally and convincing its provincial counterparts to do the same. Given the different responses from various levels of government in terms of accepting and acting on intelligence in managing the pandemic, these are significant hurdles to overcome when reacting to such an event.

At the same time, intelligence priorities are not just about national security—in fact, those priorities need to be broader and support a range of policy actions by the government, including foreign, defence, security, and public safety policy. Indeed, the aims of intelligence in Canada are to avoid strategic surprise, provide long-term expertise, and support the policy process (PCO 2021, 20). As our experience with COVID-19 has demonstrated, health issues like a global pandemic can impact all aspects of society, including what we see as traditional national security issues. For instance, the pandemic is believed to have increased radicalization among ideologically motivated violent extremists and encouraged the spread of conspiracy theories (see Argentino and Amarasingam, this volume; Babb and Wilner, this volume; CTED 2020). Indeed, global pandemics, along with other international events, can certainly impact Canadian national security (Carvin and Davis 2020).

Health issues like disease outbreaks are a collective-action problem and require the international community to track the spread and use data collected to benefit the general population (Youde 2012, 83). While classified intelligence may provide early warning of an impending pandemic, and this information could easily be shared among the Five Eyes (P. F. Walsh 2020, 598), the classified nature of that information may hinder the global sharing necessary for a successful response. This hesitation stems from the need to protect sources and methods, while states are also reluctant to share information that could provide decision advantages to their adversaries. Still, states have a moral and legal international obligation to share this information broadly and quickly (WHO 2016; Youde 2012, 83). For this reason, health intelligence collected through classified means has some utility.

Privacy and Health Intelligence for Canada

There are other concerns about adopting health intelligence as a priority, ranging from the practical (like Canada's limited intelligence resources) to the ethical. As Buzan, Wæver, and de Wilde note, successfully labelling an issue a security (or intelligence) issue removes it from the realm of ordinary political discourse and permits the undertaking of exceptional actions (1998, 24). The exceptional circumstances created by the pandemic (and other crises) enable emergency measures and allow the suspension of normal politics (Kamradt-Scott and McInnes 2012, 96). A number of countries, such as Singapore, China (Kharpal 2020), Russia (Rainsford 2020), and Israel (Davis 2020), have used their intelligence-collection capabilities in an attempt to limit the spread of the pandemic within their borders. These actions have raised significant concerns about privacy, the lawful use of these powers and information collected through these mechanisms, and the authority used to collect that information, etc. (Davis 2020; see also West, this volume).

For instance, it has now come to light that the Singaporean government has and will continue to leverage its TraceTogether contact tracing program for law enforcement investigations after previously stating that data would only be used for tracking COVID-19 exposure (Illmer 2021). In Israel, the Shin Bet's role in contact tracing came under scrutiny after civil rights organizations brought a petition before the Supreme Court and a state comptroller's report showed that the Shin Bet app is not effective enough when compared with investigations carried out by the Israeli Health Ministry (Bandel 2020). The Shin Bet is now only permitted to use digital tracking to find contacts of coronavirus patients when they refuse to take part in epidemiological investigations (Estrin 2021).

Certainly, surveillance systems are necessary to detect the spread of infectious diseases, but it is also critical to note that these systems can be used in discriminatory ways, such as to abrogate freedom of movement and speech (Youde 2012, 83). As intelligence scholars Omand (2006) and Bellaby (2012) note in their respective work on ethics, surveillance and the recourse to secret intelligence should be a last resort.

So, the question becomes: Do we really need health intelligence, or is this a solution looking for a problem? Certainly, the intelligence community has a role to play in providing any relevant intelligence to decision-makers on a host of intelligence issues, including those that relate to public safety, as intelligence relating to a pandemic clearly does. But are there better mechanisms to collect and share information about pandemics and to respond to this type of international event, both with our close allies and the wider international community?

The Way Forward

It is difficult to argue that states would not benefit from better early warning of a pandemic or other natural events and the associated responses by other governments that will have an impact on national security. As other chapters in this book illustrate, Canadian security and intelligence agencies' work has clearly been impacted by the pandemic, both in terms of their day-to-day function and the threats that they are investigating, mitigating, and disrupting. While it is still early to assess the federal government's performance during the pandemic, there are a few points of near universal agreement when it comes to assessing how Canada could have better managed the pandemic.

Adequate PPE

The Canadian government had insufficient levels of PPE during the early days of the pandemic, and little in the way of a plan to secure more, particularly in a competitive environment (Dyer 2020; Carvin et al., this volume). While early warning could help Canada gain a competitive advantage in terms of securing PPE when a pandemic is imminent, that preparedness could also be maintained on a continual basis. In addition, as other states adopt early warning systems for pandemics, any advantage that a Canadian system would have on this front would be diminished by increased competition.

Implementing or Bolstering the Capabilities of the Global Public Health Intelligence Network

Scientists within the Global Public Health Intelligence Network (GPHIN) accused the government of placing a higher priority on information provided by China and the WHO than the information held by GPHIN during the early days of the COVID-19 pandemic (Robertson 2020; Lee and Piper, this volume). Information provided by the intelligence community to GPHIN and public health decision-makers could have been used to verify, provide context for, or clarify information held by other government departments and agencies regarding the situation in other countries and the responses of other governments. Reviving a 2004 proposal to develop a mechanism that would allow the Public Health Agency of Canada, which houses GPHIN, to incorporate classified intelligence would be an appropriate place to begin (Brewster 2021).

Increased Coordination and Engagement with the Global Health Security Agenda

Launched in February 2014 and endorsed by the G7 in June of that year, the Global Health Security Agenda (GHSA) was established to address the global threat posed by infectious diseases such as SARS and COVID-19.[4] Among the GHSA's objectives are enhancing countries' capacities to address infectious disease, emphasizing global health security at the national level, and promoting multi-sectoral collaboration. As a member of the GHSA, Canada has committed to a number of 2024 targets, including investing in health security to strengthen national and global responses

(GHSA n.d.). Through the GHSA, Canada has also committed to distributing $5 million to international partners to bolster capacity in the area of global health security. An improved public health capacity in Canada could enhance Ottawa's contribution to the GHSA, and Canada's support to international institutions and developing countries.

Conclusion

Since the outset of the global pandemic, commentators have criticized the Canadian response to the crisis on various grounds. One of the propositions to improve our response to future pandemics and similar events is to include health intelligence as an intelligence priority. Certainly, enhancing existing Canadian health intelligence institutions such as GPHIN and contributing to international initiatives like the GHSA would improve the possibility of a more coordinated and proactive Canadian response. However, expanding health intelligence into the mandate of the broader intelligence community may not yield the desired results of early warning and better response. Warning intelligence, to be effective, must be listened to and acted upon by decision-makers. To be credible, that warning needs to come from experts who work within Canada's existing health intelligence infrastructure.

Without a doubt, better coordination and information sharing between health intelligence actors and the intelligence community would improve Canadian warning and policy responses. Whether Canada needs to dedicate some of its intelligence-collection efforts, such as its limited HUMINT and SIGINT capacities, is another question entirely. This proposition has not been sufficiently supported, particularly in the absence of a robust review of Canada's existing tools and responses to the COVID-19 pandemic. Pandemics certainly have national security implications. However, a move to broaden the scope of the Canadian intelligence community's collections efforts, dilute existing collection on national security threats, and duplicate efforts within the existing health intelligence framework may not lead to better warning and policy responses.

NOTES

1   Diseases or infections that are naturally transmissible from vertebrate animals to humans. For more information, see WHO (2020).

2   The Quadripartite Medical Intelligence Committee was established during the Second World War and facilitates the sharing of military medical intelligence between member countries Canada, the United States, Britain, Australia, and New Zealand.

3   This unclassified, for-official-use report was released by the PCO to the authors upon request in January 2021.

4   P.F. Walsh (2020) has put forward the idea of linking the work of the GHSA to the Five Eyes intelligence community. Others, such as Bowsher, Bernard, and Sullivan (2020), have argued that this should be expanded to include NATO countries.

REFERENCES

Bandel, Netael. 2020. "Israeli Government Tells Court It May Reduce Shin Bet Role in Contact Tracing." *Haaretz*, 16 December 2020. https://www.haaretz.com/israel-news/.premium-israeli-government-tells-court-it-may-reduce-shin-bet-role-in-contact-tracing-1.9373050.

Barnes, Alan. 2020. "Getting It Right: Canadian Intelligence Assessments on Iraq, 2002–2003." *Intelligence and National Security* 35, no. 7 (May): 1–29. https://doi.org/10.1080/02684527.2020.1771934.

Bellaby, Ross. 2012. "What's the Harm? The Ethics of Intelligence Collection." *Intelligence and National Security* 27, no. 1 (February): 93–117. https://doi.org/10.1080/02684527.2012.621600.

Bowsher, Gemma, Rose Bernard, and Richard Sullivan. 2020. "A Health Intelligence Framework for Pandemic Response: Lessons from the U.K. Experience of COVID-19." *Health Security* 18, no. 6 (December): 435–43. https://doi.org/10.1089/hs.2020.0108.

Brewster, Murray. 2021. "Public Health Agency Failed to Cite Military Intelligence in Pandemic Bulletins." *CBC News*, 11 January 2021. https://www.cbc.ca/news/politics/covid-military-medical-intelligence-1.5866627.

Buzan, Barry, Ole Wæver, and Jaap de Wilde. 1998. *Security: A New Framework for Analysis*. London: Lynne Rienner.

Carvin, Stephanie, and Jessica Davis. 2020. "National Security and Pandemics: The Limits of Early Warning." *Policy Options*, 24 April 2020. https://policyoptions.irpp.org/magazines/april-2020/national-security-and-pandemics-the-limits-of-early-warning/.

CSE (Communications Security Establishment). 2020. "Joint CSE and CSIS Statement— May 14, 2020." Government of Canada, last modified 28 May 2020. https://www.

canada.ca/en/security-intelligence-service/news/2020/05/joint-cse-and-csis-statement.html.

CTED (Counter Terrorism Committee Executive Directorate). 2020. "The Impact of the COVID-19 Pandemic on Terrorism, Counter-Terrorism and Countering Violent Extremism." United Nations Security Council, December 2020. https://www.un.org/securitycouncil/ctc/sites/www.un.org.securitycouncil.ctc/files/files/documents/2021/Jan/cted_paper_the-impact-of-the-covid-19-pandemic-on-counter-te.pdf.

Davis, Jessica. 2020. "Intelligence, Surveillance, and Ethics in a Pandemic." *Just Security*, 31 March 2020. https://www.justsecurity.org/69384/intelligence-surveillance-and-ethics-in-a-pandemic/.

Dilanian, Ken. 2020. "How U.S. Spies Predict Pandemics like Coronavirus." *NBC News*, 13 March 2020. https://www.nbcnews.com/health/health-news/spying-coronavirus-little-known-u-s-intel-outfit-has-its-n1157296.

Dyer, Evan. 2020. "The Great PPE Panic: How the Pandemic Caught Canada with Its Stockpiles Down." *CBC News*, 11 July 2020. https://www.cbc.ca/news/politics/ppe-pandemic-covid-coronavirus-masks-1.5645120.

Elbe, Stefan. 2006. "Should HIV/AIDS Be Securitized? The Ethical Dilemmas of Linking HIV/AIDS and Security." *International Studies Quarterly* 50, no. 1 (March): 119–44. https://doi.org/10.1111/j.1468-2478.2006.00395.x.

Estrin, Daniel. 2021. "Israel's Supreme Court Ends Spy Agency Cellphone Tracking Of COVID-19 Infections." *NPR*, 1 March 2021. https://www.npr.org/sections/coronavirus-live-updates/2021/03/01/972560038/israels-supreme-court-ends-spy-agency-cellphone-tracking-of-covid-19-infections.

FINTRAC (Financial Transactions and Reports Analysis Centre of Canada). 2018. *Terrorist Financing Assessment*. Ottawa: FINTRAC, 2018. https://www.fintrac-canafe.gc.ca/intel/assess/tfa-2018-eng.pdf.

GHSA (Global Health Security Agenda). n.d.. "Member Commitments." Global Health Security Agenda, accessed 21 June 2021. https://ghsagenda.org/member-commitments/.

Gill, Peter, Stephen Marrin, and Mark Phythian. 2008. *Intelligence Theory: Key Questions and Debates*. London: Taylor and Francis.

Herman, Michael. 2001. *Intelligence Services in the Information Age*. 1st ed. London: Routledge.

Huggard, Natan, and Kevin Sachs. 2020. "Technosurveillance Mission Creep in Israel's COVID-19 Response." *TechStream*, (Brookings Institute) 9 June 2020. https://www.brookings.edu/techstream/technosurveillance-mission-creep-in-israels-covid-19-response/.

Illmer, Andreas. 2021. "Singapore Reveals Covid Privacy Data Available to Police." *BBC News*, 5 January 2021. https://www.bbc.com/news/world-asia-55541001.

Kahana, Ephraim. 2020. "Intelligence against COVID-19: Israeli Case Study."
    International Journal of Intelligence and CounterIntelligence 34, no. 2 (August): 1–8.
    https://doi.org/10.1080/08850607.2020.1783620.

Kamradt-Scott, Adam, and Colin McInnes. 2012. "The Securitisation of Pandemic
    Influenza: Framing, Security and Public Policy." *Global Public Health* 7, no. 2
    (January): 95–110. https://doi.org/10.1080/17441692.2012.725752.

Kharpal, Arjun. 2020. "Use of Surveillance to Fight Coronavirus Raises Concerns about
    Government Power after Pandemic Ends." *CNBC*, 26 March 2020. https://www.
    cnbc.com/2020/03/27/coronavirus-surveillance-used-by-governments-to-fight-
    pandemic-privacy-concerns.html.

Lancet Planetary Health. 2021. "A Pandemic Era." *Lancet Planetary Health* 5, no. 1
    (January): 1. https://doi.org/10.1016/S2542-5196(20)30305-3.

Lustgarten, Abrahm. 2020. "How Climate Change Is Contributing to Skyrocketing Rates
    of Infectious Disease." *ProPublica*, 7 May 2020. https://www.propublica.org/article/
    climate-infectious-diseases?token=rbkATiWFlr_lTtppXfPWnGWasHsL0evu.

Mangan, Kevin, and Dan Breuninger. 2020. "Coronavirus Deaths Projected to Hit 3,000
    per Day by June, Internal Trump Administration Analysis Says." *CNBC*, 4 May
    2020. https://www.cnbc.com/2020/05/04/coronavirus-trump-administration-
    projects-3000-deaths-per-day-by-june.html.

Margolin, Josh, and James Gordon Meek. 2020. "Intelligence Report Warned of
    Coronavirus Crisis as Early as November: Sources." *ABC News*, 8 April 2020.
    https://abcnews.go.com/Politics/intelligence-report-warned-coronavirus-crisis-
    early-november-sources/story?id=70031273.

Mykhalovskiy, Eric, and Lorna Weir. 2006. "The Global Public Health Intelligence
    Network and Early Warning Outbreak Detection." *Canadian Journal of Public
    Health* 97, no. 1 (January–February): 42–4. https://pubmed.ncbi.nlm.nih.
    gov/16512327/.

NSICOP (National Security and Intelligence Committee of Parliamentarians). 2019.
    "Annual Report 2018." Government of Canada, 9 April 2019. https://www.nsicop-
    cpsnr.ca/reports/rp-2019-04-09/intro-en.html.

Omand, Sir David. 2006. "Ethical Guidelines in Using Secret Intelligence for Public
    Security." *Cambridge Review of International Affairs* 19, no. 4 (December): 613–28.
    https://doi.org/10.1080/09557570601003338.

PCO (Privy Council Office). 2021. "Canadian Intelligence Prioritization." Government of
    Canada. Unpublished report in authors' possession.

Rainsford, Sarah. 2020. "Russia Uses Facial Recognition to Tackle Virus." *BBC News*, 4
    April 2020. https://www.bbc.com/news/av/world-europe-52157131.

Reuters. 2021. "Trump Administration Had No Coronavirus Vaccine Distribution Plan:
    White House." *Reuters*, January 24, 2021. https://www.reuters.com/article/us-
    health-coronavirus-usa-klain-idUSKBN29T0FY.

Riechmann, Deb. 2020. "Medical Intelligence Sleuths Tracked, Warned of New Virus." *Associated Press*, 16 April 2020. https://apnews.com/article/da45eec432d6ff4cc9e0825531e454a6.

Riehle, Kevin P. 2013. "Assessing Foreign Intelligence Threats." *American Intelligence Journal* 31 (1): 96–101. https://www.studocu.com/row/document/technical-university-of-kenya/journalism-and-mass-communication/tutorial-work/assessing-foreign-intelligence-threats/8136941/view.

Robertson, Grant. 2020. "What Happened with Canada's Pandemic Alert System? The GPHIN Controversy Explained." *Globe and Mail*, 5 October 2020. https://www.theglobeandmail.com/canada/article-what-happened-with-canadas-pandemic-alert-system-the-gphin/.

Shapira, Itai. 2020. "Israeli National Intelligence Culture and the Response to COVID-19." *War on the Rocks*, 12 November 2020. https://warontherocks.com/2020/11/israeli-national-intelligence-culture-and-the-response-to-covid-19/.

SIRC (Security and Intelligence Review Committee). 1997. "SIRC Annual Report 1996–1997." Government of Canada, 30 September 1997. http://www.sirc-csars.gc.ca/anrran/1996-1997/index-eng.html.

Summers, Juana. 2020. "Timeline: How Trump Has Downplayed the Coronavirus Pandemic." *NPR*, 2 October 2020. https://www.npr.org/sections/latest-updates-trump-covid-19-results/2020/10/02/919432383/how-trump-has-downplayed-the-coronavirus-pandemic.

Walsh, Nick Paton. 2020. "Leaked Documents Reveal China's Mishandling of the Early Stages of Covid-19 Pandemic." *CNN*, 30 November 2020. https://www.cnn.com/2020/11/30/asia/wuhan-china-covid-intl/index.html.

Walsh, Patrick F. 2020. "Improving 'Five Eyes' Health Security Intelligence Capabilities: Leadership and Governance Challenges." *Intelligence and National Security* 35, no. 4 (April): 586–602. http://www.tandfonline.com/doi/abs/10.1080/02684527.2020.1750156.

Wark, Wesley K. 2020. "Pandemic Gives Security and Intelligence Community an Urgent New Mission." *Policy Options*, 14 April 2020. https://policyoptions.irpp.org/magazines/april-2020/pandemic-gives-security-and-intelligence-community-an-urgent-new-mission/.

Warner, Michael. 2002. "Wanted: A Definition of 'Intelligence'—Central Intelligence Agency." *Studies in Intelligence* 46 (3). https://www.cia.gov/static/72b2d4c0d01e4e05c60ff7d37fdd68b1/Wanted-Definition-of-Intel.pdf.

WHO (World Health Organization). 2016. *International Health Regulations (2005)*. 3rd ed. Geneva: World Health Organization. https://www.who.int/publications/i/item/9789241580496.

———. 2020. "Zoonoses." World Health Organization, 29 July 2020. https://www.who.int/news-room/fact-sheets/detail/zoonoses.

Wu, Tong, Charles Perrings, Ann Kinzig, James P. Collins, Ben A. Minteer, and Peter Daszak. 2017. "Economic Growth, Urbanization, Globalization, and the Risks of Emerging Infectious Diseases in China: A Review." *Ambio* 46, no. 1 (August): 18–29. https://doi.org/10.1007/s13280-016-0809-2.

Youde, Jeremy. 2012. "Biosurveillance, Human Rights, and the Zombie Plague." *Global Change, Peace and Security* 24, no. 1 (January): 83–93. https://doi.org/10.1080/1478 1158.2012.641278.

Canadian National Security Operations during COVID-19

Stephanie Carvin

Introduction

The COVID-19 pandemic hit shortly after a profound period of change for the Canadian national security and intelligence community. Between 2017 and 2019, the Trudeau government engaged in the most extensive overhaul of the community's architecture since 1984. In this sense, many departments and agencies were still coming to grips with new authorities, legal regimes, and requirements as the lockdown took hold in March 2020.

This chapter uses interviews with members of the Canadian national security and intelligence community (or what I refer to as "the community") to examine how departments and agencies managed their operations during the COVID-19 crisis. It provides insight into how the community dealt with and responded to changes in the work environment and the threat environment. It concludes by examining how senior-level members of the national security and intelligence community think the pandemic experience may affect their future operations.

Methodology

This chapter is based on semi-structured interviews with ten senior management-level individuals in the Canadian national security and intelligence community, ranging from the Director General to the Assistant Deputy Minister levels. The advantage of interviewing senior managers is that they were generally familiar with the organization-wide response of their department or agency. Four interviewees were part of their organization's COVID-19 task force, established to manage employee safety while ensuring the continued operation of their organization's critical functions. The organizations represented in this study include the Canada Border Services Agency (CBSA); the Communications Security Establishment (CSE), including its outward-facing entity, the Canadian Centre for Cyber Security, or "Cyber Centre"; the Canadian Security Intelligence Service (CSIS); the Privy Council Office's Intelligence Assessment Secretariat (PCO IAS); and Public Safety Canada (PSC).[1]

Limitations

For reasons of time and availability, this study has certain limitations that the reader should bear in mind. First, I did not interview working-level employees of the agencies. Thus, it is essential to note that these individuals' experiences may be different from that of management. Second, I conducted interviews for this project in January and February of 2021. At this time, a second wave was cresting in Ontario and Quebec, where all of the organizations in this study are headquartered; this fact was captured in the interviews. However, the National Capital Region was also hard hit by a third wave in April and May 2021. Therefore it is important to note that the information in this article reflects the views of interviewees during a specific time during the pandemic, which may have evolved later. Finally, the small number of interviews means that this study provides a window into how national security organizations managed this crisis rather than a comprehensive overview.

National Security Organizations in "Phase Zero"

Unsurprisingly, one of the first significant challenges for the community as they turned to face a radically new working environment was their inability to access the classified networks necessary to send or receive intelligence products. This restriction made it impossible to hold basic conversations about classified or sensitive issues as regular telephone and internet communication channels are not secure. Even when employees could work in a secure compartmented information facility (SCIF), they often did so with reduced staff operating on a rotating schedule. These rotations meant that urgent messages sent to employees might not be read as soon as necessary if they were not scheduled to work in the SCIF that day. This section looks at how the community dealt with these challenges and the rapidly evolving technology issues by adapting business continuity plans, managing staffing, and addressing the stress and anxieties of employees.

Business Continuity

The majority of interviewees indicated that their department or agency had some kind of business continuity plan (BCP) in the case of a major disruption. Unfortunately, such plans proved to be inadequate almost immediately. In particular, many BCPs assumed that incidents preventing access to classified networks would be temporary, and that it would be possible to establish themselves at an alternative location within a few days or weeks. No organization had plans for a long-term disruption of employee access to classified networks or spaces to hold secure conversations. Therefore, as employees were sent home on the evening of 13 March 2020, plans to adapt existing BCPs to new realities were set in motion.

Even if existing BCPs were inadequate, organizations with BCPs benefited from the fact that their plans clearly identified which employees are "critical" and "essential." As one interviewee noted, at the very least, BCPs are good at "identifying critical systems and critical services." Therefore, while existing BCPs were often "not the correct playbook," the work of designating the agencies' critical functions was already complete. Other organizations seem to have relied on their ability to assess a worsening situation. Two interviewees reported situations where managers took it upon themselves to begin purchasing cleaning supplies by early March. As one interviewee noted, "Managers went out to find hand sanitizer at Walmart to ensure that critical staff had it."

After identifying the inadequacy of existing BCPs, organizations took various approaches to managing the business of national security in the early days of the pandemic, or, as several organizations referred to this period, "Phase Zero." CBSA, CSE, CSIS, and PSC interviewees reported that their organizations quickly set up a pandemic management committee, often including representatives from human resources, occupational health and safety, IT security, and senior executives. While most interviewees added that they incorporated the advice provided by the Public

Health Agency of Canada (PHAC) and the Treasury Board, some felt that the advice about procedures was "very slow" in terms of dissemination, leading them to establish their own processes to keep critical functions operating. One interviewee expressed frustration that there was sometimes an effort to ensure that things were done evenly across agencies, even if responsibilities may differ across units. In one case, an interviewee noted that there was pressure to conform to universal policies, even if units had vastly different tasks, responsibilities, and operating environments, or had put in place their own mitigation measures to reflect the working conditions in their office. In this sense, the interviewee felt that senior leadership wanted managers to "be creative," "but there was not a lot of serious options given."

Interviewees indicated that some organizations also turned to their international partners to exchange information on best practices. In particular, two interviewees noted that CSIS stayed in contact with international allies to "compare notes" as to how to function and maintain operations. As one observed, "We've stayed in close touch with all of our partners around the world. And I would say that all of us are tracking with the same challenges and the ways of being able to address them." CBSA stayed in contact with its "Border 5" (Five Eyes) partners to share advice on border management.

Staffing

Interviewees indicated that the most immediate critical task was figuring out staffing. According to one interviewee, maintaining "critical" functions at CSIS required 25 per cent operational capacity. Maintaining this capacity did not require 25 per cent of staff in the building at once, but over shifts, including evenings and weekends. Ultimately, every organization represented in this study adopted some kind of shift/rotation approach to staffing as it allowed staff to more safely access classified networks. Beyond this, individual organizations adopted other unique approaches to overcome this problem. One interviewee reported they were able to use their personal contacts with other government entities to use their SCIFs, augmenting the number of people that could access classified systems at one time. PSC looked at the jobs performed by staff and recombined them according to those that could be done entirely at home in an unclassified environment and those that required access to classified networks. Relocating tasks in this way allowed PSC to reduce the number of individuals who required access to a SCIF to do their work.

Managing Stress and Anxieties

Beyond being physically safe, a major concern reported by all interviewees was the mental health and well-being of the employees in their organizations. As one interviewee noted, individuals in the intelligence community "are used to uncertainty. But this was about their own circumstances and their work environment." Another noted, "it's not like a sustained crisis where it's a terrorism attack . . . and you're working on adrenaline. It's something outside our control."

Of course, the national security and intelligence community is not exceptional in this regard. Many of the issues and concerns are the same as those faced by other Government of Canada employees. These include anxieties about whether their workplaces were safe and having to work while home-schooling their children. However, the nature of some employees' work, especially those who needed to continue in-person meetings with sources or clients, raised additional concerns, particularly if they lived with vulnerable people at home.

Additionally, employees working on highly classified files still needed to come into the workplace. As one interviewee noted, sensitive discussions around cabinet conversations and most national security issues are, at a minimum, classified at the secret level. While top secret phones exist, interviewees described them as limited in their usefulness and connectivity. Moreover, some employees, such as client relations officers, have jobs that require them to meet with different people in secure locations across the government. This facet of their work increased their risk of coming into contact with someone who may have COVID-19. In such cases, interviewees indicated they needed to make sure that individuals undertaking this work did not put their families at risk.

Employees who were not coming into work also felt stressed. Interviewees from three organizations noted that staff told to stay home felt anxiety about their inability to do their jobs. Indeed, while their work may have been important, it was not required for the most critical functions of their respective agencies. "Some people were feeling like 'I need to get into the office. I need to do my job.' And they were really not feeling happy about being told, 'No, stay at home until we call you in.' "

On the other hand, some employees were "resentful" of their critical status. For example, there were cases where administrative assistants to senior managers were deemed critical, but senior managers overseeing high-level counterterrorism operations were not. In describing this issue, one interview said, "Even though you were essential in the BCP, we don't really need you. And even though you are not essential in the BCP, we do need you. That was a really, really tough thing to manage."

Different organizations took different steps to at least partially address these issues. Within the first few weeks of the pandemic, leadership sent frequent messages to staff about what was happening in the organization and different plans and procedures for moving ahead. CSIS set up unclassified speaking events and workshops on various topics, such as the 1918–19 Spanish flu, cyber vulnerabilities that come from working at home, and food supply chains, and child psychologists address how to handle working at home with kids and dealing with home-schooling. PSC reportedly surveyed individual employees about their personal circumstances and preferences to help re-prioritize and redistribute work. A high response rate to the surveys "helped us figure out what we have to tackle to get where we need to be." Where employees worked in a unionized environment, managers worked with the unions and labour relations to try and ensure that employees felt safe.

IT Services

Of note is the fact that almost all interviewees commented on the efforts of their IT teams to get individuals set up with equipment that allowed them to work with at least a very basic level of security. This equipment included phones, safes, secure video links, and computers secure to the "Protected B" level in most cases, and to the "Secret" level in others. One interviewee remarked that 99 per cent of their organization is now working with a protective device. "Once the pandemic hit, [IT Services] were shovelling out laptops very quickly. . . . It was a phenomenal ramp-up that worked really well." However, beyond being secure, these devices also meet archival requirements for oversight and review, so there continues to be a record of activities and decision-making while employees are working remotely.

It is not possible to come to definitive conclusions about the success of the efforts made to adjust to working in a pandemic environment. However, certain organizations appear to have been able to quickly return to a level of normalcy. PCO IAS returned to between 50 and 60 per cent capacity in the office within a month of the initial shutdown. CSIS reported that they returned to 80 per cent capacity by the beginning of January and, as noted above, a quick IT response meant that the Canadian Centre for Cybersecurity was able to adapt to a work-from-home environment within a few weeks.

A Different Kind of Threat Environment

As the pandemic continued, intelligence and national security agencies found themselves having to adjust to a new operating environment that impacted how they collected and assessed intelligence, raised new intelligence questions, and brought about a sudden surge in threat-related activities. In the words of one interviewee, the pandemic "amplified" vulnerabilities in Canada's critical infrastructure. Therefore, departments and agencies had to adapt quickly to an evolving threat landscape.

Collection Challenges

Intelligence collection is dependent on a number of sources, including information exchanged in meetings and via the movement of people and goods within Canada and across the border. In the immediate aftermath of the imposition of travel bans and lockdowns, the movement of illicit goods and intelligence targets slowed considerably. In some ways, these restrictions were an immediate security benefit: it became very difficult to engage in threat-related activities as malicious actors and contraband could not move about quickly or easily. As one interviewee noted, "our adversaries also dealt with COVID." For example, targets could not meet up in person, impacting their capacity to advance their operations. As another interviewee observed, "Certainly, a lot of the adversary behaviour, whether it's state actors or terrorists, if you can imagine, they can't travel. . . . That impacts us, and it impacted our adversaries equally."

However, interviewees pointed out that this positive side effect of the lockdowns also had two downsides, both of which manifested quickly. First, it is hard to target individuals who are not doing very much. As one interviewee noted, fewer people involved in activities means "that there is less intelligence. It is harder to fill in patterns and do risk assessments." Second, despite initial setbacks, actors involved in threat-related activities did not waste much time adapting to the new environment. "Eventually, malicious actors find new ways as a result of the pandemic." In the view of one interviewee, there are fewer malicious actors entering the country as a result of the pandemic. However, there has been an increase in the flow of many types of goods entering the country, raising a new set of security challenges. In particular, a significant increase in the volume of goods being shipped into the country means there is more to inspect and more opportunities for contraband to get through. Criminals realize this and try to take advantage of the situation.

Securing the Supply Chain

Related to the change in the flows of illicit goods is a series of challenges to the supply chain. In the first instance, there was concern that items coming into Canada, particularly personal protective equipment (PPE), were counterfeit. Unfortunately, while CBSA officers are trained in recognizing contraband, in the spring of 2020, they were less prepared to recognize fraudulent medical and health-related supplies. As one interviewee asked, "How do you know if PPE and testing kits coming into the country are fraudulent? We didn't have this expertise at first." The second issue of concern is the integrity of supply chains, especially as they relate to vaccines. At the time of writing, there was concern that malicious actors may seek to steal vaccines or damage or destroy them. In addition, given the urgency under which authorities are trying to bring vaccines into the country, there is a risk that malicious actors may attempt to exploit this process and use it to bring in contraband.

Cybersecurity

Most interviewees highlighted the pandemic's negative impact on cybersecurity as a particularly urgent threat. As one noted, "If there's a second pandemic, it is cybercrime." Importantly, interviewees pointed out that there was not necessarily an increase in the number of threat actors operating in this domain, but the methods they employed nonetheless became far more effective. As many individuals were worried about the pandemic and shortages, they were more likely to click on malicious links promising information on COVID-19, which then compromised their computers, networks, and/or data. Of particular and immediate concern in the initial weeks and months of the pandemic were techniques that impersonated Government of Canada websites and news outlets, and spam emails that appeared to contain urgent information about the virus, lockdowns, food and supply shortages, or other pandemic-related information. The effort to detect false information was complicated by the sudden and unprecedented transformation in how Canadians were now working—remotely, away from their IT departments and protected systems, on their home networks with unsecured Wi-Fi devices. This new environment created more opportunities for individuals to be targeted by malicious cyber actors while logging on to their work networks from home.

New Partners and Clients

The nature of the threat to medical goods and devices during the pandemic meant that national security and intelligence departments and agencies had to work with new and unconventional partners in the government, research, and private sectors. Although the PHAC has been recognized as a member of the broader national security and intelligence community for some time, there were few interactions between it and, for example, CBSA or CSIS. In addition, some departments that are wholly outside the community, such as Public Services and Procurement Canada, needed intelligence to guide their pandemic response.

Consequently, one of the obstacles to overcome was the fact that some of the core audiences for intelligence in the pandemic were unfamiliar with the products and how intelligence might inform policy-making. As one interviewee noted, "Some partners were very new at trying to manage this." Another interviewee noted that many of the new partners in the government sector did not have points of contact with collection agencies and had few employees with top secret clearance who could be briefed. "There's these new [client] departments, but we're probably not consumers of intelligence five years ago that sure need to be consumers of intelligence now."

However, working together is about more than providing intelligence analysis—some departments and agencies were actively involved in managing the transition to operating online. For example, CSE is responsible for the defence of Government of Canada systems. As such, they were responsible for assisting in the acceleration and acceptance of technological modernization, including cloud computing. They also provided support to departments and PHAC, who suddenly required a new set of tools and communication mechanisms.

The problem was arguably worse outside of the government sector. New threats put industries that had seldom been in contact with national security agencies and that employ few individuals with security clearance in the immediate spotlight. Intelligence collected in the early weeks of the pandemic indicated a surge in cyber attacks and interest from foreign governments in the biopharmaceutical and health sectors (Lathem 2020.) Companies and research institutes (both in the private sphere and at universities) did not understand the extent to which foreign governments would be interested in or target their work. However, unlike government departments and agencies, there is little support either in terms of advice or mitigation for private and academic entities. While the CSE may provide cybersecurity support to systems deemed critical to the Government of Canada with certain authorizations, most of the private sector falls outside this protection. Moreover, while the Cyber Centre can provide advice on threat mitigation, small and medium-sized enterprises may not have the resources to quickly or efficiently implement that advice.

Response

Given the changes to both the physical work environment and the threat environment, how did the Canadian national security and intelligence community respond? Interviewees indicated that although there was no overarching or coordinated strategy for the community, there were similarities in at least three respects: re-prioritization and adjustment, the development of new products, and reaching out to new audiences.

"Ruthless Prioritization" and Readjustment

One interesting finding of this study was that interviewees felt that their organizations had the appropriate mandates and authorities to counter the main threats posed by the pandemic. Although there was some discussion of the need for clarification in some respects (discussed below), no interviewee indicated that their organization required a new or enhanced mandate to cover their activities specifically related to the pandemic.[2]

Instead, interviewees indicated that from an intelligence-requirements perspective, the authorities to collect intelligence on the pandemic already existed while requirements shifted in significance. In this sense, the pandemic "was a new area to explore in terms of what the government was interested in . . . so we did shift to that."

However, the sudden "surge" in pandemic-related intelligence collection and analysis in a novel area required "ruthless prioritization." As one interviewee noted, "we have a whole production line and we had to go through an exercise of 'what do we really need'?' " Another interviewee noted, "we had to drop certain things because the most important thing was for senior executives to know what was going on. It went back to normal as the summer went on." As an example of such a compromise, PCO IAS turned a product typically distributed daily into one distributed every two to three days. CBSA analysts found themselves writing pieces that were more tactical than strategic, a transition described as "hard" but necessary.

In addition, to support these new priorities, there were changes in the kinds of information that clients wanted and, in turn, what units provided. One interviewee noted that senior clients were not necessarily looking for highly classified intelligence so much as briefings on what was happening from people expert at synthesizing information. More than usual, analytical intelligence units were valued for their skills, not just the intelligence they could provide.

New Products

Given the above-noted difficulties accessing classified spaces, most interviewees indicated that their department or agency developed new open-source intelligence products for their clients. The first kinds of products provided synthesized information for consumers. For example, PSC temporarily designed products to help amalgamate all of the different reports coming from the community to make the information more useful and accessible. CSIS's Academic Outreach and Stakeholder Engagement branch also created an open-source product that was a "two-page" roundup of think tank reports, podcasts, webinars, and various scholarly sources called "Need to Know." After it reportedly "exploded in popularity," CSIS turned the roundup into an official product put out every couple of weeks.

Open-Source Intelligence

However, the real transformation came with the increased use of open-source information to inform intelligence analysis. Even agencies that typically work at lower classification levels, such as CBSA, developed new open-source products. Products included a bi-weekly COVID-19 "snapshot," focused on border issues, written by the strategic intelligence team for senior management, and shared with partners.

One of the biggest shifts in this area was made by PCO-IAS. As one interviewee noted, "We had always tried to be all-source," but "many analysts believe that if it is not classified it is not an assessment." The pandemic forced a cultural transformation on this front: "Our ability to use open source meant that we had more information and that it was more timely." As the interviewee noted, "80 per cent of what we do is well covered in [open-source]. Twenty per cent of intelligence adds depth and colour to the understanding of an issue," but very little is truly unique information. As such, PCO IAS developed "commentaries" on topics such as the pandemic's impact on the economy, geopolitics, "mask diplomacy," and disinformation that were well-received and ultimately expanded its client base.

CSIS's intelligence assessment unit, the Intelligence Assessment Branch (IAB), was required to go through a similar transformation, particularly as senior leaders emphasized the need for outreach to the broader research and life sciences communities and their supply chains to help mitigate threats. As one interviewee noted, the Branch is very good at providing classified information or briefings but "they are maybe a little bit less comfortable doing the open-source stuff." The interviewee noted that IAB is "getting really good at [such work]," but that most of the unclassified briefings ultimately were provided by CSIS's Academic Outreach and Stakeholder Engagement branch.

Similarly, the Canadian Centre for Cyber Security worked to produce more content at the unclassified level. They adopted the "Traffic Light Protocol" for many of their products. Designed to facilitate information sharing between the government, the private sector, and other key stakeholders, the Traffic Light Protocol uses four colours to indicate expected sharing boundaries for recipients of the information. Used by national security agencies in other countries, such as the United States, it enabled the Cyber Centre to pass on sensitive information. Information flagged as "red" may not be shared beyond the direct recipient; "yellow" is information that may be shared within an organization and certain clients on a need-to-know basis; "green" information may be shared with peers and partner organizations; and "white" information may be distributed without restriction. Adopting this protocol enabled the Cyber Centre to provide more meaningful advice and information to those outside the government.

Similarly, interviewees indicated that CSE developed lower-classified products (Protected B) that built on knowledge informed by intelligence that could be distributed to clients in order "to remain relevant and helpful and to really find out where our value added is." These products have reportedly received good feedback from clients who are working from home: "They appreciated it, they could use it, they could communicate it, they could make decisions based on it. . . . There was a benefit to folks to receive those things, so absolutely we want to continue that work." However, it was also clear that there were limits to the open-source transformation. In the view of one interviewee, the clear and obvious specific value proposition of CSE for the Government of Canada is the provision of information from the global information infrastructure. "I'm very mindful that our business is special," reported one interviewee, "and we should . . . make sure we maximize that."

Educating and Understanding New Audiences

As noted above, most national security agencies made efforts to reach new audiences within the government and the private sector. An increase in the number of intelligence products and briefings that are unclassified or of low classification appears to have helped drive this interest. However, the process of serving new clients can generate certain challenges. Interviewees spoke of a need to "educate stakeholders, both in government but also in the private sector." According to one interviewee, "Initially, it was, frankly, ensuring that decision-makers know that intelligence plays a role. That may not be their first instinct, typically." As such, agencies needed to expend time to "better inform key stakeholders, government stakeholders, of the type of intelligence that can be produced and why it would play such a key role."

Importantly, interviewees stressed that the developing relationship between national security and intelligence agencies, non-traditional government partners, and the private sector is mutually beneficial. Interviewees indicated that there were at least three benefits for the community from these exchanges. First, one interviewee noted, "for us, it is a two-way street," meaning that meeting with new partners helped provide a better understanding of what and where the vulnerabilities are and allowed agencies to tailor their intelligence requirements. Providing threat briefings also helped intelligence-collection agencies better understand their policy clients' needs: "When they see what we can bring, it's really a partnership because they explain their processes, the procedures, and then we can help fill those gaps."

Second, knowledge from the policy community helped educate and better prepare the community for certain tasks or fill intelligence gaps. An example of this is the need to protect the integrity of supply chains. As noted above, intelligence and law-enforcement individuals did not have training or expertise in recognizing fraudulent medical devices. Therefore, a lot of effort in the first weeks of the pandemic went toward finding the expertise necessary to stop goods at the border, often from non-traditional or policy partners.

Finally, following briefings and exchanges with non-traditional partners, clients better understood and recognized threat-related activities. Armed with this new knowledge, clients would often contact intelligence and national security agencies when they spotted something suspicious. An interviewee noted that collection agencies were also "getting leads from those organizations" due to these exchanges. Once educated on what threat-related activities are and whom they should contact, new partners were "phoning us because they've come across information of concern and they want our feedback on it. They benefit, we benefit."

Conclusion: Future Implications

Findings from the interviews indicate that—as is almost certainly the case in other areas of government—senior managers and executives within the Canadian national security and intelligence community are evaluating the future implications of the pandemic in terms of how their organizations will fulfill their mandates. This final section provides an overview of these assessments, beginning with trends in how threat information is conveyed, followed by expectations for the working environment, and concluding with challenges the community is likely to face.

Acceleration

One of the most consistent findings is that the pandemic accelerated changes that were already taking place in the community. As one interviewee noted, all of the changes planned for 2023 were in place by April 2020. In the case of the CSE/Cyber Centre, interviewees identified three key areas of acceleration: accepting and modernizing new technology; the kinds of advice the centre provides to Canadians; and engagement with critical infrastructure and private sector stakeholders in the face of sophisticated cyber threats.

Out of the Shadows

Whether it was interest driven by new open-source, unclassified, or low-classification products, outreach to new partners in the private sector, official statements and speeches, or engaging with the media, the community has arguably never engaged so thoroughly with others. In 2020, CSIS's Academic Outreach and Stakeholder Engagement branch gave threat briefings to over 400 companies, representing over two thousand people. These numbers include briefings to over forty universities in each of the ten provinces. The branch also gave an interview to discuss its activities to the Public Policy Forum (Lathem 2020). In February 2021, CSIS's Director gave a speech hosted by the Centre for International Governance Innovation (CIGI) in which he publicly acknowledged China and Russia as threat actors engaged in economic espionage and foreign influence activity (CSIS 2021). This was the first time in decades—if ever—that someone in his position made such a declaration. Early in the pandemic, CSE also publicly noted that it was involved in taking down websites involved in COVID-19 fraud—the first public acknowledgement of this kind of action (Tunney 2020). Additionally, CSE publicly attributed a cyber-espionage campaign to Russia (CSE 2020).

There are several reasons for this increase in the level of public interaction. First, in recent years, as the targets of threat-related activities moved from the government to the private sector, there has been a gradual recognition that there is a need for the community to be more publicly engaged and to speak clearly to stakeholders. Building on the point made above, this, too, has been accelerated by the pandemic. As one interviewee noted, "The media stuff is just stuff we do now. It's just life. It's weird and we live with it." Second, interviewees noted that when intelligence agencies make statements or attribute malicious activities, it generates media attention and interest from members of the private sector, who become concerned that they may be targeted. This concern makes public outreach to the private sector easier and more likely to continue.

Exploiting Open-Source Resources

To facilitate more engagement with non-traditional partners and the private sector, to augment their capabilities, and to produce products that can reach a larger number of clients, it is very likely that many parts of the intelligence and national security community will continue to use more open-source information. While interviewees noted that there are still pockets of resistance in intelligence analysis units, open-source information means simply having more resources and often more timely information since analysts do not have to wait on collection. One interviewee noted that Canada's allies are opening centres of excellence to exploit this information, which will likely increase the incentive to develop similar capabilities in Canada and to increase the legitimacy of open-source information as a resource more generally. Importantly, this does not necessarily mean that agencies are switching to producing unclassified products; open-source assessments often remain classified because they have foreign policy implications. However, this will likely make the sharing of such products easier. In this regard, the Cyber Centre's use of the Traffic Light Protocol may be a model for the rest of the community.

Spying from Home?

An interesting finding is the extent to which most interviewees felt that national security and intelligence departments and agencies operate will change. In particular, many of the interviewees felt that the work environment would be far more flexible in the future. The main reason they gave for this is that the private sector is heading in a similar direction, and so national security and intelligence agencies will need to offer more flexible conditions to attract and maintain talent. As one interviewee asked, "How does the service remain competitive? Our Intelligence Officers are probably going to still come in the door and our analysts, maybe. But human resources, finance, policy people. . . . How do I recruit a really good policy person who is getting a similar job offer at the Department of Fisheries and Oceans and just would prefer to be able to have time to be able to work from home?"

Indeed, it seems clear that working from home or a more flexible workday/workweek is very popular in some parts of the national security and intelligence community. A survey conducted by PSC in July 2020 found that only 9 per cent of employees wanted to return to working in an office full-time. As an interviewee noted, "the work situation will never return to the way it was, and this is a great thing. It will free people to be more productive." They noted, for example, that many employees were spending less time commuting.

However, not everyone interviewed was convinced that this would happen. One interviewee noted that they were hopeful that the more flexible arrangements would remain but said that "this experience should change the way things work, but I am cynical." Another remarked that there were advantages to adopting a more flexible approach to work, such as the ability to recruit talent from across the country more easily, but that it will ultimately depend on the preferences of high-level officials, such as Deputy Ministers. Given that many senior managers like having their people around them, "in a lot of other areas we will see business as usual." Of note, even where individuals were optimistic about change, they suggested that the community has been "slow off the mark" because "it does require a significant investment of resources, time, and energy." Thus, while there is a clear desire for change, what the future of work looks like for the Canadian intelligence and national security community remains to be seen.

Widening National Security?

A final trend identified through the interviews concerns the belief of many in the community that the scope of national security and the kinds of intelligence that they collect should expand. As noted above, all agencies interviewed faced new requirements (or a change in priorities) to support government decision-making and to counter threats related to the pandemic. Yet, interviewees overwhelmingly indicated that they had the mandate and authorities to collect the intelligence needed by the government. So, what is the case for expansion?

First, information from the interviews indicates that conversations are taking place within their organizations about the need to change the way the community is managed. In an age marked by hyperconnectivity, increasing threats to critical infrastructure, and our dependencies on the Internet, interviewees argue that the government needs to improve the integration and enhance the centralization of the national security and intelligence community. One interviewee noted that the community needs to review how it manages early warning, how intelligence assessment informs policy-making, and how the community works with non-traditional partners. However, the community's future success also depends upon whether it can improve the way its intelligence products inform decision-making. This will require efforts to maintain the ad hoc relationships and arrangements created during the pandemic so that they are carried forward into the future.

Other interviewees felt that Canada needs to widen the scope of its intelligence activities from a narrow threat focus to one more closely tied to Canada's broader national interests. In the words of one interviewee, "the discussion needs to be about what are, and how do we protect, our national interests and get away from a security-service mentality to an intelligence-service discussion. What do we want from our intelligence service? What do we want from intelligence? What do we need as policy-makers from an intelligence service?" In other words, to be more relevant to government decision-making and to better understand future threats, the community needs to move beyond its current approach of (mostly) focusing on threat intelligence and instead adopt a wider approach that looks at future disruptive challenges coming over the horizon.

At What Cost?

As noted above, interviewees confirmed that the pandemic required the community to collect intelligence and/or develop expertise in new areas or areas that had not been the focus of much attention in the past. However, they also noted that this came with a price: long-term strategic planning was dropped in favour of generating immediate tactical information. One interviewee offered the following observation: "You're just, like . . . 'We're going to do the things that are the most important, and that's the way it's going to be.' . . . The downside of that is clearly that those other things, like nice-to-do things . . . had to drop off because they require time, attention. . . . I think those are the things that we had to let drop that folks are anxious to get back to." As such, while there may currently be interest in widening the mandate of the intelligence and national security community to look at issues such as health intelligence, or other larger strategic issues, if this is done without community coordination and an allocation of appropriate resources, there may be a cost in terms of losing focus on other more traditional areas of concern. This may be a positive change for some, but re-prioritization without care may leave new gaps where old requirements once existed.

A widened approach that draws the community's focus away from threats toward interests—the latter being a more contestable concept given that the former is defined in law—is a significant, if not radical, step for Canada. It would almost certainly require new legislation, new authorities, and, ultimately, a new debate about what we want our national security and intelligence agencies to do. I have already expressed concerns that widening the community's mandate to include areas like health and the environment could entail the securitization of these issues—political problems that require political solutions (Carvin and Davis 2020). Nevertheless, this chapter's findings are indisputable: a widening of mandates is on the minds of community leaders. Although it is far from clear whether the Canadian government wishes to tread such a path, it will be an important post-COVID-19 development to observe in the coming months and years.

NOTES

1   This project was subject to ethics approval by Carleton University's Office of Research Ethics (Project #115056). Interviewees were promised anonymity, but permission was sought to identify organizations where it was deemed important for clarity.

2   However, it should be noted that in interviews and in public statements, CSIS officials have indicated that they believe that, generally speaking, their authorities are increasingly out of date and that this is a problem when it comes to fulfilling their mandate. In interviews, CSIS officials confirmed they believed they could collect for the new intelligence requirements related to the pandemic. Nevertheless, they stress that there are presently challenges that need to be addressed, such as technological limitations on intelligence collection that was not foreseen by the drafters of the *CSIS Act* in 1984. See CSIS (2021).

REFERENCES

Carvin, Stephanie, and Jessica Davis. 2020. "National Security and Pandemics: The Limits of Early Warning." *Policy Options*, 24 April 2020. https://policyoptions.irpp.org/magazines/april-2020/national-security-and-pandemics-the-limits-of-early-warning/.

CSE (Communications Security Establishment). 2020. "CSE Statement on Threat Activity Targeting COVID-19 Vaccine Development." Government of Canada, last modified 16 July 2020. https://www.cse-cst.gc.ca/en/media/2020-07-16.

CSIS (Canadian Security Intelligence Service). 2021. "Remarks by Director David Vigneault to the Centre for International Governance Innovation." Government of Canada, last modified 9 February 2021. https://www.canada.ca/en/security-intelligence-service/news/2021/02/remarks-by-director-david-vigneault-to-the-centre-for-international-governance-innovation.html.

Lathem, Catherine. 2020. "A Pivotal Moment: CSIS Steps Out of the Shadows to Protect Canada's Biopharmaceutical and Healthcare Sectors during the COVID-19 Pandemic." *Public Policy Forum*, 23 November 2020. https://ppforum.ca/publications/a-pivotal-moment-csis-steps-out-of-the-shadows/.

Tunney, Catharine. 2021. "Canada's Cyber Spies Taking Down Sites as Battle against COVID-19 Fraud Begins." *CBC News*, 23 March 2021. https://www.cbc.ca/news/politics/cse-disinformation-spoofing-1.5504619.

Collection and Protection in the Time of Infection: The Communications Security Establishment during the COVID-19 Pandemic

Bill Robinson

Introduction

For the Communications Security Establishment (CSE), Canada's national cryptologic agency, the COVID-19 pandemic has presented great challenges, but it has also presented opportunities. A free-standing department housed in the portfolio of the Minister of National Defence, CSE has two primary missions: protecting the electronic communications, data holdings, and information-processing activities of the federal government and other designated institutions from theft or interference (known as information technology security [ITSEC], or more recently cyber security); and providing intelligence on the electronic communications, data holdings, and information-processing activities of foreign governments and other foreign entities of interest (known as signals intelligence [SIGINT]). Like all government institutions, CSE has faced the simultaneous challenges of maintaining essential operations and protecting its workforce from the pandemic. But COVID-19 also posed the urgent new task of ensuring the electronic security of public servants across the government who were suddenly directed to work from home. Protecting the country's health system and research institutions from pandemic-related cyber threats also became a top priority. Meanwhile, the demands for intelligence production levied on the SIGINT side of the agency remained as high as ever, while new pandemic-related intelligence concerns arose and pressure to exploit the intelligence-gathering opportunities presented by COVID-19 was probably also high.

This chapter looks at the challenges that the COVID-19 pandemic has posed for CSE, focusing first on the agency's cybersecurity role and then on its signals intelligence role. It then looks at the special problems of workforce protection posed for CSE by the fact that much of its work cannot be performed outside the office. The concluding section considers whether CSE's experience during the pandemic holds lessons for the agency's future operations.

When the COVID-19 pandemic arrived, CSE was already in the midst of adapting to major changes in its mission and operating environment. Among other measures, Bill C-59, adopted in mid-2019, included the *Communications Security Establishment Act*, a sweeping overhaul of the statute governing the agency's operations that added to its mission the conduct of offensive and defensive cyber operations. C-59 also replaced the oversight and review mechanisms for the agency, establishing entirely new organizations with broadened mandates (see Bill C-59, *An Act Respecting National Security Matters*, S.C., 2019, c. 13). The agency was also still adjusting to the 2018 creation of the Canadian Centre for Cyber Security, which amalgamated under CSE the IT security branch of the agency and most of the cybersecurity elements of Shared Services Canada[1] and Public Safety Canada (CSE 2018). The Cyber Centre, as it is often called, was still in the process of consolidating these disparate elements into a unified organization and moving its core operations to a new headquarters when the pandemic struck. CSE had to accommodate these changes and adjust to continuing technological flux across the agency's mission areas while absorbing ongoing staff and budget growth in both the cybersecurity and SIGINT programs. CSE has tripled in size since 2001, and it may still be growing (Robinson 2021a). The arrival of COVID-19 added an entirely new set of challenges with respect to operational priorities, operational tempo, and workforce safety.

Cybersecurity Operations

The most obvious effects of the pandemic have been on the cybersecurity side of CSE's operations. The federal government's March 2020 decision to quickly transition as much of the public service as possible to working from home created an enormous increase in demand for secure online access to government IT systems. As the technical authority on cybersecurity issues for the federal government and operator of its cyber defence systems, CSE has played a key role in supporting the rollout of pandemic-related online services for the Canadian public and the efforts of Shared Services Canada to provide secure and reliable services for online meetings of cabinet, virtual meetings of Parliament, and online access to government IT systems and databases by public servants at a scale far in excess of anything previously envisaged. The government provided an additional $114 million in October 2020 to support these efforts, of which $6.3 million went to CSE (Treasury Board of Canada 2020, 1-15). The agency also received a $47 million increase in budget authority in February 2021, but the portion of that sum that was related to pandemic efforts has not been disclosed (Treasury Board of Canada 2021, 2-15).

In addition to supporting the activities of the federal government, the Cyber Centre has provided cybersecurity advice and services to Canadian public and private health institutions and other pandemic-related private-sector activities such as vaccine research and development. The kinds of threats that such entities face include

- criminal efforts to steal and sell intellectual property (IP) or to use "ransomware" to encrypt the computer systems and data of vital institutions and demand payment for their decryption;
- state-sponsored efforts to steal IP or other confidential pandemic-related information; and
- efforts by states or other malicious actors to sabotage Canadian pandemic response efforts.

In addition to issuing its own public warnings and advisories directed at the health sector (e.g., CSE 2020b, 2020e, 2020h), the Cyber Centre issued at least one joint advisory with the Canadian Security Intelligence Service (CSIS 2020). The Cyber Centre also joined its counterparts in the United Kingdom and the United States to issue a public warning in July 2020 about the efforts of Russian intelligence services to steal "information and intellectual property relating to the development and testing of COVID-19 vaccines" (CSE 2020a). To help research organizations assess whether their systems had been compromised, the accompanying advisory included technical details of the tactics, techniques, and procedures used by the Russian intelligence services. More targeted outreach was also undertaken. During the first year of the pandemic,

> the Cyber Centre established new partnerships with over 100 health sector organizations, including provincial and territorial regional health authorities, patient care facilities, and organizations involved in the development, manufacture and delivery of COVID-19 vaccines. . . . Throughout 2020 the Cyber Centre held weekly video calls with over 100 representatives from the health sector to share practical advice and answer questions about cyber threats. In 2021, these calls are continuing on a bi-weekly basis (CSE 2021a).

The Cyber Centre also assisted in the development of a "cyber-survey tool to provide health sector organizations such as hospitals, doctors' offices and long-term care facilities, among others, with an easy-to-use tool to assess the cybersecurity of their organization" (Standing Committee on Health 2020, 21).

Since the passage of the *CSE Act*, the Minister of National Defence has had the option to designate entities outside the federal government (e.g., telecommunications companies, electricity providers, other levels of government) as infrastructures of importance to the Government of Canada. This designation opens the way for the Cyber Centre to provide additional services to these entities, such as monitoring the activity on their IT networks. However, such assistance can only be provided following a formal request from the recipient and, if required by the type of assistance sought, the issuance of a valid ministerial authorization. Cyber Centre head Scott Jones has testified that such support is offered only in special cases of particular importance where commercial cybersecurity services are unlikely to be sufficient (Standing Committee on Industry, Science and Technology 2020, 15). The government will not confirm whether any organizations associated with Canada's pandemic response have received this designation or are being provided such services.[2]

Publicly available information suggests that Canada's health institutions have weathered these threats quite well. According to the Cyber Centre, "a Canadian biopharmaceutical company was compromised by a foreign cyber threat actor almost certainly attempting to steal its intellectual property" in April 2020 (CSE 2020e). The first publicly identified intrusion, minor in its effects, hit a hospital network in Montreal in October 2020 (Tu and Freeze 2020). Two months later, CSE reported that "multiple Canadian hospitals have suffered ransomware attacks in recent months," referencing the Montreal case in particular (CSE 2020d). Overall, the Cyber Centre "issued over 20 cyber alerts to health sector partners and provided incident response support in more than 85 cases affecting the sector" in 2020–21 (CSE 2021a). To date, however, no major incidents have been identified.

Another role of the Cyber Centre is to provide cybersecurity advice and guidance to the broader Canadian public. Since the start of the pandemic, this has included advice on avoiding online hazards such as malicious websites, emails, and texts that seek to exploit COVID-19 concerns to deliver malware or collect personal data, including sites imitating Government of Canada sites offering COVID-19 information or pandemic income support and other services (CSE 2020c, 2020d). The Cyber Centre has also worked proactively with industry partners, including commercial and international Cyber Incident Response Teams, to shut down such activities, and it provides lists of malicious websites to the Canadian Internet Registration Authority's "Canadian Shield" domain name server, which automatically protects users of that service from connecting to them. Between March 2020 and July 2021, the Cyber Centre contributed to the removal of "more than 8,600 websites, social media accounts, and email servers impersonating the Government of Canada" (CSE 2021b). The Cyber Centre also produced a security assessment of the COVID Alert mobile app launched by the government in July 2020 to notify users of possible exposures to the virus (CSE 2021c).

Active cyber operations (ACO) and defensive cyber operations (DCO) have been another potential avenue for action by CSE. These could be used, for example, to interfere with the computer systems of malicious cyber actors targeting Canadians. The power to conduct such activities, more commonly called computer network attack or cyber attack operations, is a new element of CSE's mandate, granted only in 2019. Each operation requires specific ministerial approvals (CSE 2020f). CSE has begun receiving such approvals (NSIRA 2020, 25), but the agency will neither confirm nor deny that ACO/DCO measures have been employed for COVID-19-related matters.[3] Cyber operations have been characterized by the Cyber Centre as a last-resort measure, and thus their use, if any, has probably been limited. For now, the agency will state only that it "continues to leverage all aspects of our mandate to ensure that Canada is protected against cyber-threats and that the Government of Canada has access to information that can help inform decisions on Canada's approach to COVID-19" (Standing Committee on Government Operations and Estimates 2020, 10). CSE's Five Eyes partners have been more forthcoming on this question, with Australia (Australia 2020) and the United Kingdom (Fisher and Smyth 2020) both confirming the use of cyber attack capabilities against COVID-19-associated targets.

SIGINT Operations

The SIGINT side of CSE accounts for about 70 per cent of the agency's staff and budget resources (Robinson 2021a). Mandated to produce intelligence in response to Canadian government priorities (and also to conduct cyber operations), this part of the agency is by necessity even less forthcoming about the details of its work. However, it is likely that the advent of the pandemic has led to a rebalancing of the agency's intelligence-collection and intelligence-production priorities.

Collecting intelligence in support of the agency's cybersecurity activities—monitoring the plans, activities, and capabilities of foreign cyber threat actors—was already an important pre-pandemic role on the SIGINT side. Given the sweeping new vulnerabilities that were created across Canada in both the public and private sectors by the shift to working from home, it is likely that cybersecurity support was given even higher priority during the pandemic. Other COVID-19-related intelligence is also likely to have been a high priority. Probable topics of interest include pandemic-related developments and plans in other countries, particularly those suspected of withholding information from the international community, and intelligence about activities that might undermine Canada's pandemic response. In addition to threats to IT systems, the latter might include theft of intellectual property or disruption operations such as cyber-enabled influence campaigns that seek to undermine Canada's COVID-19 response or leverage concerns about the pandemic to advance other agendas (CSE 2021a). CSE may also have sought intelligence in support of Canadian COVID-related procurement activities abroad, such as information about the availability and quality of supplies of personal protective equipment and, conceivably, confidential details of foreign vaccine and treatment technologies.

The likely consumers of intelligence on topics such as these would include CSE's primary customers—the Privy Council Office and Prime Minister's Office; Global Affairs Canada; the Canadian Security Intelligence Service; the Royal Canadian Mounted Police; and the Department of National Defence/Canadian Armed Forces—but also Innovation, Science and Economic Development Canada; Public Services and Procurement Canada; and of course, Health Canada. Even before the pandemic, CSE had a memorandum of understanding in place with Health Canada governing the provision of SIGINT to both the department and the Public Health Agency of Canada. The agreement, signed in 2008, specifically noted that "A key focus of [Health Canada] is to maintain a pandemic preparedness plan" (CSE 2008). CSE has not revealed, however, whether it actually collected and provided Health Canada with any information useful for pandemic warning or preparedness in the period prior to the emergence of the COVID-19 pandemic, or whether such information, if provided, was employed in any way in subsequent decision-making.

In addition to pandemic-related questions, CSE's pre-pandemic intelligence priorities—encompassing permanent concerns such as North American security, counterterrorism, diplomatic and prosperity issues, and support to military operations—have remained important. Emphasis may have been reduced on some of these priorities as a short-term measure, but it is also likely that temporary collection opportunities have arisen across many topics as a result of the global shift to working from home and other disruptions caused by the pandemic. The agency will have wanted to seize those opportunities while they existed, not only to collect information in the moment but to establish footholds in target IT systems that CSE may be able to exploit after the return to more normal conditions.

The combination of these factors—new pandemic-related priorities and persisting priorities with new opportunities—means that pressure to maintain a high operations tempo on the SIGINT side will have been high.

The agency "reinvented" the way it packaged its intelligence reports in 2020–21 "to provide critical information about the pandemic more quickly, and in a more digestible format. We also adjusted our dissemination approach to be able to securely deliver timely intelligence to a wider group of government clients, including clients working remotely." However, the number of SIGINT clients served by CSE fell significantly—from 2,100 in 2019–20 to 1,450 in 2020–21—probably reflecting a lack of secure delivery options for lower-priority clients working from home (CSE 2021a).

Another motive for maintaining operations on the SIGINT side of the agency is to sustain the large inflows of data and reporting that CSE receives from partner agencies. Canadian reports account for less than 10 per cent of the SIGINT reports typically available to Canadian SIGINT customers, with most of the remainder coming from CSE's Five Eyes partners, primarily the National Security Agency (NSA) in the United States, but also the United Kingdom's Government Communications Headquarters, the Australian Signals Directorate, and New Zealand's Government Communications Security Bureau (Robinson 2020, 105). It is also vital to CSE and the wider Canadian intelligence community that CSE maintain its own provision of data and reporting to its foreign partners. The privileged access that Canada has to the output of its intelligence partners depends ultimately on the continuing contribution that Canada makes to the collective intelligence pool. As Canada's main collector of foreign intelligence, CSE is the primary Canadian contributor to that pool, providing intelligence end product reports and other reporting produced by CSE and the Canadian Forces Information Operations Group, the military organization that collects SIGINT for CSE and the Canadian Armed Forces;

bulk metadata ("minimized" to withhold information about Canadians); and communications intercepts collected by Canada on behalf of partner agencies. Intercepts acquired for partners are collected using selectors (email addresses, phone numbers, etc.) supplied by those partners and examined by CSE collection managers to ensure they are consistent with Canadian priorities and directions on intelligence collection and do not target Canadians or persons in Canada. If approved, they are then forwarded to Canadian collection systems (CSE 2012, 21). Canada's Five Eyes partners would surely sympathize if pandemic response measures caused some disruption to these activities, but they would also take note, and the continued operation of these approval, collection, and forwarding processes has undoubtedly been given very high priority by CSE.

Workforce Protection Issues

Like other parts of the intelligence community, CSE has faced special difficulties in balancing its need to maintain a high operational tempo with its need to protect its workforce from COVID-19. Public servants across much of the federal government have been able to work from home during much of the pandemic, but this option is not available to those whose work can only be done in high-security office spaces. A large part of CSE's work, especially on the SIGINT side of the agency, cannot be done from home or even in a normal office, but must be carried out within CSE's "secure compartmented information facility" (SCIF) spaces within its headquarters, the Edward Drake Building. This is a requirement not just of the Canadian government, but also of CSE's Five Eyes partners. As noted above, much of the SIGINT data and reporting that CSE is able to draw on to support its Canadian clients originates with those partners, and the sharing of that material with CSE is contingent on Canada's continued observance of the agreed security procedures for its handling.

CSE would not provide information on the extent to which SIGINT personnel may have been directed to stay at home at various points during the pandemic, on the grounds that this would be too revealing of the agency's capabilities.[4] However, some information is available about other parts of the Canadian intelligence community. The Canadian Forces Information Operations Group reduced peak-hours staffing at its main intercept station at Canadian Forces Station Leitrim in Ottawa by as much as 40 per cent from late March to May 2020, with occupancy returning to near-normal levels only in the fall (Robinson 2021b). Similarly, the Integrated Terrorism Assessment Centre (ITAC), located next door to CSE in the CSIS building, cut back the number of people working in its offices by as much as 80 per cent during the early days of the pandemic. Even by mid-summer 2020, the number of people working in ITAC spaces was only half the normal level, while by the fall, following renovations to improve the safety of the centre, around three-quarters of personnel were back.[5] CSIS seems to have followed a broadly similar trajectory with its own personnel at its Ottawa building (Robinson 2021b).

A comparison with other Five Eyes SIGINT agencies can also be instructive. Even in New Zealand, which was highly successful in suppressing the spread of COVID-19, the Government Communications Security Bureau initially "reduced staffing levels and limited staff numbers around [its] facilities by moving to shift working, with weekly rotations" (New Zealand 2020). Similarly, NSA and GCHQ, the American and British SIGINT agencies, both implemented sharp reductions in workforce attendance around the end of March 2020, followed by a gradual return to higher occupancy over the summer and fall. Interestingly, the major COVID-19 waves of the winter of 2020–21 and the spring of 2021 do not seem to have caused a similar retreat by these agencies, possibly indicating that modifications to occupancy practices and the workspaces themselves were by that time considered sufficient to protect their workforces (Robinson 2021b). It seems likely, therefore, that CSE applied at least some reductions in office occupancy during the pandemic's first wave in the spring of 2020. CSE may also have made some changes during the second and third waves (Robinson 2021b).

The problem of secure workspaces is much less acute on the cybersecurity side of CSE, where a portion of the Cyber Centre's work must be conducted in a SCIF, but much can also be performed at lower levels of classification, including, in many cases, the unclassified level. In fact, when the pandemic hit, the Cyber Centre was in the process of moving most of its personnel from the high-security Edward Drake Building on Ogilvie Road to new leased spaces in a commercial building at 1625 Vanier Parkway. Close to 800 of CSE's 3,000 employees will eventually be housed in this building. Many of these employees have been able to work from home, communicating with the office and each other over a CSE virtual private network suitable for material up to the Protected B level. Only when higher-security matters arise have they had to come into one of the buildings, where they can work on the "high side." This has also meant there is spare space in the Vanier Parkway building where other CSE employees, such as administrative support personnel, can work if they need office accommodations but not Drake-level security. CSE has acknowledged that it was "very fortunate" to have this space available when the pandemic arrived.[6]

The combination of work from home and the shift of Cyber Centre and other employees to the Vanier Parkway building will have made it much easier for CSE to provide physically distanced workspaces for those members of the workforce who do require the Edward Drake Building for most of their work. SIGINT analysts spend part of their time staying current with news reports and other open-source information related to their SIGINT targets, and although they would have to be careful to avoid revealing those targets, they could in principle read this sort of unclassified material at the Vanier Parkway offices, or possibly at home. Still, the great bulk of SIGINT work can only be performed in the Edward Drake Building. Here, too, CSE argues that it has been fortunate in that the Edward Drake Building is a new facility (occupied only in 2015) featuring a modern and efficient ventilation system.[7] At the time of its construction, the workspaces in the building were reportedly entirely open concept, with separate rooms for meetings but no private offices (Weston 2013) (Pod 1 of the complex, CSE's high-performance computing centre, may be an exception as it was constructed as part of a separate project). The open nature of the building has probably eased the problem of ensuring appropriate physical distancing of the SIGINT workforce. According to the agency, among other measures, it has

> staggered and reconfigured workstations to ensure two metres of physical distancing. We have significantly increased cleaning and sanitization of our facilities, focusing on high-touch surfaces. There are hand sanitization stations throughout our facilities. We have closed or reconfigured many of our

common areas. Masks are mandatory any time employees are not seated at a safely distanced desk.[8]

Another way to enhance physical distancing within the Edward Drake Building is to utilize the building more intensively outside traditional office hours. A portion of the CSE workforce has always been on shift work to provide a minimal 24/7 operations capability, but this is quite small, leaving the building largely unoccupied during nights and weekends. When employees currently working primarily at home need to visit the office, the agency has sought to schedule those visits during these less crowded times.[9] CSE has also acknowledged "staggering [its] work schedules" (CSE 2021a), but it is not clear whether the agency made any effort to move a significant number of traditional day workers to other shifts. Shift work is never popular and would pose great problems for some employees, but it might be workable as a relatively limited and short-term expedient. The collective agreement CSE has with the Public Service Alliance of Canada enables the agency to schedule shift work when needed to meet its operational requirements (CSE 2015), and it is possible that it undertook some effort to transfer work outside of the normal Monday-to-Friday day-shift hours. Some agencies in the US intelligence community reportedly did this, moving "their employees and contractors into rotating shifts, where some worked from 6 a.m. to 2 p.m., and a new group came into the classified office space to work from 3 to 11 p.m." (Ogrysko 2020). The NSA may have been one of the agencies that did this at some points during the pandemic (Robinson 2021b).

Another workforce-protection measure has been the conversion of public events to an online format. For example, CSE's GeekWeek conference, an annual unclassified event designed to "foster collaboration between the Government of Canada, critical infrastructure partners and academic researchers to address vital problems facing the cyber security industry," was held entirely online in 2020 (CSE 2020g). University recruitment events have also been moved online, as have student internships. In a typical year, CSE hosts up to four hundred students on three-month internships, but during the pandemic all interns have worked exclusively from home.

CSE's workforce-protection measures appear to have been successful, as the agency reported that no cases of workplace transmission of the virus were recorded during 2020–21 (CSE 2021a). (No information is available about cases that may have occurred later in 2021, during the third and fourth waves of the pandemic.)

Work-life balance is another aspect of workforce management that CSE will have had to address. With the closure of schools and daycares for extended periods during the pandemic, employees with young children have had to juggle job requirements with the need to provide full-time child care, a task that commonly falls disproportionately on women. In 2017–18, women accounted for 37.3 per cent of the CSE workforce, with approximately half working in "a corporate function" such as policy, administration, and public communications (NSICOP 2020, 20). Such jobs are more likely than most at CSE to be at least partly transferable to home, which could ease the problem for those workers of ensuring that someone is available to supervise children or other dependents, but it also increases the probability that this task will fall more heavily to women. Meanwhile, for those members of the CSE workforce who must work at the office, flexible hours may ease the problem of meeting dependent-care requirements somewhat, but for others who may be required to work un-usual shifts, such difficulties could be exacerbated. CSE will have had to adjust its expectations of its employees' productivity to account for the effect that increased dependent-care responsibilities have had on its work-force, particularly women. In March 2021, "CSE hosted a virtual panel discussion where six employees spoke frankly about the disproportionate impact of COVID-19 along gender lines" (CSE 2021a). The agency will also have had to consider the mental health needs of its workforce and remain alert to the consequences of pandemic-related stress. In response to such concerns, CSE reports that it "held training courses and speaker events on topics such as self-compassion, managing anxiety and parenting in the pandemic" (CSE 2021a).

Assessing Performance and Looking to the Future

Whatever the exact menu of measures applied by CSE to maintain its operations, at the end of 2020 the agency asserted that it had succeeded in remaining fully operational during the pandemic (CSE 2020i). The secrecy surrounding the agency's activities makes judging the success of those operations difficult. The COVID-19-related cybersecurity incidents made public to date have been minor in scope and consequences, with no evidence of any significant effect on Canada's federal or non-federal pandemic response. CSIS has confirmed that the intelligence community is "aware of the efforts of state adversaries to spread disinformation about pandemic responses in an attempt to discredit government efforts and diminish confidence in vaccine rollout efforts" (CSIS 2021), but these threats, while concerning, appear to have been marginal in their effects. Hostile intelligence-gathering activities against Canadian targets are more difficult to assess. The rapid move to working from home across the public and private sectors is likely to have opened new opportunities for hostile exploitation, but many of these intrusions may go undetected or otherwise remain unreported. The success of CSE's own intelligence-gathering efforts is even less likely to be revealed.

In some ways, the COVID-19 pandemic may have served as a preview of the issues the Cyber Centre will face in the future as work migrates outside the traditional office. Are there lessons from the current experience that can be applied to the design of more permanent, secure remote-work capabilities? The pandemic period may also have accelerated the agency's understanding of how best to operationalize the cybersecurity authorities it was granted in 2019 to work with entities outside the federal government. Was the Cyber Centre's advice and guidance used effectively by the organizations that needed it? Is the voluntary participation model laid out in the *CSE Act* sufficient for the most vital elements of Canada's critical infrastructure?

One lesson that CSE and other essential elements of government might draw from the COVID-19 pandemic is that they need to develop the infrastructure and procedures to securely perform work outside of existing high-security office spaces when emergencies require it. Such an option would improve the agency's resilience against a wide range of threats that might constrain the use of CSE facilities in the future, not just pandemics. However, it would likely require the relaxation of certain security requirements, which would need to be negotiated with the other members of the Five Eyes partnership. The time to do that is before the next emergency arises. The agency might also want to examine greater use of remote work even under normal circumstances, as Gioe, Hatfield, and Stout (2020) have suggested for the US intelligence community.

NOTES

1   Shared Services Canada is the Canadian government agency responsible for providing information technology services to the federal government.

2   Christopher Williams, Director General, Public Affairs at CSE, email message to author, 22 February 2021.

3   Email from Christopher Williams.

4   This information was provided during a 23 October 2020 online meeting between members of the Canadian intelligence community and authors for this book.

5   23 October 2020 meeting.

6   23 October 2020 meeting.

7   23 October 2020 meeting.

8   Email from Christopher Williams.

9   23 October 2020 meeting.

REFERENCES

Australia. Department of Defence. 2020. "On the Offensive against COVID-19 Cyber Criminals." 7 April 2020. https://www.minister.defence.gov.au/minister/lreynolds/media-releases/offensive-against-covid-19-cyber-criminals.

CSIS (Canadian Security Intelligence Service). 2020. "Joint CSE and CSIS Statement—May 14, 2020." Government of Canada, last modified 28 May 2020. https://www.canada.ca/en/security-intelligence-service/news/2020/05/joint-cse-and-csis-statement.html.

———. 2021. "Remarks by Director David Vigneault to the Centre for International Governance Innovation." Government of Canada, 9 February 2021. https://www.canada.ca/en/security-intelligence-service/news/2021/02/remarks-by-director-david-vigneault-to-the-centre-for-international-governance-innovation.html.

CSE (Communications Security Establishment). 2008. "Memorandum of Understanding between the Communications Security Establishment and Health Canada." 12 February 2008. Released to the author in redacted form under Access to Information request A-2017-00017.

———. 2012. *OPS-1: Protecting the Privacy of Canadians and Ensuring Legal Compliance in the Conduct of CSEC Activities*. 1 December 2012. Released to the author in redacted form under Access to Information request A-2017-00017.

———. 2015. "Collective Agreement between the Communications Security Establishment and the Public Service Alliance of Canada." 11 February 2015. http://negotech. labour.gc.ca/eng/agreements/12/1292005a.pdf.

———. 2018. "The Minister of National Defence Announces the Launch of the Canadian Centre for Cyber Security." Government of Canada, last modified 16 October 2018. https://cyber.gc.ca/en/news/minister-national-defence-announces-launch-canadian-centre-cyber-security-0.

———. 2020a. "CSE Statement on Threat Activity Targeting COVID-19 Vaccine Development." Government of Canada, last modified 16 July 2020. https://www. cse-cst.gc.ca/en/media/2020-07-16.

———. 2020b. "Cyber Security for Healthcare Organizations: Protecting Yourself against Common Cyber Attacks." Government of Canada, September 2020. https://cyber. gc.ca/sites/default/files/publications/itsap00131-e.pdf.

———. 2020c. *Cyber Threat Bulletin: Impact of COVID-19 on Cyber Threat Activity*. Government of Canada, last modified 10 June 2020. https://cyber.gc.ca/en/ guidance/cyber-threat-bulletin-impact-covid-19-cyber-threat-activity.

———. 2020d. *Cyber Threat Bulletin: The Continued Impact of COVID-19 on Cyber Threat Activity*. Government of Canada, last modified 21 December 2020. https://www. cyber.gc.ca/en/guidance/cyber-threat-bulletin-continued-impact-covid-19-cyber-threat-activity.

———. 2020e. *Cyber Threat Bulletin: Impact of COVID-19 on Cyber Threats to the Health Sector*. Government of Canada, last modified 25 June 2020. https://cyber.gc.ca/en/ guidance/cyber-threat-bulletin-impact-covid-19-cyber-threats-health-sector.

———. 2020f. "Foreign Cyber Operations." Government of Canada, last modified 27 October 2020. https://www.cse-cst.gc.ca/en/inside-interieur/cyberoperations-cyberoperations.

———. 2020g. "GeekWeek 7." Government of Canada, last modified 21 October 2020. https://cyber.gc.ca/en/events/geekweek-7.

———. 2020h. "Renewed Cyber Threats to Canadian Health Organizations," Alert AL20-026. Government of Canada, 30 October 2020. https://cyber.gc.ca/en/alerts/ renewed-cyber-threats-canadian-health-organizations.

———. 2020i. "#YearInReview: In just a few short months . . ." Twitter post (@ cse_cst), 31 December 2020, 12:59 p.m. https://twitter.com/cse_cst/ status/1344704764223889408.

———. 2021a. *Communications Security Establishment Annual Report 2020–2021*. Government of Canada, last modified 28 June 2021. https://www.cse-cst.gc.ca/en/ accountability/transparency/reports/communications-security-establishment-annual-report-2020-2021.

——. 2021b. *Cyber Threats to Canada's Democratic Process: July 2021 Update.* Government of Canada, July 2021. https://cyber.gc.ca/sites/default/files/2021-07/2021-threat-to-democratic-process-3-web-e.pdf.

——. 2021c. *Security Assessment of the COVID Alert Exposure Notification Service.* ITSP.10.003, 14 January 2021. https://raw.githubusercontent.com/cds-snc/covid-alert-documentation/main/CCCS_SecurityAssessment.pdf.

Fisher, Lucy, and Chris Smyth. 2020. "GCHQ in Cyberwar on Anti-vaccine Propaganda." *Times* (London), 9 November 2020. https://www.thetimes.co.uk/article/gchq-in-cyberwar-on-anti-vaccine-propaganda-mcjgjhmb2.

Gioe, David V., Joseph M. Hatfield, and Mark Stout. 2020. "Can United States Intelligence Community Analysts Telework?" *Intelligence and National Security* 35 (6): 885–901. https://doi.org/10.1080/02684527.2020.1767389.

New Zealand. Government Communications Security Bureau. 2020. "Speech: Cyber Security in a Covid-19 World." Wellington, 3 August 2020. https://www.gcsb.govt.nz/news/cyber-security-in-a-covid-19-world/.

NSICOP (National Security and Intelligence Committee of Parliamentarians). 2020. *Annual Report 2019.* Ottawa, 12 March 2020. https://www.nsicop-cpsnr.ca/reports/rp-2020-03-12-ar/annual_report_2019_public_en.pdf.

NSIRA (National Security and Intelligence Review Agency). 2020. "2019 Annual Report." 11 December 2020. https://www.nsira-ossnr.gc.ca/wp-content/uploads/2020/12/AR-NSIRA-Eng-Final.pdf.

Ogrysko, Nicole. 2020. "Could the Pandemic Force the Intelligence Community to Reconsider Workplace Flexibilities?" *Federal News Network*, 21 May 2020. https://federalnewsnetwork.com/workforce/2020/05/could-the-pandemic-force-the-intelligence-community-to-reconsider-workplace-flexibilities/.

Robinson, Bill. 2020. "From 1967 to 2017: CSE's Transition from the Industrial Age to the Information Age." In *Big Data Surveillance and Security Intelligence: The Canadian Case,* edited by David Lyon and David Murakami Wood, 89–111. Vancouver: University of British Columbia Press.

——. 2021a. "The Communications Security Establishment." In *Top Secret Canada: Understanding the Canadian Intelligence and National Security Community,* edited by Stephanie Carvin, Craig Forcese, and Thomas Juneau, 72–89. Toronto: University of Toronto Press.

——. 2021b. "Spy agencies, COVID-19, and parking lots." *Lux Ex Umbra* (blog), 28 March 2021. https://luxexumbra.blogspot.com/2021/03/spy-agencies-covid-19-and-parking-lots.html.

Standing Committee on Government Operations and Estimates. 2020. Evidence. 1st Sess., 43rd Parliament, Meeting No. 14, 25 May 2020. https://www.ourcommons.ca/Content/Committee/431/OGGO/Evidence/EV10768227/OGGOEV14-E.PDF.

Standing Committee on Health. 2020. Evidence. 1st Sess., 43rd Parliament, Meeting No. 32, 7 July 2020. https://www.ourcommons.ca/Content/Committee/431/HESA/Evidence/EV10823064/HESAEV32-E.PDF.

Standing Committee on Industry, Science and Technology. 2020. Evidence. 1st Sess., 43rd Parliament, Meeting No. 16, 20 May 2020. https://www.ourcommons.ca/Content/Committee/431/INDU/Evidence/EV10761671/INDUEV16-E.PDF.

Treasury Board of Canada. 2020. "Supplementary Estimates (B), 2020-21." https://www.canada.ca/content/dam/tbs-sct/documents/planned-government-spending/supplementary-estimates/supplementary-estimates-b-2020-21.pdf.

———. 2021. "Supplementary Estimates (C), 2020-21." https://www.canada.ca/content/dam/tbs-sct/documents/planned-government-spending/supplementary-estimates/supplementary-estimates-c-2020-21.pdf.

Tu Thanh Ha, and Colin Freeze. 2020. "Quebec Health Network Targeted by Cyberattack." *Globe and Mail*, 29 October 2020. https://www.theglobeandmail.com/canada/article-quebec-health-network-targeted-by-cyberattack/.

Weston, Greg. 2013. "Inside Canada's Top-Secret Billion-Dollar Spy Palace." *CBC News*, 8 October 2013. https://www.cbc.ca/news/politics/inside-canada-s-top-secret-billion-dollar-spy-palace-1.1930322.

8

COVID-19 as a Constraint on the CAF? As Always, the Mission Matters

Stephen M. Saideman, Stéfanie von Hlatky, and Graeme Hopkins[1]

Introduction

COVID-19 presented the Canadian Armed Forces (CAF) with personnel, training, and operational challenges, but there is variation in how the CAF has responded. While the government and the public's primary focus may have been on operations at home, first with the troops replacing depleted staffs in long-term care facilities (LTCFs) and later, in helping with the vaccine rollout, the CAF continued to be involved in several international missions. These missions varied in terms of how exposed troops were to the virus, and as a result the CAF entirely halted some operations while adapting others. In this chapter, we discuss the increased focus on domestic operations and provide an assessment of international operations, highlighting which ones mainly continued as planned, which ones were modified, and which ones were largely frozen. The domestic efforts produced more controversy than the deployments abroad. For the international efforts, the key variable was how much contact with foreign troops the CAF had, although other factors mattered. We conclude with a consideration of the implications of the pandemic for the future of the CAF.

The CAF Enters the Fight at Home

Domestic operations are integral to what the CAF does and are highlighted in every defence review as one of its core missions, even if the focus of politicians, the media, and the budget tends to be more on expeditionary operations. Before the Afghanistan mission, one of the most prominent operations on many senior officers' biographies was the 1998 ice storm in Ontario and Quebec.[2] The increased frequency of natural disasters—floods, fires, extreme storms—has increased the pace of CAF operations at home. Lieutenant-General Wayne Eyre, then the Commander of the Army, noted just before the pandemic struck Canada that the pace of domestic operations had increased, creating challenges and imposing trade-offs for the CAF (Berthiaume 2020b). Therefore, it should not be surprising that the government looked to the CAF to respond to the pandemic. Unlike any other government agency, the CAF has large numbers of trained individuals who can be quickly deployed to a new mission and who have experience in planning and coordinating the logistics of complicated and sudden tasks. Below, we discuss the two key missions—support to LTCFs and helping with vaccine distribution—before noting how the CAF's day-to-day work in Canada has been affected by the pandemic.

As the CAF reacted to the pandemic, it stood up Operation LASER to protect the force, assist governments at all levels, and maintain readiness (DND 2021c).[3] Phase 3 (pandemic response) of Operation LASER was activated on 13 March 2020 after Phase 2 (pandemic alert).[4] The most visible manifestation was the deployment of soldiers into fifty-four eldercare facilities in Quebec and Ontario after the pandemic depleted their staffs (Berthiaume 2020c). This effort drew the media's attention for a few reasons. It was surprising—the public might expect the CAF to provide logistical support to distribute protective gear, but replacing nursing staff was not something most people had anticipated. Soldiers in uniform entering LTCFs provided the media with dramatic pictures. It was also controversial as the soldiers observed neglect and abuse of the elderly in some of these facilities, ultimately reporting that abuse up their chain of command; that report eventually made its way into the media (Brewster and Kapelos 2020; Treble 2020).[5] Because the provinces are ultimately responsible for these facilities, their request to the CAF to assist civil authorities came back to bite them with these revelations (CBC News 2020). At the same time, the desire by the CAF to pull the troops out as quickly as possible became a point of contention with the provinces (Canadian Press 2020). While this effort almost certainly gained the CAF goodwill with the public, it may have created some tensions with the leadership of the relevant provinces. We further discuss these push-pull dynamics below.

The CAF gained attention again in the fall and winter of 2020–21 as it played a significant role in supporting the vaccine rollout in the form of Operation VECTOR. Vaccinating the entire population poses significant logistical challenges, especially as the first vaccine distributed in Canada required extremely cold storage. A first move in this effort involved the CAF delivering five freezers to northern communities in December 2020. Major-General Dany Fortin also became one of the key players in this effort in his role as Vice-President of Logistics and Operations at the Public Health Agency of Canada (PHAC), and CAF personnel assisted PHAC in planning the vaccines' distribution.[6] While there has been significant criticism of the rollout, with major problems tied to the reliability of supply chains, none focused on the CAF.[7]

Less visible efforts by the CAF at various stages of the pandemic included assistance to more remote communities across Canada. Early on, for example, Canadian Rangers were asked to do wellness checks, provide transportation, distribute food and supplies, provide shelter, and assist emergency operation centres (DND 2021c).[8] Rangers provided similar assistance in remote communities as winter approached in November and December 2021. These latter efforts included more medical assistance and help with quarantining the sick.

Lastly, the pandemic has affected the daily business of how the CAF operates in Canada. The need to work from home applied to almost 85 per cent of the CAF, similar to what the Defence Team and the rest of the government experienced (MacDonald and Vance 2020, 3). Most training efforts, exercises, and the like were cancelled, altered, or postponed at the outset of the pandemic. Search and rescue missions had a longer window to act in the spring before resuming normal alert levels in late June. Additionally, recruitment was put on hold.

Contagion within the CAF has been relatively limited. Since the CAF has roughly 100,000 members (including reservists), contagion within the force was less than 1 per cent—and therefore less than the rate among the broader Canadian public. As some troops deployed into what was the pandemic equivalent of harm's way—LTCFs—the relatively low contagion rate can be considered a successful adaptation to the pandemic. By scaling back meetings, exercises, and training, and through the application of COVID-19 protocols (masks, social distancing), the CAF has mostly mitigated the direct impact of the pandemic. Harder to measure will be the impact on service families during school closures and the inaccessibility of the usual forms of assistance (family, base communities), especially for those with kin deployed abroad. It is also difficult to ascertain how the pandemic and the CAF's adaptation has affected readiness and effectiveness. Could the CAF fight as well in January 2021 as it could in January 2020? The level of activity abroad suggests that the CAF is still capable of carrying on with its international operations, as we show below. While readiness is hard to measure even in the best of times, the lack of personnel renewal and a reduced training tempo are likely to have lasting effects.

Before moving on to the CAF's expeditionary efforts, it is worth considering the politics of the home game. The provinces got more and less than they wanted from the aid they received from the CAF. Quebec and Ontario were embarrassed by the CAF's reports of neglect and abuse in their long-term care facilities. On the other hand, not only did the CAF fill vital positions in the LTCFs, but they almost certainly saved the provinces money. While the CAF can ask for cost recovery—getting reimbursed for the expenses of giving aid to the provinces—this rarely happens because of the optics of such a request (Leuprecht and Kasurak 2020). As Minister of National Defence Harjit Sajjan said before the pandemic, "I also want to emphasize that the CAF will not be doing any cost recovery and we have not done so for any disasters" (Global News 2019). Unsurprisingly, like in past CAF emergency efforts, the provinces wanted the CAF to stay longer. Ontario and Quebec were saving money by having federally paid troops in the LTCFs rather than provincially paid nursing staff. This tension arises frequently when the CAF assists civil authorities. However, in this case, the key difference is that most CAF assistance to the civil power missions do not reveal quite so dramatically the extent of provincial shortcomings. This one did in a very public way and at a time when the pandemic response was monopolizing headlines. The conflicting imperatives—bad publicity, saved money—means that there may not be clear lessons to be learned by provincial leaders about whether to ask the CAF for help in the future. Politicians who are more concerned with budget challenges will likely be quicker to ask for CAF help. However, those politicians who are either more concerned about bad news stories or are more politically vulnerable may find the COVID-19 experience to be a warning against involving the CAF in their province's affairs. As the CAF was again sending troops into pandemic hot zones during the first few months of 2021, the lesson may be that desperation crowds out other concerns.

Capacity-Building On Ice

For the CAF's operations abroad, the impact of the pandemic has varied. Maritime and air operations adjusted to the pandemic mostly with modest alterations. On the other hand, land operations were often curtailed abroad because of their large capacity-building component—training other countries' troops—which represented a higher risk of COVID-19 transmission when compared to other mission tasks.

Operations at Sea, Limited at Shore

Canadian maritime operations are the less obvious case of relatively successful COVID-19 operations: there were no major COVID-19-related crises despite ships being perfect breeding grounds for the disease. Cruise ships were not the only vessels to make the news, as the spread of COVID-19 disabled the USS *Theodore Roosevelt*, one of the most powerful warships in the world.[9] The crew's experience shook the US Navy, ultimately leading to the firing not just of the ship's captain but also of the Secretary of the Navy (Vanden Brook 2020). The pandemic reveals that naval vessels present both safety and risk. Alone at sea, a ship is essentially a bubble that can socially distance for months on end. However, any port visit risks exposing not just a few sailors but ultimately the entire crew. As a result, while Canadian naval or joint exercises continued, albeit at a reduced pace, the port visits that usually go along with such missions did not. Indeed, crews could no longer go ashore wherever they docked and were required to stay near their ships. Visitors to these docked ships were restricted and screened.[10]

In 2020, the CAF continued to participate in most multilateral maritime exercises as these could proceed with minimal interaction with the crews of other vessels. Operation CARIBBE, in which Canada assists US-led counter-narcotics operations in the Caribbean and eastern Pacific, ended early as the ports in the Caribbean closed in the first months of the pandemic, making it hard to sustain logistics. Also, Canada's partners cancelled some of the exercises, such as the US-led TRADEWINDS. Two Canadian ships—HMCS Winnipeg and HMCS Regina—also participated in a slimmed-down RIMPAC 2020 (the largest multilateral maritime exercise, taking place annually in the Pacific), as the shore-based component was cancelled. HMCS Winnipeg's tour continued afterwards, with the ship participating in Operation NEON, which seeks to deter and detect North Korean sanction-busting. Operation REASSURANCE, aimed at building confidence in NATO defence commitments in eastern Europe and making more credible deterrent posture towards Russia, has sea, air, and land components, with the deployment of ships continuing to the Baltic Sea. HMCS Halifax began its six-month deployment in January 2021 as part of this operation, and it is the flagship of Standing NATO Maritime Group 1, the NATO fleet in the Baltic.

Less Friction Above

Compared to the army and navy, the air force was the least exposed to the risks of COVID-19, with the fewest operations or capacity-building efforts abroad. The most notable mission is the Air Task Force in Romania, part of Operation REASSURANCE. Lasting from September to December 2020, the deployment of six CF-18s and a support team, a total contingent of 135 personnel, made almost no news. The mission's primary aim was to take part in the larger NATO activities intended to deter Russia and reassure NATO allies. Along the way, the pilots helped train the Romanian Air Force and participated in several NATO exercises. Because of a concurrent Russian exercise, KAVKAZ 2020, the Canadian contingent was busier than usual, with more Russian planes approaching allied airspace requiring interceptions by Canadian CF-18s (Thatcher 2020). However, the planes and pilots could not participate in as many events, such as air shows and exercises in the region, that would have required their support team to move beyond the base in Romania. Keeping the support staff in

Romania was a COVID-19 mitigation measure, which ultimately limited the RCAF's presence in eastern Europe. To prevent the contingent from contracting COVID-19, they were not allowed to go outside the base unless necessary for operations and only with permission. Interactions with non-Canadians at the Romanian air base were also restricted.[11]

The CAF also had a series of air missions in Africa in support of various peacekeeping efforts. In the summer of 2020, Operation FREQUENCE supported France by helping to transport materiel to the Sahel region via an RCAF CC-177. Operation PRESENCE was scheduled to provide tactical airlift out of Uganda but was delayed as that country required isolation for foreign aircrews.

Just as ships at sea from different countries could operate without their personnel ever meeting, so did these air missions proceed with minimal contact with personnel from other countries. The planes do not involve mixed aircrews, unlike NATO airborne warning and control aircraft. Additionally, most of the interactions would be either on the tarmac of air bases or in large buildings—where planes are maintained—so that the risks of infection are much lower. All of this makes it easier to mitigate risk and continue with training and operations. The concern then shifts to what happens when personnel are off-duty. Since these missions involve short rotations, it was less difficult to create policies that kept Canadian aviators and support crews on base at all times. However, had these been much longer missions, it would have been more challenging to keep everyone restricted to base.

A Grounded Army

In a pandemic, the land forces face entirely different challenges from those operating in the air or at sea. Many of the CAF's overseas operations are "capacity-building" efforts, which involve training other countries' troops. These missions require sustained interactions with individuals from other states, with disruptive personnel rotations on the trainer side and turnover on the trainee side, as trained units roll out and new units roll in. As a result, the CAF placed most of these missions on operational pause during the first stages of the pandemic; some have not been resumed. The one exception is Canada's role as a Framework Nation in the Enhanced

Forward Presence in Latvia, which is not a capacity-building mission per se but involves a lot of multinational training and exercises.

For Operation UNIFIER, the training mission in Ukraine, Canada opted to hedge its bets by not replacing all two hundred soldiers training the Ukrainian armed forces in March 2020 as part of the regular rotation, deploying only sixty troops instead as placeholders. The training itself stopped as neither side wanted to expose their forces to the virus. In June, ninety soldiers went to Ukraine to start again in July, and this training, with COVID-19 mitigation protocols, has continued since (DND 2021a).

The CAF had already altered its primary capacity-building mission, Operation IMPACT, before the pandemic due to the American assassination of Iranian Major-General Qassem Soleimani. Operation IMPACT involves different Canadian missions in the Middle East and Canada's contribution to the NATO mission in Iraq. On 3 January 2020, a drone strike targeted Soleimani while he was visiting Iraq. His death led to Iranian retaliatory strikes and fears of additional attacks on foreign troops in Iraq. Consequently, most Canadian troops were repositioned outside Iraq before the pandemic struck. They were in the process of returning to Iraq when the World Health Organization declared COVID-19 a global pandemic, which caused changes to the operation once again. Major-General Jennie Carignan, the commander of the NATO mission at the time, reported that "We basically had to collapse our train-the-trainers activities in our satellite sites outside of Baghdad starting on 11 March. . . . We had to take specific actions and adapt to the pandemic context. So, they had to cease training for a while to protect the force. They had to operate differently" (Brewster 2020). Ultimately, the CAF trainers returned home. The CAF also paused Operation IMPACT's smaller and less visible training missions in Lebanon and Jordan.[12]

Some of the smaller missions supporting peacekeeping operations were also affected by COVID-19. Operation KOBOLD in Kosovo had a four-week delay as rotations were interrupted, but then the mission continued. This effort involves 5 CAF members in the headquarters of the NATO mission in Kosovo. Operation CALUMET, involving about 55 CAF members participating in the Multinational Force and Observers in the Sinai, had its rotations interrupted, but now the mission continues. Operation CROCODILE, with 9 CAF members supporting the United

Nations in the Democratic Republic of the Congo, was largely unaffected. For Operation SOPRANO, on the other hand, the 10 CAF members in South Sudan supporting the UN mission were relocated. Rotations were later suspended (DND 2021a).

With 540 soldiers in Latvia, the biggest Canadian land operation has been more like the naval and air operations than the other army missions.[13] That is, since the focus is less on training a series of different units and more on operating as a single unit, there are fewer interactions with foreign troops. Even though units from nine countries populate the base in Latvia, all countries treated the base like a bubble, not unlike the National Basketball Association's 2020 summer season. Canadian troops quarantined both before and after the deployment into the bubble (more on that below).

According to Colonel Eric Laforest, commander of Task Force Latvia, "training keeps on going, as you would suspect, with the full battle group of nine nations" (Berthiaume 2020a). The units cancelled various events where they would have interacted with the Latvian public and cut off recreational opportunities such as visits to bars, restaurants, and other outings. Most interestingly, because the CAF leads a force that includes soldiers from Italy and Spain, two countries that got hit very hard early in the crisis, Canadian officers learned quickly and adopted the rules that Spanish and Italian troops used to minimize the risks of infection. These measures allow the NATO forces in Latvia, led by the Canadians, to continue their efforts to train themselves and work together to reassure the population in the Baltics and Poland and deter Russian forces.

Before arriving, all troops quarantined before they entered the NATO base bubble in Latvia. In the summer rotation, some Canadian troops violated these procedures, leading to exposure and their return to Canada mid-flight (Berthiaume 2021). Toward the end of 2020, there was also an outbreak, including among the CAF contingent, producing some controversy as the Spanish were displeased with the quarantine arrangements for those who were exposed or infected. The union representing Spanish soldiers issued a letter denouncing the COVID-19 containment policies as insufficient (ATME 2021). While the Spanish media picked up this story (20 minutos 2021), the Canadian media did not report the complaints. The scope of the outbreak and its impact on operations has not been publicly addressed and remains unclear. Thus, while the Canadian military tends to present the Latvian mission and its leadership as a success even amid the pandemic, the mission was not immune from the pandemic nor alliance displeasure.

Conclusion

COVID-19 tends to reveal pre-existing conditions, not just in people but in governments and societies as well. The reverse is also true—that strengths become more obvious amid adversity. The CAF has managed to play an important role at home while projecting force and continuing many, but not all, of its operations abroad. In times of national emergency, the CAF is not just the force of last resort but often the country's early responder. When the provinces could not act, the CAF sent in their people at the provinces' request. With the large but temporary needs tied to the planning and distribution of the vaccine, the CAF was the obvious solution. Less obvious at the time of writing are the costs to the CAF and Canada regarding additional expenses, mental health challenges, and readiness.

The pandemic created more stress for everyone, but it has also altered how people deal with adversity. This affects military personnel in unique ways. Sports, visits to bars, and other social activities are reduced or eliminated, removing ways to blow off steam. Military personnel and their families usually rely heavily on their base communities to deal with the stress of military life. However, in this pandemic, these safety nets are largely missing. Moving forward, then, managing the aftermath of the pandemic will be a concern for the CAF. Some personnel need to recover from the physical effects of the disease, while some of the veterans of the deployments to LTCFs may suffer from post-traumatic stress (Thompson 2020). At the same time, the CAF response during the pandemic has increased its visibility among the general population. This profile might inspire Canadians to consider joining the CAF or improve overall support for the military.

Conversely, decisions regarding expeditionary operations are unlikely to have long-lasting impacts. Resuming training cycles after responsible pauses should not be problematic, with some adjustments. Indeed, the trainers and the trainees in various capacity-building exercises have more in common now as survivors of the COVID-19 pandemic. The navy and air force can resume port calls and air shows without much difficulty, and the Latvian mission can increase outreach within the region once it is safe to do so. By mostly carrying on, the CAF has shown itself to be resilient not just at home but abroad as well. While there have been cases of COVID-19, no mission received anything like the bad public relations hit that the US Navy suffered due to the USS *Theodore Roosevelt* outbreak.

There will undoubtedly be lessons-learned exercises. The obvious lesson is that capacity-building is different and more fragile than presence operations and efforts where the CAF trains itself. The CAF should study the impact of disruptions on training. At home, the politics of providing assistance to civil authorities will make it harder to adopt lessons learned. For instance, academics may think it would be better if the CAF advertised more clearly to the public what it can and cannot do when it is aiding municipal and provincial governments (Canadian Defence and Security Network 2020). However, a moral hazard presents itself: being more explicit about what the CAF can do might result in the Forces being asked to do more (Leuprecht and Karusak 2020). That said, DND/CAF leadership has routinely communicated with the Forces and the public about their domestic operations during the pandemic, notably via weekly messages by the Chief of the Defence Staff and weekly Twitter threads by the Deputy Minister.[14]

Nevertheless, before the crisis, CAF leadership lamented the increased pace of domestic operations. One lesson from this emergency is that requests for CAF assistance to civil authorities might increase in the future. The CAF should examine its training cycles and the resources it expends to re-calibrate in the face of this increased tempo of operations at home. It is time to reset priorities amid changing realities. While the Strong, Secure, and Engaged policy includes responding to domestic emergencies as a core mission, the media, politicians, and the Forces themselves see these missions as less of a priority than overseas deployments.[15] If the CAF and DND do not want to invest more time and resources in domestic operations, an alternative is to develop the equivalent of the American Federal Emergency Management Agency (FEMA) with a robust reserve capacity. While other government agencies have some capacity, Canada has nothing like FEMA. Unless and until this happens, the CAF will remain an early responder to major domestic crises.

NOTES

1   The authors are most thankful for the assistance we received from Cornel Turdeanu of the Department of National Defence's Public Affairs group. We are also grateful to Carleton University for its COVID Response Research Assistance funds and for its Paterson Chair funds.

2   The Department of National Defence used to post the biographies of all officers at the rank of colonel/captain (N) and above on an easily accessible webpage. That, alas, is no longer the case.

3   For more see chapter 9.

4   Phase 1 is the normal state of preparedness for a pandemic.

5   To read the report, see Headquarters 4th Canadian Division Joint Task Force (Central), "3350-Op LASER 20-01 (COS)," Government of Canada, 26 April 2020, https://www.macleans.ca/wp-content/uploads/2020/05/JTFC-Observations-in-LTCF-in-ON.pdf.

6   Fortin was subsequently removed due to an investigation into accusations of past sexual misconduct.

7   For more, see chapter 3.

8   For a good discussion of who the Rangers are and what they have done during the pandemic, see Moon (2021).

9   For an assessment of the pandemic's impact on the ship's crew, see Malone (2020).

10   Email with staff of the Department of National Defence's Public Affairs group, 30 December 2020.

11   Email correspondence with staff of the Department of National Defence's Public Affairs group, 26 January 2021.

12   There are discussions with the two countries on how to restart those training efforts, but as far as we can tell, training remained on hold at the time of writing.

13   This paragraph is based on comments made by a senior CAF officer at an event held under the Chatham House Rule in December 2020.

14   For instance, see the Chief of the Defence Staff's letters of 27 March (DND 2020a) and 15 May 15 2020 (DND 2020b) announcing the resumption of some of the CAF's ordinary business.

15   Anonymous junior officers have told us that domestic deployments are not as valued as foreign ones, and the benefits are much less.

REFERENCES

ATME (Asociación de Tropa y Marinería Española). 2021. "Militares españoles del eFP VII, que deberían haber vuelto el 15 de enero, continúan aislados en tiendas de campaña en Letonia por COVID-19." Asociación de Tropa y Marinería Española, 20 January 2021. https://www.atme.es/covid-efpvii/.

Berthiaume, Lee. 2020a. "Canadian Troops in Latvia Stay on Target as COVID-19 Upends Other Missions." *CTV News*, 21 May 2020. https://www.ctvnews.ca/canada/canadian-troops-in-latvia-stay-on-target-as-covid-19-upends-other-missions-1.4947986.

———. 2020b. "Disaster Relief a Threat to the Canadian Army's Fighting Edge, Commander Says." *National Post*, 20 January 2020. https://nationalpost.com/news/canada/disaster-relief-threatens-to-hinder-canadian-armys-readiness-for-combat-commander.

———. 2020c. "What You Need to Know about the Military's Assistance to Long-Term Care Homes." *CTV News*, 23 April 2020. https://www.ctvnews.ca/canada/what-you-need-to-know-about-the-military-s-assistance-to-long-term-care-homes-1.4909490.

———. 2021. "Canadian Troops Test Positive for COVID-19 in Latvia and Kuwait." *CTV News*, 5 January 2021. https://www.ctvnews.ca/politics/canadian-troops-test-positive-for-covid-19-in-latvia-and-kuwait-1.5254597.

Brewster, Murray. 2020. "Battle Diary: A Canadian Soldier Looks Back on a Year Commanding NATO Troops in Iraq." *CBC News*, 19 December 2020. https://www.cbc.ca/news/politics/carignan-iraq-nato-1.5848191.

Brewster, Murray, and Vassy Kapelos. 2020. "Military Alleges Horrific Conditions, Abuse in Pandemic-Hit Ontario Nursing Homes." *CBC News*, 26 May 2020. https://www.cbc.ca/news/politics/long-term-care-pandemic-COVID-19-coronavirus-trudeau-1.5584960.

Canadian Defence and Security Network. 2020. "CDSN COVID Response Recommendations and Future Directions." *Canadian Defence and Security Network*, 7 May 2020. https://www.cdsn-rcds.com/news/cdsn-covid-response-recommendations-and-future-directions-covid-recommandations-de-rponse-du-cdsn-et-orientations-futures?rq=rapid.

Canadian Press. 2020. "Feds Looking to Pull Military Out of Care Homes, Quebec Appeals for Them to Stay." *National Observer*, 29 May 2020. https://www.nationalobserver.com/2020/05/29/news/feds-looking-pull-military-out-care-homes-que-appeals-them-stay.

CBC News. 2020. "Ford Faces Blowback after Military Report Reveals' Horrific' Conditions at Ontario Long-Term Care Homes." *CBC News*, 26 May 2020. https://www.cbc.ca/news/canada/toronto/COVID-19-coronavirus-ontario-update-may-26-1.5584665.

DND (Department of National Defence). 2020a. "27 March: Letter from Chief of the Defence Staff (CDS) regarding COVID-19." Government of Canada, 27 March

2020. https://www.canada.ca/en/department-national-defence/maple-leaf/
defence/2020/03/march-27-letter-from-cds-regarding-covid-19.html.

———. 2020b. "15 May: Letter from Chief of the Defence Staff (CDS) regarding
COVID-19." Government of Canada, 15 May 2020. https://www.canada.ca/en/
department-national-defence/maple-leaf/defence/2020/05/may-15-cds-letter.html.

———. 2021a. "Changes to Military Operations in Response to COVID-19." Government
of Canada, last modified 26 March 2021. https://www.canada.ca/en/department-
national- defence/services/operations/military-operations/covid-19.html.

———. 2021b. "Military Response to COVID-19". Government of Canada, last modified 12
April 2021. https://www.canada.ca/en/department-national-defence/campaigns/
covid-19-military-response.html.

———. 2021c. "Operation Laser." Government of Canada, last modified 13 March 2021.
https://www.canada.ca/en/department-national-defence/services/operations/
military-operations/current-operations/laser.html.

Global News. 2019. "CAF Not Doing Any Cost Recovery in Atlantic Canada after Dorian."
Global News, 10 September 2019. https://globalnews.ca/video/5882712/canadian-
armed-forces-not-doing-any-cost-recovery-in-atlantic-canada-after-dorian/.

Leuprecht, Christian, and Peter Kasurak. 2020. "The CAF and Humanitarian Assistance
and Disaster Relief: Defining a Role." *Centre for International Governance
Innovation*, 24 August 2020. https://www.cigionline.org/articles/canadian-armed-
forces-and-humanitarian-assistance-and-disaster-relief-defining-role.

MacDonald, Adam, and Carter Vance. 2020. "COVID-19 and the CAF: Overview,
Analysis, and Next Steps." *CDA Institute: Vimy Paper* 44 (2020): 1–21. https://
cdainstitute.ca/wp-content/uploads/2020/04/Vimy-Paper-Word-Version-Editted.
pdf.

Malone, John D. 2020. "USS Theodore Roosevelt, COVID-19, and Ships: Lessons
Learned." *JAMA Network Open* 3, no. 10 (2020): 1–3. doi:10.1001/
jamanetworkopen.2020.22095.

Moon, Peter. 2021. "Canadian Rangers Overcome the Challenges of COVID-19 in 2020."
Wawatay News, 6 January 2021. https://wawataynews.ca/feature-stories/canadian-
rangers-overcome-challenges-COVID-19-2020.

Thatcher, Chris. 2020. "How Canada's Air Task Force-Romania Is Adapting and Evolving."
Skies, 27 November 2020. https://skiesmag.com/news/canada-air-task-force-
romania-rcaf/.

Thompson, Nicole. 2020. "Mental Health Supports Brought In For Soldiers at Long-Term
Care Homes, Commission Hears." *CTV News*, 12 November 2020. https://toronto.
ctvnews.ca/mental-health-supports-brought-in-for-soldiers-at-long-term-care-
homes-commission-hears-1.5186494.

Treble, Patricia. 2020. "What's Inside the Disturbing Report on Ontario's Long-Term-Care
Homes." *Maclean's*, 26 May 2020. https://www.macleans.ca/news/canada/whats-
inside-the-disturbing-report-on-ontarios-long-term-care-homes/.

20 minutos. 2021. "Denuncian que militares españoles están aislados en Letonia por la Covid en "durísimas condiciones" y a -20 grados". *20 minutos*, 21 January 2021. https://www.20minutos.es/noticia/4551549/0/denuncian-que-militares-espanoles-estan-aislados-en-letonia-por-la-covid-en-durisimas-condiciones-y-a-20-grados/?autoref=true.

Vanden Brook, Tom. 2020. "Acting Navy Secretary Is Out after Bungled Firing of USS Theodore Roosevelt's Captain." *USA Today*, 7 April 2020. https://www.usatoday.com/story/news/politics/2020/04/07/coronavirus-navys-modly-out-after-mishandling-virus-plagued-ship/2963986001/.

Defence Intelligence and COVID-19

James Cox

Introduction

Did the Defence Intelligence Enterprise ever lose its effectiveness as a result of constraints imposed during the COVID-19 pandemic? Throughout
2020, the Department of National Defence (DND) and the Canadian
Armed Forces (CAF) conducted over thirty missions at home and abroad.
Some were short-term. Others continue in or near conflict zones around
the world. Many operations were adjusted to varying degrees as a result
of the effects of COVID-19 (Government of Canada 2020c). Despite constraints, all missions received effective intelligence support.

This chapter explores the impact of the COVID-19 pandemic on the
Defence Intelligence Enterprise (DIE) active across DND and the CAF at
the strategic and operational levels during 2020. It shows that the DIE,
despite having to adopt novel personnel and systemic work practices to
meet mandated public health requirements, continued to meet all priority
intelligence requirements set by government and delivered operational intelligence products to deployed CAF missions. However, such continued
effectiveness was not easy.

The DIE is an enabling function that provides strategic and operational intelligence to deployed military missions at home and abroad,
and to government decision-making related to the defence of national
interests and pursuit of national objectives. It co-operates extensive-
ly with other government intelligence organizations across the broader

Canadian intelligence community, as well as with the intelligence agencies of Canada's closest allies and partners. Canadian Forces Intelligence Command (CFINTCOM) is the institutional lead of the DIE, but it also has a corporate role that contributes to defence policy development, provides all-source intelligence analysis, generates deployable intelligence capabilities, and conducts training and professional development programs. Within CFINTCOM, throughout the pandemic, capability generation enjoyed the same primacy of effort as intelligence production, while other activities became less urgent.[1]

In early 2020, when COVID-19 arrived in Canada and authorities imposed decisive public health restrictions across DND and the CAF, defence intelligence activity was initially—and dramatically—slowed and reduced. Nonetheless, DND and CAF attention remained focussed on what *must be* done, particularly the provision of intelligence products to senior decision-makers, ongoing missions, and prioritized intelligence support to allies and partners. By the end of the summer, the DIE had found its "sea legs" and, thanks to a number of procedural and workforce adjustments, had returned to a more comfortable, but no less hectic, level and pace of activity.

In the sections that follow, I first outline the general effects of COVID-19 at the national strategic level within National Defence Headquarters (NDHQ), which sets the stage for a more detailed look at what happened within CFINTCOM and the impact of COVID-19 on defence intelligence generally. Concluding material follows.

There are three principal reasons why the DIE continued to function effectively during the pandemic. First, it was never a question whether defence intelligence production would continue, requirements would be met, or deployed missions supported. Military personnel in particular are trained to operate in various threat environments, and COVID-19 was just another threat environment to be tolerated and mitigated. Intelligence products have continued to flow throughout the pandemic, although their presentation was not always as polished as had been the custom before.

Second, military doctrine and DND instructions placed a high priority on workforce protection. Any organization is unlikely to operate at full effectiveness if personnel fall ill or become subject to unmitigated risks that divert attention and effort from the main mission. With the warning of COVID-19 in early 2020, DND/CAF leaders at all levels set their minds to implementing force protection protocols that conformed to regional and local public health measures.

Third, the defence team is well acquainted with adaptation and change, so DIE leaders at all levels were alert to the need to monitor performance and change work habits as required. Throughout the pandemic, restrictions and practices were modified to meet operational requirements. Some weeks were slower than others, but local "battle rhythms" eventually stabilized, and work continued.

CFINTCOM is one of a number of military commands headquartered in Ottawa, and the DIE is systemically integrated in the defence operational planning process, so a general review of the overall NDHQ reaction to COVID-19 will help understand what happened within CFINTCOM and how the pandemic affected the DIE.

COVID-19 in National Defence Headquarters

Long before warnings of COVID-19 began to surface in late 2019, the DND/CAF already had a counter-pandemic contingency plan in place—Contingency Plan (CONPLAN) LASER. It described the intended response to a worldwide pandemic of an influenza-like disease. This contingency plan had been drafted as a result of the recognition of a pandemic as one of the eight modern potential threats to Canadian national security listed in the 2004 National Security Policy (Government of Canada 2004). When activated, CONPLAN LASER became Operation (OP) LASER (Government of Canada 2021c).

The four phases of OP LASER cover measures to protect defence personnel and reduce the impacts of a pandemic in order to sustain operational capabilities and readiness in support of national objectives and requests for assistance. It is important to note that there are two aspects to this operation. The first is focussed on military force protection, integrity, and effectiveness. The second provides for military support to civil authorities. Phase 1 (pandemic preparedness) was ongoing in late 2019, with routine monitoring of world pandemic threats and mitigation planning. During this phase, in February 2020, the CAF were already supporting government activity by opening a quarantine centre at Canadian Forces

Base Trenton to receive Canadians evacuated from Wuhan in China and Canadian tourists evacuated from a cruise ship in a Japanese port. As COVID-19 continued to spread and related risks were better understood, in part due to medical intelligence (MEDINT) reports dealing with probable COVID-19 effects on CAF troops generally and deployed missions in particular, the Deputy Minister (DM) and Chief of the Defence Staff (CDS) activated Phase 2 (pandemic alert) on 2 March 2020. This phase involved continued monitoring of COVID-19 and the adoption of protective measures as directed by local commanders.

On March 4, Prime Minister Justin Trudeau announced the creation of a Cabinet Committee to lead the federal response to COVID-19 (Prime Minister's Office 2020). On March 11, the World Health Organization (WHO) declared the crisis to be a global pandemic (World Health Organization 2021). Then on March 13, Parliament agreed to adjourn for five weeks because of COVID-19. That same day, the DM and CDS activated Phase 3 (pandemic response) of Operation LASER (Colonel Orest Babij, pers. comm. 2020). Phase 3 formally recognized widespread and continuous transmission of COVID-19 in the general population and the imminent threat of its impact on military personnel and missions. Responses to civil authorities' requests for assistance continued to be received and, where approved by government, actioned.

Within NDHQ, complementary direction from the DM and CDS imposed a virtual lockdown. People were sent home and only essential personnel remained in their offices or at their worksites. Direction was given to activate command-level business continuity plans. Out of an abundance of caution, the immediate intent was to adopt force protection measures based on guidance by regional and local public health officials (Colonel Orest Babij, pers. comm. 2020; Colonel Steven Desjardins, pers. comm. 2020).

Two priorities were set. First, a deliberate strategic prioritization of work ensued so as to identify what *must* be done. This included responding to requests for assistance from civil authorities. What *should* be done was tackled as best it could be, usually from home offices. What *could* be done would be addressed later. Second, staff who were required to do work that *must* be done continued to work in their offices in NDHQ. Others worked remotely from home. According to Marie-Hélène Chayer, the Assistant

Chief of Defence Intelligence at the time, all operational and deployed force protection requirements continued to be met, but longer-term, less important non-operational activity was put off for another day.

Personal routines changed. Those who continued to work in their offices had their work environment regulated by a number of new protocols, including one-way traffic arrows on the floor, copious amounts of hand sanitizer located on tabletops, and maximum limits on the number of personnel allowed on any level, conference room, or elevator at any one time. Everyone had to wear a mask when not at their desks. Custodial staff increased the frequency with which they cleaned office furniture. Personnel dispatched to work at home proceeded to organize their home offices and personal work routines, shaped by family circumstances.

As March turned into April, there was considerable experimentation with various online video conference platforms and email connections at the unclassified level. Local commanders and civilian managers adopted measures that suited their situations. These challenges were interesting enough within Canada, but with travel being cancelled, international co-operation brought its own set of problems. Face-to-face meetings with allies and partners are important for relationship dynamics, but adverse effects of the pandemic were not as grim in this area as might have been expected because allies and partners were facing their own pandemic challenges and force protection restrictions. Mutual understanding and empathy prevailed.

With over thirty different operations at home and abroad, DND/CAF had to conduct a detailed analysis of each mission to determine the adjustments required to protect deployed personnel while ensuring the achievement of critical mission objectives. Adjustments ranged from delaying deployment of some capabilities and amending the number of military personnel deployed to modifying operational and training activity within deployed missions, all of which sought to achieve a balance between acceptable risk factors for personnel, the ability to sustain the mission, and the impact any change would have on the mission. In some cases, adjustments came because of a pause in operational activities by host or partner nations (Government of Canada 2020c). For example, as a result of the effects of COVID-19, the United States Pacific Fleet restricted the timing and scope of Rim of the Pacific (RIMPAC) 2020, a large multinational maritime exercise usually conducted over two months, to just the last two weeks of August with no training events ashore (Government of Canada 2020f; see also Saideman, von Hlatky, and Hopkins, this volume). In Latvia, Canada's battle group deployed as part of Operation REASSURANCE adjusted how it trained and cut most contact with the general public outside its barracks (Berthiaume 2020).

Throughout April 2020, NDHQ settled into something of a routine. The to-and-fro of various force protection initiatives abated somewhat but never completely stopped. On May 1 the DM and CDS were able to issue their first of many regular DM/CDS Joint Directives that served to control defence work across the department and throughout all CAF commands, formations, and units. This first Joint Directive was clear regarding its applicability

> to all employees of the Department of National Defence (DND employees) [as] an order that applies to all officers and non-commissioned members of the CAF, and any other persons granted access to defence establishments in accordance with the Defence Controlled Access Area Regulations, SOR/86-957 (ref A) and the Inspection and Search Defence Regulations (ref B). Members of the Defence Team (DT) on named domestic or international missions will follow the direction and guidance issued in relevant operational tasking orders. (Government of Canada 2020e)

In early autumn, DND/CAF had accepted that they would have to continue to function safely in a COVID-19 threat environment for the foreseeable future. On 22 October 2020, things had settled to the extent that the DM and CDS could issue a "CDS/DM Directive for Sustained Activities in a COVID-19 Environment," which was updated in December 2020. In outlining guiding principles, the directive stated that,

> Notwithstanding COVID-19 transmission rates, DND/CAF will ensure unfettered continuity of operations for critical capabilities and services to include designated operational force elements . . . military support and advice to government,

command and control, intelligence. (Government of Canada 2020b)

The directive went on to define enabling priorities, including the direction to "continue to execute all aspects of the intelligence function." As well, given DND/CAF experience adapting to the COVID-19 environment and the need to enhance its intelligence practices, CFINTCOM was specifically tasked with "work[ing] with the Privy Council Office and other intelligence organizations to explore the feasibility of establishing a joint intelligence fusion team to better harmonize COVID-19 specific requirements." There is no public information on whether or how this last direction has been actioned, but since cabinet formed a committee to deal with the pandemic, it would not be unusual for the Privy Council Office to establish something of a COVID-19 intelligence working group under the National Security and Intelligence Advisor to the Prime Minister.

CFINTCOM

The Commander of CFINTCOM is the functional authority for defence intelligence and, as such, reports directly to the Chief of the Defence Staff. Concurrently, he also holds the appointment of Chief of Defence Intelligence, which reports directly to both the CDS and the DM (Government of Canada 2020d). CFINTCOM's principal role is to provide credible, timely, and integrated defence intelligence capabilities, products, and services to support Canada's national security objectives (Government of Canada 2016). Within that role, CFINTCOM has three key responsibilities. First, it provides multi-source intelligence analysis, strategic warning, and threat assessments, while also conducting integrated collection management and managing the defence intelligence cycle, including coordination of defence intelligence requirements. Second, in its "force generator" mode, CFINTCOM trains, prepares, and deploys intelligence capabilities to meet DND/CAF intelligence requirements. Third, the command develops policies and directives governing defence intelligence activities and leads compliance reviews of intelligence activity throughout the DIE. The detailed organization of CFINTCOM is not publicly available, it is generally organized as shown in figure 9.1:

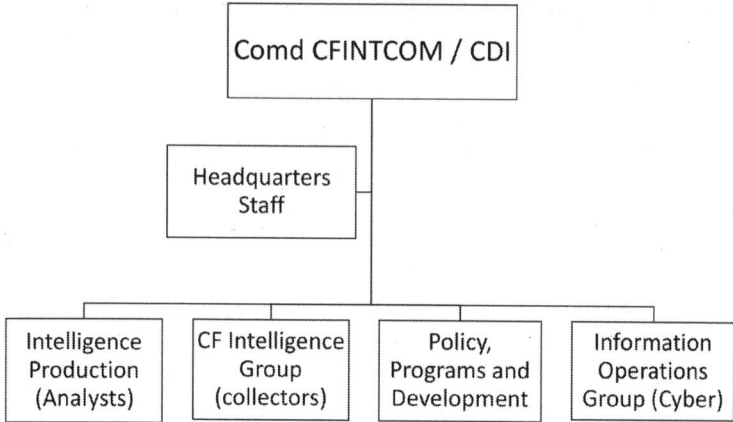

FIGURE 9.1: Outline of CFINTCOM organization

CFINTCOM has an integrated civilian-military staff, one branch of which is responsible for intelligence production and led by a senior public servant. The intelligence production branch includes a Directorate of Scientific and Technical Intelligence (DSTI), with a senior civilian defence scientist at its head. A MEDINT cell is located within DSTI, led by a military Health Services Officer. Far from being "tucked away on the edges of the country's security and defence establishment," as claimed in some media reporting, the leader of the MEDINT cell provided frequent input to intelligence analysis in early 2020 on the existence, effects, and likely spread of COVID-19 (Brewster 2020; Marie-Hélène Chayer, pers. comm. 2020).

Media stories tended to either misinterpret the role of MEDINT or misunderstand it altogether. The CFINTCOM MEDINT cell was seldom more than one person working within DSTI. Its role was to monitor and report on disease and other health threats that would impact CAF personnel, both at home and abroad on deployed missions. It contributed to CFINTCOM strategic and operational analyses. The cell did not have a mandate to report findings outside DND/CAF. It is not a "central" intelligence agency.

The head of the MEDINT cell routinely collected open-source information from the WHO, other countries, and relevant public websites, and she often had classified liaison with equivalent offices across the Five Eyes and NATO, particularly with US military MEDINT elements. MEDINT products were not disseminated as sole-source assessments, but were crafted into all-source intelligence products reported to the DM and CDS, which enabled effective DND/CAF decision-making, as all intelligence should.

DND/CAF MEDINT reports would have been shared, as is routine, among other intelligence assessment offices in government, such as the Intelligence Assessment Secretariat in the Privy Council Office, or with Global Affairs Canada. Research found no indication that CAF MEDINT was requested by, or shared with, the Public Health Agency of Canada, which had its own pandemic surveillance capability and was regularly in contact with the WHO and other governments.

When the NDHQ lockdown came in mid-March 2020, the strategic intelligence production staff immediately prioritized the assessments they were in the process of completing.[2] People working on those assessments that *must* be done and requiring frequent access to classified information systems continued to work from the office. Other less urgent assessments were completed by staff at home, who came back into the office only when they absolutely had to have access to classified material. Risk-management decisions were delegated down to mid-level managers, who tweaked staff working hours to achieve an effective workflow and manage a work/home balance that was different for every individual.

Somewhat unexpectedly, human resource management became the most challenging issue. No one questioned the need to continue producing intelligence assessments, but trying to manage who was needed where and when required engaged leadership at all levels. Supervisors had to remain attentive to a workforce sometimes stressed by complex family issues at home or nervous about returning to work in a pandemic environment. The synchronization of work activities needed to meet the different expectations of missions, clients, and senior leaders (who were now always in the building), allies, health-care officials, spouses, and kids was tricky, but eventually found its own rhythm in the different staff offices across CFINTCOM.

Over time, supervisors became aware of possible adverse effects on people's mental health, perhaps caused by social isolation at home. As it turned out, many analysts apparently enjoyed working from home, alone, where they could think and work at their own speed, without undue distraction or interruption, family life notwithstanding.

With their attention directed to the new personnel management issues, there was less opportunity for supervisors to provide analysts with the usual detailed instructions for the completion of various assessments. Some analysts may have momentarily faltered without such direction, but, in a pleasant surprise, it soon became apparent that many analysts relished the opportunity to fill the instructional void with their own novel ideas and inclinations about how to proceed on certain issues. This development allowed senior leaders to identify those with talent and potential who "bloomed" during a stressful period and to "mark" those who might develop into future effective intelligence managers.

Interestingly, co-operation with intelligence allies seemed to improve during this period because everyone was in the same boat. Not only were various parties more inclined to connect online, assessment burden-sharing among partners picked up because, alone, no one could continue to do what they had been doing at the same level. "Tag-teaming" became common as co-operative allied groups shared analytical projects to the benefit of all. For example, in a NATO context, in "normal" times, a working group of allied analysts might meet to collaborate on a joint analysis of a certain issue, but now, with time and availability at a premium, close allies more readily accepted products developed by one nation and subsequently shared with all. The Canadian cadre, being smaller than that of its principal allies, enjoyed some agility in switching from subject to subject as prioritization demanded. It was often hectic, but throughout the year, assessment products remained actionable, relevant, and timely, even if they were not presented in as polished a format as had been the case before the pandemic.

Another component of CFINTCOM, the CF Intelligence Group, provides a range of specialist intelligence collection capabilities, including imagery from the Canadian Forces Joint Imagery Centre, human intelligence in Joint Task Force X, counter-intelligence in the Canadian Forces National Counter-Intelligence Unit (CFNCIU), the Joint Meteorological

Centre (JMC), and the Mapping and Charting Establishment. It also oversees the CF School of Meteorology and the CF School of Military Intelligence (CFSMI). The Commander and staff of the CF Intelligence Group are located in NDHQ, but the units have personnel deployed across the country and on missions abroad.

Some military officers with command responsibility were unsatisfied with their ability to remotely exercise command influence. Command is an intensely personal endeavour and when both commanders and subordinates are working remotely from a laptop at home, personal presence and influence are missing. Some found video-teleconferencing useful, but not everyone had access to such a capability. Not surprisingly, this issue was felt more acutely by leaders than by their subordinates.

At a personal level, in the course of a day, COVID-19 restrictions had one senior officer with command responsibilities going from working in the office all the time, when not travelling, to working from home exclusively. Within a week it became apparent that he and his key staff could not effectively continue remote work because communicating via a Blackberry and the intermittent Defence Virtual Private Network Infrastructure connection was ineffective. The network was eventually upgraded (Government of Canada 2020a). CF Intelligence Group leadership initially returned to the office about one to two days a week, then increased to three to four days when needed. At the time of writing, their "battle rhythm" remains about two to four days a week in the office, with some days seeing reduced work hours.

Significantly, in March 2020, as part of the original lockdown, the CDS decisively ordered the cessation of all CAF training activity. Courses stopped running and candidates were returned to their home units. Field exercises were abruptly ended, and units redeployed back to garrisons. Imperative training for senior officers about to be posted abroad as defence attachés had to be completed via a distance learning module.

At the non-commissioned member level, not only were candidates already in training at the CFSMI ordered to go home before completing their training, but personnel waiting to commence training would be held up for even longer, creating a projected shortage of future junior ranks in the training pipeline. The situation was not so dire in the junior officer ranks, which were largely up to strength before the pandemic hit.

More broadly, when training ceased in March 2020, CFSMI had been in the middle of a multi-year plan to increase training capacity, with the objective of bringing the Intelligence Branch up to its permitted manning level. The plan was set back because of the shutdown. Even when training was allowed to start up again in the summer, capacity remained lower than usual because of imposed physical distancing. At the time of writing, in early 2021, centralized CAF recruit training is still operating at considerably less than full capacity, so the flow of entry-level personnel to CFSMI for primary intelligence training also remains low. However, the reduction in primary intelligence training allowed CFSMI to increase the number of more senior training courses, a development that is serving to reduce the backlog, built up in recent years, of those requiring more advanced intelligence training (Colonel Orest Babij, pers. comm. 2020).[3]

It can also be noted that while in-house training was suspended, CFSMI instructional staff turned their minds to adapting training courses to online formats, which have been subsequently instituted for a number of courses (Colonel Orest Babij, pers. comm. 2020). This will allow for more flexible training of more Intelligence Branch personnel in the future.

Between April and June 2020, NDHQ began planning for the resumption of "normal" business activity, and the leadership spent much time and effort ensuring a safe working environment for those returning to the office. During this time and later into the summer, the CF Intelligence Group met all of its force generation requirements. Production, however, was adversely affected, particularly at the CF Joint Imagery Centre, where a very high percentage of the work is highly classified, and at the Mapping and Charting Establishment, where tremendously large data files could not be efficiently accessed remotely. On the plus side, many analysts at both units took advantage of newly created online training opportunities provided by Canada's intelligence allies and sought to adapt as best they could. The CF National Counter-Intelligence Unit, for its part, took a hit in terms of its activity. Details are not publicly available, but one might imagine the constraints experienced by this largely HUMINT-oriented endeavour. Despite all this, it was "business as usual" at the Joint Meteorological Centre, where staff continued to provide 24/7/365 meteorological support to the CAF. On balance, though, at the end of 2020, the

CF Intelligence Group had still not returned to its full, pre-COVID-19 posture or capacity.

Overall, as a force employer, CFINTCOM continued to meet its strategic intelligence-production requirements, but perhaps with less polish than it, or its clients, had been accustomed to. It might be that a senior leader who would normally receive a personal briefing, presented by a briefer with a practiced script and polished set of PowerPoint slides, might now get only an email with slides attached, or just the slide deck itself, or just a verbal briefing without notes or slides. The CFINTCOM force generation role was slowed somewhat but continued to work to catch up. At the time of writing in early 2021, defence intelligence at the national strategic level continued to meet all requirements, and as time goes on, it moves steadily closer to regaining the operating level it had before the arrival of COVID-19.

Conclusion

The 2004 National Security Policy recognized a pandemic as one of eight significant potential threats to Canadian national security. Accordingly, DND/CAF had a counter-pandemic contingency plan in place when COVID-19 arrived. When it hit, defence leaders immediately prioritized essential work and related staffing requirements. DND/CAF also adopted force protection measures ordered by public health authorities. Those who did not have to work in the office were ordered to work at home. Despite the disruption, the DIE continued to meet prioritized intelligence production and force generation responsibilities. Mandatory intelligence products were delivered as required, but they were not as aesthetically pleasing as they once were. In these circumstances, substance trumped looks.

Leaders, managers, and staff alike found the effort to gain effective balance and rhythm in workflows, at all levels, to be a significant early challenge, as personnel juggled work in the office or at home—the latter for some or all of the time, depending on the individual's role. Family circumstances influenced who could do how much, and when. However, as leaders and their staff members settled into workable routines, people became more comfortable with communications technology and remote work. Some staff are keen to continue working remotely where it is appropriate to do so.

In the end, it was never a question of whether the DIE could or would continue to work effectively in support of deployed missions and government decision-making requirements. COVID-19 just made the work more difficult, but it was nothing CFINTCOM and the DIE could not overcome. In fact, the lessons learned regarding new technical tools and processes will likely benefit the DIE in the long run (Marie-Hélène Chayer, pers. comm. 2021).

NOTES

1   I owe a debt of gratitude to Colonel (Retired) Steven Desjardins and Lieutenant-Colonel (Retired) Greg Jensen, both of whom are experienced military intelligence officers who now provide contracted intelligence policy advice at both the strategic and operational level in DND/CAF. Their help in understanding "the big and long picture" is truly appreciated.

2   I am indebted to Mme Marie-Hélène Chayer, Assistant Chief of Defence Intelligence in CFINTCOM for the information regarding intelligence production in this section.

3   I thank Colonel Babij for his information about the CF Intelligence Group, and also for his perceptive insights into the complexities of the CF Intelligence Branch generally.

REFERENCES

Babij, Colonel Orest. 2020. Canadian Armed Forces. Personal interview via Zoom. Ottawa, 26 October 2020, with follow-up email 4 January 2021.

Berthiaume, Lee. 2020. "Canadian Troops in Latvia Stay On Target as COVID-19 Upends Other Missions." *CTV News*, 21 May 2020. https://www.ctvnews.ca/canada/canadian-troops-in-latvia-stay-on-target-as-covid-19-upends-other-missions-1.4947986/.

Brewster, Murray. 2020. "Canadian Military Intelligence Unit Issued Warning about Wuhan Outbreak Back in January." *CBC News*, 10 April 2020. https://www.cbc.ca/news/politics/coronavirus-pandemic-covid-canadian-military-intelligence-wuhan-1.5528381.

Chayer, Marie-Hélène. 2020. Assistant chief of defence intelligence, Department of National Defence. Personal interview via Zoom. Ottawa, 10 November 2020, with follow-up email 4 January 2021.

Desjardins, Colonel Steven (Retired). Contract adviser to CFINTCOM. Personal interview via Zoom. Ottawa, 22 October 2020.

Government of Canada. 2004. *Securing an Open Society: Canada's National Security Policy*. Ottawa: Privy Council Office, April 2004. http://publications.gc.ca/site/eng/9.686980/publication.html.

———. 2016. "Canadian Forces Intelligence Command." Last modified 12 August 2016. https://www.canada.ca/en/department-national-defence/corporate/organizational-structure/canadian-forces-intelligence-command.html.

———. 2020a. "Ask Anything: ADM (IM), Len Bastien Answers Questions about Defence O365, Wi-Fi Connectivity, GPNet Stations." Lat modified 25 August 2020. https://www.canada.ca/en/department-national-defence/corporate/video/leadership/2020/08-25-dtnews.html.

———. 2020b. "CDS/DM Directive for Sustained Activities in a COVID-19 Environment." Last modified 17 December 2020. https://www.canada.ca/en/department-national-defence/corporate/policies-standards/cds-dm-directive-fall-2020-posture.html.

———. 2020c. "Changes to Military Operations in Response to COVID–19." 18 September 2020. https://www.canada.ca/en/department-national-defence/services/operations/military-operations/current-operations/list.html.

———. 2020d. "Commander Canadian Forces Intelligence Command—Rear Admiral Scott Bishop." Defence 101—Transition Binder, last modified 11 March 2021. https://www.canada.ca/en/department-national-defence/corporate/reports-publications/transition-materials/defence-101/2020/03/defence-101/cfintcom.html.

———. 2020e. "DM/CDS Joint Directive—DND/CAF COVID-19 Public Health Measures and Personal Protection." 1 May 2020. https://www.canada.ca/en/department-national-defence/corporate/policies-standards/dm-cds-joint-directive.html.

———. 2020f. "Exercise Rim of the Pacific (RIMPAC)." 26 June 2020. https://www.canada.ca/en/department-national-defence/news/2020/09/canadian-armed-forces-successfully-complete-rimpac-2020.html.

———. 2020g. "Joint CDS/DM Update on Defence Team COVID-19 Fall Posture." 6 October 2020. https://www.canada.ca/en/department-national-defence/maple-leaf/defence/2020/10/joint-cds-dm-update-dt-covid-19-fall-posture.html.

———. 2021a. "Defence Team—COVID-19." Last modified 13 April 2021. https://www.canada.ca/en/department-national-defence/campaigns/covid-19.html.

———. 2021b. "Military Response to COVID-19." Accessed 21 June 2021. https://www.canada.ca/en/department-national-defence/campaigns/covid-19-military-response.html.

———. 2021c. "Operation LASER." Last modified 28 June 2021. https://www.canada.ca/en/department-national-defence/services/operations/military-operations/current-operations/laser.html.

Jensen, Lieutenant-Colonel Greg (Retired). Contracted adviser, Canadian Joint Operations Command. Personal interview via Zoom. Ottawa, 16 October 2020.

Prime Minister's Office. 2020. "Prime Minister Creates Committee on COVID-19." News release, 4 March 2020. https://pm.gc.ca/en/news/news-releases/2020/03/04/prime-minister-creates-committee-covid-19.

World Health Organization. 2020. "WHO Director-General's Opening Remarks at the Media Briefing on COVID-19." 11 March 2020. https://www.who.int/director-general/speeches/detail/who-director-general-s-opening-remarks-at-the-media-briefing-on-covid-19---11-march-2020.

Reviving the Role of GPHIN in Global Epidemic Intelligence

Kelley Lee and Julianne Piper

Introduction

Effective surveillance, monitoring, and reporting are essential pillars in any global system of disease prevention, control, and response. Identifying public health events of concern quickly and accurately, to provide early warning of outbreaks and new pathogens, is particularly critical. Epidemic intelligence prompts timely action to prevent such events from becoming more severe and potentially spreading internationally (Murray and Cohen 2017).

The World Health Organization (WHO) is mandated with the responsibility for global epidemic intelligence gathering under the remit of the International Health Regulations (IHR), an internationally binding legal instrument that governs how national governments and the WHO respond to international health emergencies. Historically, this UN specialized agency relied on paper-based reports from official government sources. When developed and launched by Canadian public health officials in the late-1990s, the Global Public Health Intelligence Network (GPHIN) proved to be a ground-breaking initiative for expanding capacities to rapidly gather and disseminate epidemic intelligence. Within a decade, however, GPHIN's role would become less prominent, and was indeed downgraded by the Canadian government. Technological advances, new data platforms, and a shift in the political climate away from multilateralism led to the sidelining of GPHIN. This decline in support mirrored WHO's struggle with chronic underfunding at a time of increasing risks from emerging pathogens and outbreaks, notably from zoonotic diseases (Smith et al. 2014).

This chapter begins by briefly tracing the creation and integration of GPHIN, as a technically and politically innovative tool for strengthening outbreak intelligence capacities nationally and globally. We then explain the factors leading to the decline of support for GPHIN and its neglect during a period of withdrawal from global engagement and co-operation under the Stephen Harper government (2006–15). We consider the implications for the replacement of GPHIN with alternative arrangements for national and global health security, notably in relation to the emergence of SARS-CoV-2 and the COVID-19 pandemic. We conclude with lessons learned for GPHIN and the future role of early warning systems amid anticipation of new revisions to the IHR (2005) and reform of WHO and potentially of global health governance more broadly.

Background: Creation and Expansion of GPHIN

Several critical trends at the turn of the twentieth century led to the creation and refinement of GPHIN, which offered a cutting-edge contribution to international disease surveillance. First, the rapid transformation and growth of communication technologies significantly changed how information could be collected and shared. Second, in response to accelerating globalization, the security sector's traditional focus on issues of national economic or military importance expanded to encompass a wider range of social and political issues. The emerging framework of "human security" in the 1990s sought to shift focus from the security of the state to that of individuals and communities, reframing basic human needs such as access to education and health care as security concerns (UNDP 1994). Amid the HIV/AIDS pandemic, the reframing of health by WHO and other global health actors became increasingly common, contributing to the popularization of the concept of "global health security." Third, as a prominent voice in the global health landscape, Canada was a respected champion for both multilateralism and a broadly defined global health agenda. It was against this backdrop and at the nexus of security, global public health, and information technology that the first iteration of GPHIN (GPHIN I) was established in 1997.

GPHIN I was created by Canadian public health officials with financial support from the Nuclear Threat Initiative based in Washington, DC. Initially a prototype, GPHIN was a leader in the yet-to-be-explored field of Internet-based disease surveillance (Mykhalovskiy and Weir 2006). It served as a national early warning and situational awareness network designed to detect potential public health threats worldwide through real-time, events-based monitoring of media reports from around the world (Mawudeku et al. 2016). In 2000, GPHIN was then integrated by WHO as one of the centrepieces of its Global Outbreak Alert and Response Network (GOARN). GOARN was a global "network of networks," serving as a repository of global epidemic intelligence and a reserve of experts that could be deployed by WHO in response to identified public health events. Supplementing traditional reporting and co-operation with member states, GOARN enhanced WHO's ability to detect potential international public health threats. The historically novel reporting relationship between GPHIN and WHO prompted comparisons with Canada's formative contribution to international peace and security through its championing of UN peacekeeping (Wenham 2016).

The post-9/11 world saw a broader framing of security issues to include biological, bioterrorist, and chemical threats, all of which contributed to the growing prominence of the global health security paradigm. Amid renewed efforts to further strengthen early warning and rapid response to outbreaks following the severe acute respiratory syndrome (SARS) outbreak in 2002–03, GPHIN II was launched in November 2004. The Minister of Health at the time, Ujjal Dosanjh, exemplified the tone of Canada's approach, noting that "such incidents as SARS and avian influenza have demonstrated the importance of a strengthened network of international cooperation and communications. GPHIN is an example of the benefit of this increased collaboration" (Government of Canada 2004). The launch of GPHIN II was among several significant investments made by the Canadian government in its health emergency preparedness and response capacities during this period, including the creation of the Public Health Agency of Canada (PHAC) in 2005. These developments coincided with the revision of the International Health Regulations (IHR) by WHO member states as the international legal framework for preventing and controlling the international spread of disease. The embedding of non-government information sources in the IHR's functions, as provided by GPHIN II and similar systems, was especially seen as a substantial strengthening of national and global epidemic intelligence in an increasingly interconnected world.

The prototype of enhancements for GPHIN II was developed in collaboration with Nstein Technologies, in recognition of the "need to make the most of the tools of modern communication . . . for the earliest threat detection possible" (Ted Turner quoted in Government of Canada 2004). This second iteration of GPHIN brought a new level of sophistication, marked by an expansion to operations in seven languages, the adoption of an all-hazards approach, and a greatly increased data-processing capacity. Maintained by PHAC as a hub of surveillance and response, GPHIN II performed secure web-based system searches of news wires with more than twenty thousand daily news reports and websites, on a wide range of topics including disease outbreaks, bioterrorism, chemical exposures, product and drug safety, and natural disasters. Information was then filtered for relevance and made available via electronic international alerts to GPHIN users, including WHO, government authorities worldwide, and NGOs, as well as daily reports for use within Canada. If the automated filtering by the system's algorithms determined an event met a certain threshold of significance, an alert would be sent to GPHIN users automatically. Events at a lower threshold of significance, or deemed irrelevant by the automated process, would be examined by GPHIN analysts from a wide range of disciplinary backgrounds (e.g., journalism, public health, medicine, social sciences) to check their accuracy. Any potential alerts erroneously dismissed would be actioned appropriately.

The incorporation of GPHIN into global health surveillance systems was a critical contribution to WHO's capacity to identify disease events, sometimes even before states reached a comprehensive understanding (Davies 2015). In the mid-2000s, GPHIN was providing approximately 40 per cent of WHO's early warning information on disease outbreaks. Perhaps even more significantly, the creation and success of GPHIN helped revitalize and transform the global impetus for international monitoring of disease outbreaks and other health threats (Mykhalovskiy and Weir 2006).

Overall, initially envisioned as an early warning system to strengthen Canadian responses to potential public health threats, GPHIN became recognized as "one of the most imaginative and creative additions to global disease detection . . . [and] a key tool for the detection of significant new epidemics, wherever in the world they may occur" (Government of Canada 2004). Yet while GPHIN's contributions were celebrated at the global level, its role remained to inform Canada's responses to global health crises including SARS (2002–03), H1N1 (2009) and MERS (2012) (Dion, Abdelmalik, and Mawudeku 2015). Indeed, in a world of increasingly permeable borders and mobile populations, distinctions between "global" versus "national" public health risks became somewhat blurred.

The Displacement of GPHIN

The accolades given to GPHIN for its early contributions to addressing issues of data scarcity and access to enhance global public health surveillance systems through the increased use of open-source and unofficial data sources have been well earned. The early detection of SARS by GPHIN in 2002, in particular, put it at the forefront of a new era with the coming into force of the revised IHR (2005). However, two developments since this period led to the decline of GPHIN. The first concerned dynamics at the global level. On the heels of GPHIN's success came the advent of other platforms, such as ProMED and HealthMap. Launched in 2006, HealthMap is an automated system based on algorithms for data collection, filtration, and assessment. The HealthMap system expanded open-source disease surveillance by integrating "disparate data sources, including online news aggregators, eyewitness reports, expert-curated discussions and validated official reports, to achieve a unified and comprehensive view of the current global state of infectious diseases and their effects on human and animal health" (cited in Roberts 2020). The importance of HealthMap was demonstrated in March 2014 when it issued a health alert regarding a hemorrhagic fever in Guinea, which was reported to WHO by the government nine days later as a rapidly evolving Ebola virus outbreak.

In principle, these additional platforms should have strengthened WHO's GOARN, expanding available intelligence sources. In practice, GOARN shifted over this period from its original mandate of global coordination of early warning public health intelligence to a stronger focus on response. One reason for this shift was the increased workload of reviewing and analyzing incoming intelligence from a growing number of traditional and digital sources. This increase in demands on staff coincided with funding pressures on WHO caused by decades of zero real and absolute growth in the assessed contributions of member states, policies upheld amid the global financial crisis (Lee and Piper 2020). The decision by GOARN to shift focus to response activities led surveillance platforms to work more directly with governments and each other. As part of their commitments under the 2005 IHR, many States Parties also invested in strengthening core capacities during this period, including disease surveillance. Many countries began to develop direct relationships with other countries, often circumventing WHO. Instead of a globally coordinated network of networks, therefore, epidemic intelligence became increasingly fragmented. GPHIN maintained its close working relationship with GOARN but found itself operating amid multiple, even competitive, systems of epidemic intelligence (Roberts 2020).

The second factor leading to the decline of GPHIN stemmed from domestic policy decisions. The emergence of a more fragmented global epidemic intelligence environment coincided with rapid technological change and expanding "big data" sources (e.g., social media), which required platforms to continually invest in updates. However, amid increased austerity measures under the Harper government (2006–15), the necessary financing for updates was not forthcoming and GPHIN failed to keep pace (Carter, Stojanovic, and de Bruijn 2018).

In 2013, an evaluation of epidemic intelligence systems revealed that the GPHIN "system design did not allow the extraction or collection of data in a format compatible" with the needs of the Global Health Security Initiative, a prominent Ottawa-based international partnership formed in 2001 to strengthen global public health preparedness (Barboza et al. 2013). The impacts of insufficient investment in GPHIN were compounded by changes in PHAC management. Efforts to align bureaucratic processes with other federal departments, and to reduce spending, ultimately resulted in an undervaluation of and subsequent departure of relevant public health expertise from PHAC's senior management. While these developments originated under the Harper government, the Trudeau government (2015–) has not reversed this trend. This has contributed to institutionalized misunderstandings of how to effectively leverage GPHIN's capacity. In a renewal process undertaken from 2015 to 2019, driven in part by efforts to bring GPHIN into compliance with government IT policies, PHAC and the National Research Council replaced GPHIN with a "modular platform that incorporates modern natural language processing techniques to support more ambitious situational awareness goals" (Carter, Stojanovic, and de Bruijn 2018). As noted in the interim report by the independent review of GPHIN launched by the Government of Canada in 2020, "while the [renewal] led to some enhancements, some potential opportunities might not have been realized and not all were satisfied with the amount of improvement that resulted" (External Review Panel 2021).

However, this description suggests a continued lack of understanding of the important role played by a system like GPHIN. The renewal resulted in a significant curtailing of certain GPHIN functions, prompting internal dissent and resignations. In practice, this meant that GPHIN alerts have not been issued for public health events in Canada since 2014, and changes to reporting procedures meant that GPHIN analysts could no longer issue alerts about detected public health threats without senior management's approval (External Review Panel 2021). This requirement undermined GPHIN capacity to provide rapid early warning. As described in a *Globe and Mail* investigation, "as a result of this edict, the alert system went silent, which had a cascading effect inside the department. Soon after, international surveillance and intelligence-gathering activities were also cut back. Analysts were told to focus on domestic issues that were deemed more valuable to the department" (Robertson 2020a).

Overall, at both the global and domestic levels, governments have failed to invest sufficiently in up-to-date and coordinated epidemic intelligence systems since SARS-1. GPHIN suffered as part of this broader pattern of neglect. From a flagship platform celebrated internationally, lack of investment by successive federal governments over time saw it struggle to keep pace with technological change (PHAC 2018). Most importantly, at a time when risks of major public health events evolved and grew amid intensified globalization, Canada's epidemic intelligence system became increasingly neglected.

The Role of GPHIN in Early Warning on COVID-19

The scale of global devastation resulting from COVID-19 is testament to a collective failure to act on lessons learned from previous global health emergencies, both in terms of repeated calls from experts to strengthen the authority of WHO in its global coordination role, and the need to enhance preparedness and response capacities at the national level. Unfortunately, GPHIN's trajectory and the degree to which it was leveraged to support national and global responses to the COVID-19 pandemic are no exception.

Canada's Chief Public Health Officer, Theresa Tam, confirmed that GPHIN was the body responsible for informing her of a cluster of coronavirus cases in Wuhan in late December 2019 (Gilmore 2020). Government records confirm that data on the outbreak was first shared by GPHIN on 31 December 2019 (PHAC 2020). When questioned on the role of GPHIN in Canada's COVID-19 response, Health Minister Patty Hajdu underscored that Canadian officials were aware of the risks to human health and "watching it very carefully" in late 2019 and early 2020. However, she also acknowledged that greater intelligence provided by GPHIN would have likely contributed to a better and earlier understanding of the situation (Gilmore 2020). Indeed, the critical value added of a tool like GPHIN is that its reliance on unofficial sources like local news outlets and social media means that it should, in theory, outpace the data-collection and information-sharing processes of official government sources.

Analyses of the beginning of the COVID-19 pandemic contend that GPHIN was not leveraged to its full potential in the earliest days and weeks of the outbreak, nor in the period from early January to mid-March 2020, during which Health Canada's assessment of the risk of COVID-19 to Canadians was persistently maintained as "low" (Wark 2020). At least three early warning platforms—BlueDot, HealthMap, and ProMED—have been credited for alerts on 30 December 2019 regarding a cluster of "unidentified pneumonia cases" in Wuhan, several days ahead of WHO's first public notification of the outbreak via Twitter on 4 January 2020

(WHO 2020). Key questions surrounding the role of GPHIN in responses to COVID-19 extend beyond whether or not the threat could have been identified a few days or weeks earlier. That GPHIN was not issuing global alerts throughout 2019 and 2020 and, equally importantly, that it was not being drawn upon for situational awareness as the COVID-19 pandemic unfolded suggest that critical opportunities were missed. For example, if GPHIN had been operating at optimal capacity, it is difficult to imagine that the intelligence network would not have picked up on red flags around the global spread of SARS-CoV-2 and its impacts, which were being signalled at escalating rates by late January and throughout February (Wark 2020). Similar questions could be asked about what intelligence informed Canada's preparedness and response to the new COVID-19 variants that subsequently emerged during the pandemic.

There was widespread disappointment with GPHIN's failure to provide timely Canadian intelligence or global early warning alerts. Simply put, "the Global Public Health Intelligence Network was meant to perform a critical warning task with regard to the COVID-19 outbreak. This was its job" (Wesley Wark quoted in Brewster 2020). Considerations of the role of GPHIN and epidemiological intelligence gathering in national and global responses to COVID-19 must extend beyond questions of what information was collected and how, to how this information was made use of once available. Notwithstanding the potential benefits that earlier intelligence could have had, why did the early warning signs not trigger a sufficiently robust national public health response to prevent (or mitigate) the pandemic? The failure in Canada to prevent the devastating impacts of COVID-19 suggests deeper structural and institutional challenges, including an inadequate incident-management system. For future events, how can Canada better leverage its intelligence gathering capacity to support timely and evidence-informed decisions? What investments will be required from Canada and others to sustainably advance global health security? The next and final section expands on these dimensions, presenting some of the lessons learned so far with respect to the role of GPHIN.

Lessons Learned

According to the 2018 *Joint External Evaluation of Canada Self-Assessment Report*, which assessed the country's core capacities to carry out its commitments under the IHR (2005), "Canada has strong public health surveillance systems in place to detect and monitor existing and emerging disease and events of significance to human health, animal health and health security. These systems are able to act upon, communicate and share information across authorities, jurisdictions and sectors" (PHAC 2018). However, against the backdrop of the COVID-19 pandemic, many have raised questions about the effectiveness of existing epidemic intelligence to provide early warning from major public health events (Robertson 2020b). The focus has understandably been on the weakened role of GPHIN, which "should have been at the heart of a Canadian and indeed a global early warning system" (Wesley Wark quoted in Brewster 2020). Its neglect and decline over many years points to important lessons for preparing more effectively for future public health events that pose major risks to the country's health and well-being.

First, the exponential increase in data sources, variety, and volume since GPHIN's launch in the 1990s has proven both a blessing and a curse. Improvements to data access and scarcity, through open and unofficial sources, have undoubtedly strengthened early warning systems. The SARS, MERS (or Middle East respiratory syndrome), Ebola, and other outbreaks have been detected using similar sources prior to official government confirmation of such events. However, the explosion of "big data" poses new challenges. The capacity to gather ever more data and identify significant events amid more "noise" is increasingly difficult. If investments to update and support epidemic intelligence systems are not forthcoming, more data can slow down, rather than speed up, required action.

Second, this points to the need to recognize that epidemic intelligence goes far beyond ever-expanding data gathering. GPHIN and other digital platforms have continued to increase their data sources. However, it is how data are processed, analyzed, and shared that determines how useful these systems are for informing timely responses. These latter functions are invariably labour intensive and cannot be replaced entirely by automation. Some filtering of data is possible, using machine learning and other forms of artificial intelligence, but turning data into usable intelligence to guide action depends on skilled analysts and efficient reporting mechanisms. These functions must be supported, in turn, by appropriate resources and systems that include clear protocols for risk assessment. Systems for rapid reporting of identified risks to appropriate authorities are also essential. Thus, any failure to act quickly during the earliest stages of the COVID-19 pandemic are unlikely due to a few days' delay in early intelligence gathering. Rather, analyses of this data and the reporting of the assessed risk to appropriate decision-makers, along with clear procedures within government to act quickly and decisively on this intelligence, is where the delays are likely to have occurred.

Third, clear structural challenges have hindered the role of GPHIN. This points to the clear need to prioritize investments in an epidemic intelligence system that ensures access to the most up-to-date data sources, support for data analysts, and upgrading on a regular basis. The cost of such a system is not insubstantial but it is far less than that incurred from the failure to act in a timely manner to emerging events. The system for Canada may draw upon the many platforms now available for gathering data and need not replicate them. Investment may be focused instead on analysis of data for Canadian needs. Moreover, public health intelligence systems cannot be stand-alone operations; rather, they must be integrated with other parts of the Canadian health system. The decentralized nature of the health system in Canada, however, poses some structural problems. For example, variation in data collection and barriers to data sharing across provinces/territories (e.g., genomic sequencing) appear to be a hindrance to rapid action (Flood and Philpott 2020). Epidemic intelligence must also be better integrated with other parts of government, including the national security and intelligence community. In its early years, GPHIN analysts recognized this need and often collaborated, at the working level, with relevant units in the RCMP and CSIS, for example. These types of interdepartmental working relationships need revisiting as part of Canada's post-COVID-19 reflections. This suggests the need to consider what type of intelligence is needed for early warning for epidemic intelligence. For example, conflict, displacement of populations, terrorist threats, and environmental factors can be predictive of potential public health risks. Thus, a whole-of-government approach based on an "all-hazards" framework may be warranted to "connect the dots" across different risks to Canadian interests, including national security.

Finally, the effectiveness of any national-level system of epidemic intelligence is dependent on the quality of global health governance. Major public health events, by definition, go beyond individual countries in terms of both cause and effect. The chronic underfunding of WHO and, by extension, the weakening of GOARN's early warning function also need urgent attention in the wake of the COVID-19 pandemic (Gostin, Moon, and Meier 2020; Lee 2020). Any effort to strengthen national-level systems must thus support, and not undermine, global systems for gathering and sharing epidemic intelligence.

Conclusion

Early warning systems and epidemic intelligence capacities need to be reviewed as part of Canada's post-COVID-19 lesson-learning process. Any approach to strengthening health emergency preparedness and response capacities, both nationally and globally, should sensibly leverage existing knowledge and experience. However, future Canadian contributions to global public health intelligence gathering, and considerations of how to integrate these functions across different government agencies, must recognize the unique and often hidden attributes of GPHIN. First, GPHIN's historical successes were a result of the work of highly trained, multidisciplinary analysts with prior knowledge, specialized expertise, and judgment skills specific to identifying public health events of potential concern. The broadening of skill sets and professional backgrounds among PHAC management, to align it with other parts of government, came at the cost of critically needed specialist public health expertise. A renewal of these capacities is required, although where such expertise should best be located remains unclear. Second, GPHIN was as beneficial to Canada as it was to the rest of the world. A health intelligence system that artificially delineates between national and global risks fails to recognize the interconnected nature of such risks and the critical need for coordinated action within and across countries. Finally, GPHIN initially operated in an organizational environment that was conducive to the agility, collaboration, and technological innovation required to remain responsive in a dynamic landscape. National security, encompassing health security within Canada and globally, will benefit from renewed public health intelligence gathering that is independent of partisan politics, sustainably resourced, and linked to appropriate incident-management systems at the national and global levels.

REFERENCES

Barboza, Philippe, Laetitia Vaillant, Abla Mawudeku, Noele P. Nelson, David M. Hartley, Lawrence C. Madoff, Jens P. Linge, Nigel Collier, John S. Brownstein, Roman Yangarber, and Pascal Astagneau on behalf of the Early Alerting, Reporting Project of the Global Health Security Initiative. 2013. "Evaluation of Epidemic Intelligence Systems Integrated in the Early Alerting and Reporting Project for the Detection of A/H5N1 Influenza Events." *PLoS ONE* 8 (3): e57252. https://doi.org/10.1371/journal.pone.0057252.

Brewster, Murray. 2020. "Inside Canada's Frayed Pandemic Early Warning System and Its Covid-19 Response." *CBC News*, 22 April 2020. https://www.cbc.ca/news/politics/covid19-pandemic-early-warning-1.5537925.

Carter, Dave, Marta Stojanovic, and Berry de Bruijn. 2018. "Revitalizing the Global Public Health Intelligence Network (GPHIN)." *Online Journal of Public Health Informatics* 10 (1): e59. https://doi.org/10.5210/ojphi.v10i1.8912.

Davies, Sara E. 2015. "Internet Surveillance and Disease Outbreaks." In *Routledge Handbook of Global Health Security*, edited by Simon Rushton and Jeremy Youde, 226–38. 1st ed. Routledge. 226–38. https://doi.org/10.4324/9780203078563-20.

Dion, Marie, Phillip Abdelmalik, and Abla Mawudeku. 2015. "Big Data and the Global Public Health Intelligence Network (GPHIN)." *CCDR* 41 (9): 41–9. https://www.canada.ca/content/dam/phac-aspc/migration/phac-aspc/publicat/ccdr-rmtc/15vol41/dr-rm41-09/assets/pdf/ccdrv41i09a02-eng.pdf.

External Review Panel. 2021. "Interim Report for the Review of the Global Public Health Intelligence Network." Public Health Agency of Canada, 2021. https://www.canada.ca/en/public-health/corporate/mandate/about-agency/external-advisory-bodies/list/independent-review-global-public-health-intelligence-network/interim-report.html.

Flood, Colleen M., and Jane Philpott. 2020. "Vulnerabilities in Governance of Public Health and COVID-19." *Globe and Mail*, 9 July 2020. https://www.theglobeandmail.com/opinion/article-vulnerabilities-in-governance-of-public-health-and-covid-19/.

Gilmore, Rachel. 2020. "Hajdu: Sidelining of Pandemic Alert System an 'Administrative' Decision." *CTV News*, 10 September 2020. https://www.ctvnews.ca/politics/hajdu-sidelining-of-pandemic-alert-system-an-administrative-decision-1.5100207.

Gostin, Lawrence, Suerie Moon, and Benjamin Mason Meier. 2020. "Reimagining Global Health Governance in the Age of COVID-19." *American Journal of Public Health* 110 (11): 1615–19.

Government of Canada. 2004. "Early Warning System Tracks Global Public Health Threats 24/7." News release, last modified 17 November 2004. https://www.canada.ca/en/news/archive/2004/11/early-warning-system-tracks-global-public-health-threats-24-7.html.

Lee, Kelley. 2020. "Global Infectious Disease Governance: Getting off the Merry-Go-Round of WHO Reform." *The UN at 75: Coronavirus and Competition* (Fall 2020), Perry World House, University of Pennsylvania. https://drive.google.com/file/d/1nU7GoAkwzhlyp7sL5RKi1QQXKY7hHxQE/view.

Lee, Kelley, and Julianne Piper. 2020. "WHO and the COVID-19 Pandemic: Less Reform, More Innovation." *Global Governance* 26:523–33.

Mawudeku, Abla, Philip AbdelMalik, Richard Lemay, and Louise Boily. 2016. "GPHIN Phase 3: One Mandate, Multiple Stakeholders." In *The Politics of Surveillance and Response to Disease Outbreaks*, edited by Sara E. Davies and Jeremy R. Youde, 71–84. Farnham, UK: Taylor and Francis.

Murray, Jillian, and Adam L. Cohen. 2017. "Infectious Disease Surveillance." In *International Encyclopedia of Public Health*, edited by Stella R. Quah, 222–9. Oxford: Elsevier.

Mykhalovskiy, Eric, and Lorna Weir. 2006. "The Global Public Health Intelligence Network and Early Warning Outbreak Detection: A Canadian Contribution to Global Public Health." *Canadian Journal of Public Health* 97 (1): 42–4. https://doi.org/10.1007/BF03405213.

PHAC (Public Health Agency of Canada). 2018. "International Health Regulations—Joint External Evaluation of Canada Self-Assessment Report." Government of Canada, 20 April 2018. https://www.canada.ca/en/public-health/services/emergency-preparedness-response/international-health-regulations-joint-external-evaluation-canada-self-assessment-report.html

———. 2020. "President of the PHAC Before the Standing Committee on Health: Canadian Response to the Novel Coronavirus (March 31, 2020)." Government of Canada, 9 June 2020. https://www.canada.ca/en/public-health/corporate/transparency/proactive-disclosure/parliamentary-committee-appearances/standing-committee-health-president-covid-july-29-2020.html.

Roberts, S. L. 2020. "Incorporating Non-Expert Evidence into Surveillance and Early Detection of Public Health Emergencies." *SSHAP Case Study*, Issue 2 (April 2020). https://www.socialscienceinaction.org/resources/incorporating-non-expert-evidence-surveillance-early-detection-public-health-emergencies/.

Robertson, Grant. 2020a. "Ottawa Turned Off 'Wrong Tap' on Pandemic Surveillance, Former Intelligence Adviser Says." *Globe and Mail*, 1 October 2020. https://www.theglobeandmail.com/canada/article-ottawa-failed-to-recognize-value-of-pandemic-surveillance-former/.

———. 2020b. " 'Without Early Warning You Can't Have Early Response': How Canada's World-Class Pandemic Alert System Failed." *Globe and Mail*, 25 July 2020. https://www.theglobeandmail.com/canada/article-without-early-warning-you-cant-have-early-response-how-canadas/.

Smith, Katherine F., Michael Goldberg, Samantha Rosenthal, Lynn Carlson, Jane Chen, Cici Chen, and Sohini Ramachandran. 2014. "Global Rise in Human Infectious Disease Outbreaks." *Journal of the Royal Society Interface* 11, no. 101 (December). https://dx.doi.org/10.1098/rsif.2014.0950.

UNDP (United Nations Development Programme). 1994. *Human Development Report 1994*. New York: Oxford University Press. http://hdr.undp.org/sites/default/files/reports/255/hdr_1994_en_complete_nostats.pdf.

Wark, Wesley. 2020. "The System Was Not Blinking Red: Intelligence, Early Warning and Risk Assessment in a Pandemic Crisis." *Centre for International Governance Innovation*, 24 August 2020. https://www.cigionline.org/articles/system-was-not-blinking-red-intelligence-early-warning-and-risk-assessment-pandemic-crisis.

Wenham, Clare. 2016. "GPHIN, GOARN, Gone? The Role of the World Health Organization in Global Disease Surveillance And Response." In *The Politics of Surveillance and Response to Disease Outbreaks: The New Frontier for States and Non-state Actors*, edited by Sara E. Davies and Jeremy R. Youde, 107–20. Farnham: Taylor and Francis.

WHO (@WHO). 2020. "China has reported to WHO a cluster of pneumonia cases—with no deaths—in Wuhan, Hubei Province. Investigations are underway to identify the cause of this illness." Twitter, January 4, 2020. https://twitter.com/WHO/status/1213523866703814656?s=20.

Privacy vs. Health: Can the Government of Canada Leverage Existing National Security Surveillance Capabilities to Stop the Spread?

Leah West

Introduction

In early 2020, as COVID-19 spread across Canada, officials within and outside the national security community considered how state resources and capabilities could be retooled or redirected to manage the pandemic. One of the key debates that emerged—in this country and abroad—was whether a state's surveillance apparatus, used by federal security and intelligence agencies to detect and monitor national security threats, could be leveraged in a public health crisis. Alternatively, could the federal government mandate that individuals or telecommunication service providers share the location data generated by wireless devices—namely, cell phones—with health or security agencies? This chapter looks at these questions from a legal perspective and answers them in the negative.

Divided into three parts, the chapter explains that existing legal authorities and emergency legislation do not permit the federal government's collection of Canadian location data for public health purposes. Part 1 briefly describes the use of electronic surveillance to limit the spread of COVID-19 in other countries as well as the contact-tracing application developed by the Government of Canada. It finds that Canada's choice to use a voluntary application rather than some form of mandated collection of location data was a less effective contact-tracing tool. The application also provides no additional capacity for the enforcement of quarantine orders and public health measures.

Part 2 then canvasses the legal authorities that permit the collection of cell phone and location data by Canadian state agencies, namely, the Canadian Security Intelligence Service (CSIS), the Communications Security Establishment (CSE), and the Royal Canadian Mounted Police (RCMP). It concludes that, except for in very specific instances, existing authorities do not permit the mass collection or analysis of data necessary to trace the spread of communicable disease or enforce public health measures.

Part 3 examines Canada's emergency legislation, specifically the *Emergencies Act* and *Quarantine Act*. It refutes the arguments advanced by some scholars that the federal *Emergencies Act* in particular could be used to conduct electronic surveillance or allow cabinet to order the requisition of location data or subscriber information from Canadians or service providers. To hold otherwise would mean acknowledging property rights in personal information, a subject of debate for decades. Such a legal move would have wide-ranging implications far beyond the context of the existing pandemic and demands the full consideration of Parliament.

The chapter concludes by identifying potential legal reforms that could permit the government to leverage Canada's security apparatus to mitigate or control future public health crises. The normative question of whether the government *should* employ state surveillance tools is not addressed here but is considered by Jessica Davis and Alex Corbeil in a separate chapter in this volume.

Part 1: Surveillance to Stop the Spread?

In March 2020, the Israeli government passed emergency regulations allowing its domestic security services to conduct digital contact tracing using a classified database that compiles data provided by every telecommunications service provider in the country (Shwartz Altshuler and Aridor Hershkowitz 2020). The names of individuals who test positive are shared by health officials with the police, who then analyze the data to (1) identify and notify close contacts, and (2) enforce quarantine orders

(Landau, Kubovich, and Breiner 2020). Singapore, South Korea, and China implemented similarly sweeping surveillance measures to identify people who may be infected and to crack down on those violating public health measures (Doffman 2020). Ultimately, these measures did not prevent the spread of the coronavirus in these countries. However, they are credited with slowing the spread of the virus in Singapore (Ng et al. 2020) and South Korea (Yang 2021) in the early months of the pandemic, and with flattening the curve of infection rates in China (Sahin 2020).

Canadian privacy advocates widely decried these programs (see, e.g., CCLA 2020), but there was no robust public debate about their appropriateness or potential efficacy for slowing the spread of the virus. Ultimately, the Government of Canada chose not to implement a form of electronic surveillance or rely on security or intelligence services to assist in contact tracing. Instead, the government developed an application ("app"), COVID Alert, that users voluntarily download onto their phones. Once downloaded, users must enable the app, which then transmits a unique personal identifier via Bluetooth signal to other users. If a user tests positive for COVID-19, they can choose to enter a unique key into the app (only provided if they receive an official positive test result). The app will then notify other users whose signal crossed paths with the infected user's signal, warning them that they have come into close contact with a person with COVID-19 and encouraging them to self-isolate and get tested. At the time of its release, the app was commended by privacy experts for its strong privacy protections (see, e.g., Geist 2020). However, since then, the app's effectiveness as a public health tool has been called into question (Haggart 2020). For one, not every province and territory chose to adopt the app; the public health systems in Alberta, British Columbia, Nunavut, and Yukon do not support diagnosis reporting. Second, there is limited uptake in provinces that do support the app. By September 2020, three months after its release, less than 10 per cent of the Canadian population was using the app, and only 514 users (all within Ontario) notified the app about a positive test result; that is less than 1 per cent of the number of positive test results in the province during that period (Turnbull 2020). By March 2021, the app had been downloaded more than 6 million times, and the number of people who used it to report a positive test had increased to

20,000, yet that still only represents 5 per cent of positive cases in Canada (ISED 2021).

What is more, a flaw in the app's program identified months after its rollout requires users to ensure that the app is enabled daily. The number of notifications or contacts that have gone undetected due to the bug in the app remains entirely unknown (Daigle 2020).

Canada continues to struggle to control the spread of the virus, and the cost of the pandemic, not only in human life but to the Canadian economy, is staggering. Across the country, provinces and municipalities have undergone successive "lockdowns" to keep their health-care systems from collapsing. When the pandemic is finally behind us, we should expect policy-makers to seriously reconsider the decision to rely on citizens to volunteer their information rather than utilizing the more robust surveillance capabilities of Canada's national security and intelligence community. The need for reflection is especially important in light of the World Health Organization's warning of the likelihood of even worse pandemics in the future (WHO 2020; Dangerfield 2020).

Part 2: Canada's Domestic Surveillance Authorities

The collection of personal information by federal officials is governed primarily by the *Privacy Act* and the *Canadian Charter of Rights and Freedoms* (*Charter*). Personal information is defined as "information about an identifiable individual that is recorded in any form" (*Privacy Act*, s. 3). This includes a person's name, address, telephone number, cell phone identifier (or International Mobile Equipment Identity), and location history. The information necessary to conduct contact tracing and enforce public health orders, therefore, meets the definition of personal information.

First, under the *Privacy Act*, the government may not collect personal information unless it relates directly to an operating program or activity of the institution (*Privacy Act*, s. 4). Moreover, the government may not use personal information without informed consent (*Privacy Act*, s. 7). There are, however, exceptions to the use limitation built into the statutes governing Canada's security intelligence agencies and the Canadian *Criminal Code*. These acts give the relevant agencies the legal authority to collect and use personal information in furtherance of their mandates without notification or consent. For example, section 12 of the *CSIS Act* stipulates that

> The Service shall collect, by investigation or otherwise, to the extent that it is strictly necessary, and analyse and retain information and intelligence respecting activities that may on reasonable grounds be suspected of constituting threats to the security of Canada and, in relation thereto, shall report to and advise the Government of Canada.

Second, some—but not all—personal information collected by a government agency is subject to privacy protections under section 8 of the *Charter*. Section 8 guarantees the right to be secure against unreasonable search or seizure. This has been interpreted to mean that the *Charter*'s protections are only triggered when there is a search or a seizure that is subject to "reasonable expectation of privacy" (REP) (*R v S.A.B.*, 2003 SCC 60 at para 38). For example, one cannot reasonably claim a privacy interest in the collection of their name, the address of their workplace, or their hair colour. Rather, personal information attracting constitutional protection is "information which tends to reveal intimate details of the lifestyle and personal choices of the individual" (*R v Plant*, [1993] 3 SCR 281 at 293).

Information collected by electronic searches and seizures or through electronic surveillance will almost certainly meet the REP threshold (Forcese and West 2021, 435). Indeed, almost thirty years ago, the Supreme Court recognized that "electronic surveillance is the greatest leveler of human privacy ever known" (*R v Duarte*, [1990] 1 SCR 30 at para 22). More recently, the Supreme Court recognized that a police request for an Internet user's subscriber information might engage section 8 of the *Charter* where the police seek to link anonymous online activities to that subscriber information (*R v Spencer*, 2014 SCC 43). Likewise, collecting subscriber information or location data either from a service provider or directly from a user that reveals their physical travel patterns and personal interactions would certainly trigger the *Charter*'s protections.

Once triggered, a government search or seizure must be "reasonable" to not fall afoul of the *Charter*. A search is presumptively unreasonable if it is not pre-authorized by a neutral and impartial arbiter capable of acting judicially (*Hunter et al. v Southam Inc.*, [1984] 2 SCR 145). We typically conceive of this as the need to obtain a judicially authorized warrant. Alternatively, a warrantless search may be reasonable if it satisfies three criteria: (1) the search is authorized by law; (2) the law itself is reasonable; and (3) the search is carried out in a reasonable manner (*R v Collins*, [1987] 1 SCR 265 at para 23).

The statutes governing Canada's national security and intelligence agencies set out various criteria for obtaining prior authorization for highly intrusive searches (e.g., police wiretaps under part VI of the *Criminal Code*), and the legal parameters for conducting less intrusive warrantless searches (e.g., intelligence collection under s. 12 of the *CSIS Act*). None of these existing authorities permit the collection of personal information to conduct data analysis or electronic surveillance to stop the spread of a naturally occurring pandemic.

Before moving on, a note about the *Personal Information Protection and Electronic Documents Act (PIPEDA)*. PIPEDA regulates private-sector organizations involved in commercial activities unless ousted by applicable provincial privacy legislation. Under the Act, consent is required for collecting, using, and disclosing a person's information, particularly where subsequent use and disclosure is for a purpose other than that for which the information was collected (Forcese and West 2021, 435). *PIPEDA* binds private-sector organizations even when information is requested by federal and provincial agencies like the RCMP or Public Health Ontario.

CSIS Act

CSIS may collect Canadian datasets under section 11.05 of the *CSIS Act*. A Canadian dataset is "a collection of information stored as an electronic record and characterized by a common subject matter" that "contains personal information, as defined in section 3 of the *Privacy Act*." This data "does not directly and immediately relate to activities that represent a threat to the security of Canada," and "predominantly relates to individuals within Canada or Canadians." Location data generated from cellphone users within Canada to conduct contact tracing satisfies each element of this definition.

However, CSIS may only collect this information if it contributes to CSIS's security intelligence mandate under section 12, its security threat reduction mandate under section 12.1, or its foreign intelligence mandate under section 16 of the *CSIS Act*. The latter is not applicable to this discussion, as tracing the spread of the virus across Canada is also clearly not a foreign intelligence task.

Importantly, CSIS's security intelligence and threat reduction mandates are tied to the definition of "threats to the security of Canada." Section 2 of the *CSIS Act* defines which "threats to the security of Canada" may be investigated and reduced by CSIS. They include (1) espionage and sabotage; (2) foreign-influenced activities; (3) terrorism; and (4) subversion. Here lies the problem: the natural spread of a communicable illness does not fall into any of these categories, and therefore is not subject to investigation by CSIS.

Criminal Code

Under the *Criminal Code* of Canada, law enforcement officers may apply to judges for orders to have third parties (namely, telephone service providers) produce large quantities of data. In particular, a judge or justice may issue orders for the production of (1) "transmission data," including information about telecommunications such as the type, direction, date, time, duration, size, origin, destination, or termination of the communication, but not including the content of communications; and (2) "tracking data," or data that relates to the location of a transaction, individual ,or thing (*Criminal Code*, ss. 487.011, 487.016, 487.017).

However, to issue these orders, a judge must be satisfied that there are reasonable grounds to suspect that "an offence has been or will be committed under this or any other Act of Parliament" (*Criminal Code*, ss. 487.016(2)(a), 487.017(2)(a)). In other words, the data can only be collected if an officer can establish that there are grounds to suspect a criminal offence has or will occur in advance of requesting the information. Thus, while such an order may produce evidence of prior violations of public health measures, they cannot be issued to proactively identify if or when individuals are breaching their quarantine, gathering in large groups, etc. Moreover, production orders may not be issued for the purpose of contact tracing.

CSE Act

There is little doubt that CSE has the technical capability to collect and analyze location data generated by Canadians' cellular devices. CSE also has a mandate "to provide technical and operational assistance to federal law enforcement and security agencies, the Canadian Forces and the Department of National Defence" (*CSE Act*, s. 20). However, when CSE provides that assistance to these agencies and departments, they are bound by these bodies' legal authorities. Meaning, if CSIS or the RCMP cannot legally collect the information, neither can CSE. There is also no measure by which CSE could assist other federal or provincial agencies, (e.g., the Public Health Agency of Canada) with the collection of Canadians' personal information.

Having established that there are no regular legal authorities that would allow the federal government to leverage Canada's security and intelligence agencies' surveillance and analytical capabilities to stop the spread of an illness like COVID-19, we turn next to emergency legislation.

Part 3: Federal Emergency Legislation

This final part examines the federal *Quarantine Act* and the *Emergencies Act* and concludes that neither may be used to conduct electronic surveillance or order the requisition of location data or subscriber information from Canadians or service providers.

Quarantine Act

The federal *Quarantine Act* gives the Minister of Public Health the authority to conduct health screening when it is necessary to prevent the spread of a communicable disease. Under the Act, travellers have a duty to provide any information that a quarantine officer may reasonably require for the performance of their duties. Additionally, when the Governor in Council (essentially cabinet) issues an Emergency Order under the *Quarantine Act*, that order may subject anyone seeking to return to Canada from abroad to "any condition." Arguably, one of those conditions could be the mandatory download and use of an app that would allow quarantine officers to track travellers' movement to enforce compliance with any order issued under the Act.

Of course, there are several limits to data collection of this kind. First, it only impacts travellers coming into Canada from a foreign country. Second, collection would only be permitted for the duration of the order a traveller is subject to—for example, fourteen days from the date of their return to Canada. Third, the app would be ineffective for contact tracing as it could not capture the personal information of others in a user's vicinity who were not also subject to a quarantine order.

Emergencies Act

The *Emergencies Act* contains the stiffest government emergency powers of any emergency law in Canada. The statute defines a "national emergency" as "an urgent and critical situation of a temporary nature that . . . seriously endangers the lives, health or safety of Canadians and is of such proportions or nature as to exceed the capacity or authority of a province to deal with it, or . . . seriously threatens the ability of the Government of Canada to preserve the sovereignty, security and territorial integrity of Canada" and that cannot be addressed effectively under any other law of Canada (*Emergencies Act*, s. 3). Importantly, the caveat "any other law of Canada" means any other *federal* law (*Roberts v Canada*, [1989] 1 SCR 322).

The *Emergencies Act* anticipates four categories of emergencies: a public welfare emergency, a public order emergency, an international emergency, and a war emergency. As is the case with COVID-19, an emergency caused by "disease in human beings, animals or plants" falls within the definition of a public welfare emergency (*Emergencies Act*, s. 5). To trigger the wide-ranging powers under the Act, the Governor in Council must consult with the provincial cabinet in the affected provinces. Where the Governor in Council "believes, on reasonable grounds, that a public welfare emergency exists and necessitates the taking of special temporary measures," it may declare an emergency (s. 6(1)). At the time of writing, the Governor in Council had not declared the COVID-19 pandemic a public welfare emergency, although there is little doubt that the legal threshold has long been met. Certainly, the spread of the coronavirus disease seriously endangers Canadian lives, and the consequences, cost, and resources necessary to manage the pandemic have exceeded the internal capacities of the provinces. However, rather than invoke the Act, the Trudeau government chose not to take action that encroaches on the jurisdiction of the provinces and instead passed new legislation to take measures within its federal jurisdiction to address the crisis.

Nevertheless, the Trudeau government could have, and could still, invoke the *Emergencies Act* in response to the pandemic. Should such a declaration be made, the Governor in Council must identify the state of affairs constituting the emergency, the special temporary measures anticipated, and the area affected by the emergency. The government may only implement measures believed necessary on reasonable grounds to deal with the situation. Those orders or regulations may only pertain to a closed list of matters set out in section 8 of the Act.

Those matters include:

    (a) the regulation or prohibition of travel to, from or within any specified area, where necessary for the protection of the health or safety of individuals;

    (b) the evacuation of persons and the removal of personal property from any specified area and the making of arrangements for the adequate care and protection of the persons and property;

    (c) the requisition, use or disposition of property;

    (d) the authorization of or direction to any person, or any person of a class of persons, to render essential services of a type that that person, or a person of that class, is competent to provide and the provision of reasonable compensation in respect of services so rendered;

    (e) the regulation of the distribution and availability of essential goods, services and resources;

    (f) the authorization and making of emergency payments;

    (g) the establishment of emergency shelters and hospitals;

    (h) the assessment of damage to any works or undertakings and the repair, replacement or restoration thereof;

    (i) the assessment of damage to the environment and the elimination or alleviation of the damage; and

(j) the imposition

    (i) on summary conviction, of a fine not exceeding five hundred dollars or imprisonment not exceeding six months or both that fine and imprisonment, or

    (ii) on indictment, of a fine not exceeding five thousand dollars or imprisonment not exceeding five years or both that fine and imprisonment, for contravention of any order or regulation made under this section.

Notably absent from this list is the authority to mandate the disclosure of personal information by individual Canadians, Canadian entities regulated by *PIPEDA*, or other government departments. The Act also fails to give the government any additional authority to collect personal information from individuals or third parties.

Some have argued that the government can collect location and subscriber data from telecommunication service providers under section 8(c): "the requisition, use or disposition of property" (Flood and Thomas 2020, 112). Flood, Scassa, and Robertson suggest that this provision could be used to "access data held by telecommunications companies" (2020). Nevertheless, they note that an order or regulation made under the *Emergencies Act* issued to requisition that data would be insufficient both to overcome the protections afforded by *PIPEDA* and comply with section 8 of the *Charter*. As such, even if the government were to rely on this novel interpretation of "property" to collect the data, a new law is necessary to give service providers the authority to share the requested data.

There are three issues with the above argument.

First, while it is true that any order issued under the *Emergencies Act* for the seizure of property that is subject to a reasonable expectation of privacy must comply with section 8, and by consequence, the three criteria for warrantless searches set out by the Supreme Court in *Collins*. This much is clear from the statute's preamble.[1] However, it is not true that additional legislation is necessary to overcome the limits set out in *PIPEDA*.

When it comes to sharing or disclosing personal information, there are two key questions. First, does the entity with the desired information have the legal authority to share it? Second, does the entity requesting the information have the legal authority to collect it? If the answer to either question is "no," the information may not be shared.

Under the argument advanced by Scassa and Flood, the lawful authority to collect would be an order issued under the *Emergencies Act* to administer the Act or any number of provincial emergency regulations issued to manage a major health crisis. What they appear to overlook is that *PIPEDA* sets out several exceptions where private-sector organizations may disclose personal information without notification and consent. For example, under section 7(3)(c.1)(iii), an organization may disclose personal information to a government institution that identifies its lawful authority to obtain the information and indicates that the disclosure is requested for the purpose of administering any law of Canada or a province. This exception is the authority to share; it has already been built into *PIPEDA* for situations exactly like Scassa and Flood describe. Consequently, new legislation would not be required.

Second, under existing law, individuals do not "own" information about themselves that third parties physically compile. In *McInerney v McDonald*, the Supreme Court of Canada determined that doctors, not patients, own the physical copies of a patient's medical records ([1992] 2 SCR 138). The paper records or hard drives on which a doctor stores a patient's information are the physician's property. Therefore, a patient does not have the right to demand access to or receive copies of those records. The Court noted that, "while the doctor is the owner of the actual record, the information is to be used by the physician for the benefit of the patient," thereby giving "rise to an expectation that the patient's interest in and control of the information will continue" (para 22). Scassa herself explained that "although *McInerney* dealt with personal health information, there is no reason to expect that a Canadian court's decision would be different with respect to other types of personal information" (2018, 13).

What does this mean in the context of the location data generated by subscribers so that Rogers, Bell, and Telus can bill customers and provide them with various GPS-enabled services? For one, it means that the personal information generated by users and compiled by service providers is not the property of individual subscribers. Moreover, while Rogers, Bell, and Telus may be the physical owners of the hard drives on which they store our personal information, they do not "own" the information itself to do with it as they please. The limitations imposed by *PIPEDA* on the selling, sharing, and use of personal information held by the private sector reinforces this fact.

Even before *McInerny*, in *R v Stewart* ([1988] 1 SCR 963), the Supreme Court considered whether confidential information qualifies as property, such that it could be the subject of theft. The Court held that for anything to be property, someone must "own" it, and it must be capable of being taken or converted in a manner that results in a deprivation of its use or possession by the owner (para 35). The Court held that "except in very rare and highly unusual circumstances," information could not be taken or converted.[2] Arguably, one such exception is a trade secret. However, the accumulation of subscriber information or location data is not a trade secret, nor any other form of intellectual property. It does not satisfy the criteria to be a trade secret under IP law; it is not a plan or process, tool, research mechanism, or compound known only to the service provider and valuable only insofar as it remains a secret (Canadian Intellectual Property Office n.d.). Nor does the compilation of facts collected by service providers into an ever-changing database qualify as a copyrightable work (Scassa 2018, 7–8).

What is more, Parliament chose to amend the *Criminal Code* to capture the taking of trade secrets in 2020. However, rather than amend the *Code* so that information would qualify as "property" capable of theft, Parliament added a separate provision making it an offence to "obtain a trade secret" by deceit, falsehood, or other fraudulent means (s. 391). Here, too, bulk subscriber or location data does not satisfy the *Criminal Code* definition of "trade secret."[3]

Third and finally, any move to recognize property rights in personal information should not be undertaken lightly. This issue is subject to a long-standing debate and has wide-ranging implications for our modern, data-driven economy. Currently, none of Canada's privacy or data-protection laws expressly define who owns personal information, let alone the vast amounts of data we generate simply by living in the modern world. Before we accept that a new property right exists, numerous questions need to be considered. As Ritter and Mayer (2018) ask: When does ownership attach to data? What are the rights, privileges, and constraints vested in the owner of personal data? Can any of those rights or controls be transferred, licensed, or sold? These questions demand the full consideration of Parliament. They should not be brushed aside for the sake of expediency by fitting the square peg of electronic surveillance into the round hole that is the requisition of property.

If, however, I am wrong, and location data is property and may be requisitioned through an order issued under the *Emergencies Act,* that order would still need to comply with section 8 of the *Charter.* This is extremely complicated. We only need to look to the complex legislation surrounding the collection and use of datasets under section 11 of the *CSIS Act* for a sense of what would be required to ensure the reasonableness of collecting, retaining, and analyzing highly revealing information about an entire population. Whether such a scheme should or could be implemented via an emergency order issued by the Governor in Council is highly questionable. Moreover, it is arguable that without some sort of prior judicial authorization, the collection and use of bulk location information to enforce public health orders would never satisfy section 8 of the *Charter.*

Conclusion and Recommendations

The preceding discussion establishes that the Government of Canada has no existing legal means of leveraging the electronic surveillance and data analytics capabilities of its security and intelligence agencies to conduct contact tracing to stop the spread of a communicable illness like COVID-19. Moreover, only very narrow authorities allow for the collection and use of personal information to enforce public health measures. And, to date, reliance on a voluntary application has proven ineffective. Even if incalculable, the economic and public health costs of this choice are substantial.

In the aftermath of the pandemic, lawmakers may ultimately determine that it is appropriate to leverage the tools and techniques developed by Canada's security agencies to limit the effects of a global health crisis in a manner compliant with the *Charter.* If so, the following recommendations could serve as a starting point for a discussion on legislative reforms.

1. Expand the definition of "threats to the security of Canada" under section 2 of the *CSIS Act* to include the outbreak or spread of deadly epidemics. Such an amendment would broaden CSIS's section 12 mandate and allow for the collection of datasets to assist CSIS in fulfilling that expanded mandate.

2. Amend the *Criminal Code* to authorize the issuance of a transmission or tracking data production order to assist in the enforcement of public health measures. The threshold would need to be sufficiently circumscribed to satisfy section 8 of the *Charter* while removing the need for suspicion of a particularized offence.

3. Expand CSE's assistance mandate to include provincial health authorities where the Minister of Public Safety makes a written request to the Minister of National Defence. This request could be triggered when a province declares a provincial emergency and requests federal assistance. Under the federal *Emergency Management Act*, the Minister's responsibilities include "providing assistance other than financial assistance to a province if the province requests it" (s. 4(1)(i)).

4. Amend section 8 of the *Emergencies Act* to include a measure related to the disclosure of personal information. Currently, the measures listed in the federal *Emergencies Act* largely mirror those available to provincial governments under provincial emergency legislation, with one notable exception. Ontario's *Emergency Management and Civil Protection Act* uniquely stipulates that the Lieutenant Governor in Council may issue an order "that any person collect, use or disclose information that in the opinion of the Lieutenant Governor in Council may be necessary in order to prevent, respond to or alleviate the effects of the emergency" (s. 7.0.2(4)(13)).

Each of these recommendations comes at a cost, and that cost is the privacy of Canadians. Whether the loss of privacy resulting from enhanced surveillance and contact-tracing capabilities is worth it to stop the spread of a future pandemic is a question Canadian law and policy-makers should carefully contemplate.

NOTES

1   The text of the preamble reads: "the Governor in Council, in taking such special temporary measures, would be subject to the Canadian Charter of Rights and Freedoms and the Canadian Bill of Rights and must have regard to the International Covenant on Civil and Political Rights, particularly with respect to those fundamental rights that are not to be limited or abridged even in a national emergency."

2   The Court only considered this question in the context of criminal law. But as Scassa notes, "While the court did not consider whether it might be property in other contexts, it seems unlikely" (2018, 12).

3   *Criminal Code*, s. 391 (5). For the purpose of this section, "trade secret" means any information that (1) is not generally known in the trade or business that uses or may use that information; (2) has economic value from not being generally known; and (3) is the subject of efforts that are reasonable under the circumstances to maintain its secrecy.

REFERENCES

Canadian Charter of Rights and Freedoms, Part I of the *Constitution Act, 1982*, being Schedule B to the *Canada Act 1982* (UK), 1982, c 11.

Canadian Intellectual Property Office. n.d. "Trade Secrets Factsheet." Government of Canada, accessed 21 June 2021. http://publications.gc.ca/collections/ collection_2018/opic-cipo/Iu71-4-39-2017-eng.pdf.

Canadian Security Intelligence Service Act, RSC, 1985, c C-23.

CCLA (Canadian Civil Liberties Association). 2020. *Privacy, Access to Information, and You: The COVID-19 Edition.* Toronto: CCLA. https://ccla.org/cclanewsite/wp-content/uploads/2020/05/Privacy-Access-to-Information-and-You_-The-COVID-19-Edition.pdf.

Criminal Code, RSC, 1985, c C-46.

CSE Act (*Communications Security Establishment Act*), SC 2019, c 13, s 76.

Daigle, Thomas. 2020. "Open the Covid Alert App to Make Sure It Works, Says Developers." *CBC News*, 11 December 2020. https://www.cbc.ca/news/technology/ covid-alert-app-bug-persists-on-iphone-1.5836604.

Dangerfield, Kate. 2020. "'The Big One': WHO Warns Future Pandemics Could Be Worse than Coronavirus." *Global News*, 29 December 2020. https://globalnews.ca/news/7545830/coronavirus-pandemic-big-one-who/.

Doffman, Zak. 2020. "COVID-19 Phone Location Tracking: Yes, It's Happening Now—Here's What You Should Know." *Forbes*, 27 March 2020. https://www.forbes.com/sites/zakdoffman/2020/03/27/covid-19-phone-location-tracking-its-moving-fast-this-is-whats-happening-now/.

Emergencies Act, RSC, 1985, c 22 (4th Supp).

Emergency Management Act, SC 2007, c 15.

Emergency Management and Civil Protection Act, RSO 1990, c E.9.

Forcese, Craig, and Leah West. 2021. *National Security Law*. 2nd ed. Toronto: Irwin Law.

Flood, Colleen M., Teresa Scassa, and David Robertson. 2020. "How Invoking the Emergencies Act Could Help Canada Better Track, Contain COVID-19." *CBC News*, 27 March 2020. https://www.cbc.ca/news/opinion/opinion-covid-coronavirus-emergency-measures-act-tracking-1.5510999.

Flood, Colleen M., and Bryan Thomas. 2020. "The Federal *Emergencies Act*: A Hollow Promise in the Face of COVID-19?" In *Vulnerable: The Law, Policy, and Ethics of COVID-19*, edited by Colleen M. Flood, Vanessa MacDonnell, Jane Philpott, Sophie Thériault, and Sridhar Venkatapuram, 105–14. Ottawa: University of Ottawa Press.

Geist, Michael. 2020. "Why I Installed the COVID Alert App. *Michael Geist* (blog), 2 August 2020. https://www.michaelgeist.ca/2020/08/why-i-installed-the-covid-alert-app/.

Haggart, Blayne. 2020. "Canada's COVID Alert App Is a Case of Tech-Driven Bad Policy Design." *Conversation*, 13 August 2020. https://theconversation.com/canadas-covid-alert-app-is-a-case-of-tech-driven-bad-policy-design-144448.

Hunter et al. v Southam Inc., [1984] 2 SCR 145, 11 DLR (4th) 641.

ISED (Innovation Science and Economic Development Canada). 2021. *First Interim Report of the COVID-19 Exposure Notification App Advisory Council*. Ottawa: Ministry of Industry. https://www.ic.gc.ca/eic/site/icgc.nsf/eng/07716.html.

Landau, Noa, Yaniv Kubovich, and Josh Breiner. 2020. "Israeli Coronavirus Surveillance Explained: Who's Tracking You and What Happens with the Data." *Haaretz*, 18 March 2020. https://www.haaretz.com/israel-news/.premium-israeli-coronavirus-surveillance-who-s-tracking-you-and-what-happens-with-the-data-1.8685383?v=1613647214246.

McInerney v McDonald, [1992] 2 SCR 138, 93 DLR (4th) 415.

Ng, Yixiang, Zongbin Li, Yi Xian Chua, Wei Liang Chaw, Zheng Zhao, Benjamin Er, Rachael Pung, Calvin J. Chiew, David C. Lye, Derrick Heng, and Vernon J. Lee. 2020. "Evaluation of the Effectiveness of Surveillance and Containment Measures for the First 100 Patients with COVID-19 in Singapore—January 2–February 20, 2020. *Morbidity and Mortality Weekly Report* 69, no. 11 (2020): 307–11. https://www.cdc.gov/mmwr/volumes/69/wr/mm6911e1.htm.

PIPEDA (Personal Information Protection and Electronic Documents Act), SC 2000, c 5.

Privacy Act, RSC, 1985, c P-21.

Quarantine Act, SC 2005, c 20.

R v Collins, [1987] 1 SCR 265, 74 NR 276.

R v Duarte, [1990] 1 SCR 30, 65 DLR (4th) 240.

R v Plant (1993), 157 NR 321, [1993] 3 SCR 281.

R v S.A.B., 2003 SCC 60.

R v Spencer, 2014 SCC 43.

R v Stewart, [1988] 1 SCR 963, 50 DLR (4th) 1.

Ritter, Jeffrey, and Anna Mayer. 2018. "Regulating Data as Property: A New Construct for Moving Forward." *Duke Law and Technology Review* 16, no. 1 (2018): 220–77. https://scholarship.law.duke.edu/cgi/viewcontent.cgi?article=1320&context=dltr.

Roberts v Canada, [1989] 1 SCR 322, 57 DLR (4th) 197.

Sahin, Kaan. 2020. "The West, China, and AI surveillance." Atlantic Council, 18 December 2020. https://www.atlanticcouncil.org/blogs/geotech-cues/the-west-china-and-ai-surveillance/.

Scassa, Teresa. 2018. "Data Ownership." *CIGI Papers* no. 187. https://www.cigionline.org/sites/default/files/documents/Paper%20no.187_2.pdf.

Shwartz Altshuler, Tehilla, and Rachel Aridor Hershkowitz. 2020. "How Israel's COVID-19 Mass Surveillance Operation Works." *TechStream* (Brookings Institute), 6 July 2020. https://www.brookings.edu/techstream/how-israels-covid-19-mass-surveillance-operation-works/.

Turnbull, Sarah. 2020. "COVID Alert App Nears 3 Million Users, but Only 514 Positive Test Reports." *CTV News*, 29 September 2020. https://www.ctvnews.ca/health/coronavirus/covid-alert-app-nears-3-million-users-but-only-514-positive-test-reports-1.5125256.

WHO (World Health Organization). 2020. "The Best Time to Prevent the Next Pandemic Is Now: Countries Join Voices for Better Emergency Preparedness." World Health Organization, 1 October 2020. https://www.who.int/news/item/01-10-2020-the-best-time-to-prevent-the-next-pandemic-is-now-countries-join-voices-for-better-emergency-preparedness.

Yang, Myungji. 2021. "Behind South Korea's Success in Containing Covid-19: Surveillance Technology Infrastructures." *Items: Insights from the Social Sciences*, 21 January 2021. https://items.ssrc.org/covid-19-and-the-social-sciences/covid-19-in-east-asia/behind-south-koreas-success-in-containing-covid-19-surveillance-technology-infrastructures/.

Enforcing Canadian Security Laws through Criminal Prosecutions during a Pandemic: Lessons from Canada's COVID-19 Experience

Michael Nesbitt and Tara Hansen

Introduction

Emergencies of all kinds, pandemics being no exception, produce a host of acute challenges while simultaneously revealing and exacerbating latent systemic vulnerabilities. This chapter considers Canada's experience during the COVID-19 pandemic, focusing on illuminating those most pressing challenges and vulnerabilities associated with enforcing security threats through the criminal law.

Specifically, the chapter identifies three systemic challenges in criminal law exposed by the COVID-19 pandemic. First, Canada's criminal justice system as a whole was stress tested by the COVID-19 emergency, including through increases in certain types of criminal behaviour such as cyber scams and frauds, as well as the introduction of novel public health regulations. Investigators and prosecutors were confronted with both a broader array of enforcement obligations and an increase in distinct types of criminality. This combination created new and unforeseen challenges and increased the need for different types of professional expertise in the field. Second, Canada saw an increase in ideologically motivated extremism, particularly on the far right, and conspiracy-driven threats like QAnon (see Argentino and Amarasingam, this volume). This trend directly implicates Canada's national security apparatus, including its enforcement wings such as the Royal Canadian Mounted Police (RCMP), local and provincial police, and prosecution services. Third, this shift in criminality and extremism was layered on top of a criminal justice and national security apparatus, showing signs of being stretched to its limits. Already antiquated in terms of their use of modern technology, Canadian courts and the criminal justice system found their capacity limited during the pandemic, forcing them to make swift judgments and resort to untested technology on the fly. In the end, police and prosecutors had to make hasty decisions based on emerging and sometimes shifting information about what crimes to prioritize for prosecution, whether prosecutions could meaningfully deter public health violations, and whether extremist threats were national security threats.

The result is an uncomfortable one: an already overtaxed system must respond to *increased* security threats while operating with a *reduced* capacity to manage and prosecute such serious threats. What steps Canada takes now to modernize its system, from the process of prioritizing enforcement matters in a planned and deliberate manner to the use of technology to assist justice system participants, will go a long way in determining the system's capacity to keep a handle on democratic and extremist threats, future emergency or not.

Problem 1: The COVID-19 Pandemic Seems to Have Resulted in a Shifting Criminal Offence Landscape

Criminality and criminal-justice-associated tasks stretched resources for government departments during the COVID-19 pandemic, including that of the Canadian Security Intelligence Service (CSIS) (Bell 2020; Davey, Hart, and Guerin 2020), local police (Statistics Canada 2021), the RCMP (Roberts 2020), and prosecutors. More broadly, new health and safety restrictions under provincial authorities and federal legislation like the *Quarantine Act* required the use of additional police, prosecution, and court resources that were already heavily taxed before the pandemic (Statistics Canada 2021; Johnson 2019). Offences such as online fraud (Deveau 2020), economic crime (McGee 2020), and cyber-related crime (Canadian Centre for Cyber Security 2020), saw a significant increase in Canada (West 2020). However, Canada also saw a decrease in certain types of opportunistic crimes such as breaking and entering, robbery, and impaired driving; the most likely explanation for this decrease being that the implementation of social restrictions diminished the opportunities to commit such crimes (Statistics Canada 2021).

Rather than saying opportunistic crimes *decreased* overall, it appears more accurate to say that the types of opportunistic crimes *shifted* due to the social limitations in place due to the pandemic (Watkins 2020; Bowman and Gallupe 2020). As cities shut down, the trend moved away from traditional opportunistic crimes (such as petty subway thefts or home robberies) toward more complex scams and cybercrimes (as people spent more time working and living online) (*Canadian Security* 2020; Almazora 2021). This trend may also indicate a shift in the type of offender, from those with break-and-enter or pickpocketing skills, for example, to those with a more sophisticated technical capacity needed to engage in cyber frauds.

As Canada sees shifts in the types of opportunistic crimes and offenders, the skills needed to investigate and prosecute—and the placement of resources into the correct law enforcement teams (e.g., cyber teams versus street drug teams)—will also necessarily shift. In particular, fraud, cyber attacks, and other forms of technology-driven crimes require different knowledge and skills such as financial and technical literacy, not just to commit but also to investigate and prosecute. Given that such complex crimes are by their nature already relatively more difficult and resource-intensive to investigate and prosecute (Russel 2019), an increase in offences without a corresponding growth in state expertise and resources escalates a pre-existing systemic burden (Canadian Centre for Cyber Security 2020). Government officials would do well to monitor these trends and avenues so as to align human resourcing, hiring priorities, and skill development with the demands of prosecutions in a post-COVID-19 world.

We also see here the need to *deliberately* form policies around how to prioritize which criminal files will proceed to trial, including how and on what basis. For example, does one prioritize the prosecution of low-level *Quarantine Act* and drug offences to demonstrate statistical results (more prosecutions, better success rate), or fewer low-level frauds and extremism cases with more serious outcomes for individual victims? Prosecutors answered this question during the pandemic under the fog of an emergency, with little time for deliberation. Although this may have been necessary at the time, it is not an ideal situation and is one that Canada can and should plan to rectify going forward. The pandemic served to exacerbate an already-occurring shift to technological and financial crimes; it has also provided the opportunity to re-evaluate current prosecution priorities—and surely offered some lessons on how to do so.

Problem 2: The Pandemic Coincided with, and Almost Certainly Increased, Various Forms of Extremist Activity

Layered atop the shifting criminality and enforcement landscape was a corollary increase in extremist activity, including criminal behaviour that implicates the national security community. The COVID-19 pandemic resulted in lost jobs (Statistics Canada 2021), restricted freedoms, and a decreased sense of autonomy for many individuals and businesses (Press 2020). These outcomes, coupled with foundational shifts in political and social climates, created ideal social conditions for right-wing (and other) extremist groups to gather support and further their strategic goals (Haig 2021).

Increasingly strict government regulation of day-to-day activities, together with restrictions on movement, trade, and supply chains, likely made it more difficult for extremist groups to meet or plan in person (Bell 2020). As a result, they refocused their efforts on online platforms (see Babb and Wilner, this volume). Similar to the increase in cybercrime, this extremist move online is neither unexpected nor new. Online platforms have been rife with extremist activities for decades (Conway 2006; Amarasingam 2015), but this shift to an online presence appears to have been sped up by the pandemic and its social and political fallout (*Al Jazeera* 2020; Bell 2020; Davey, Hart, and Guerin 2020). All currently available evidence suggests that an increase in far-right activity is occurring parallel to the pandemic. Seemingly, extremist groups (or at least certain groups) are taking advantage of uncertain times to try and spread their ideology (Argentino 2020). In sum, as the shift to a virtual way of living continues and more people find themselves online more often, extremist groups have also happened into a situation where society writ large may be more cognitively receptive to their messages. Such groups are, as a result, capitalizing on the pandemic to spread their strategic goals (Bellemare 2020; UNSC CTED 2020; Amarasingam and Argentino 2020).

However, it would seem that attempts to prosecute these extremist and far-right groups have proven difficult (Quan 2020). For example, as of the time of writing, there have been only two far-right terrorism charges in Canada; the first following the murder of a women in a Day Spa in Toronto by a youth allegedly motivated by the Incel movement, and the second following a vehicle attack in London, Ontario that killed four members of a Muslim family (Nesbitt 2021).

From the perspective of criminal justice, at least two things are necessary to build law enforcement capacity to tackle this extremism, including its online and social media variants. First, a deliberate plan for prioritizing criminal investigations and prosecutions, particularly how to balance public health or other emergency-specific actions with extremism and other serious crime. Second, a re-evaluation of Canada's criminal anti-terrorism framework, with a specific need to consider the definition of terrorist activity.

A strategic plan is needed for how public health violations and low-level criminality by extremist actors—particularly those whose actions overlap with the ideologies associated with the emergency at hand (such as the organizers of anti-mask rallies)—should be investigated and prosecuted. As the state cannot prosecute everyone who commits any crime, it must look at how and when it can meet the criminal law goal of deterrence associated with those most harmful to society and identify which crimes fall into this category.

For example, one might advocate for prosecuting all protesters violating criminal laws or public health orders. However, this strategy would likely draw unnecessary attention to relatively small protests or groups and amplify their messages. Moreover, police have learned over the years—particularly after the G20 Summit in Toronto—that tactics to enforce laws and make mass arrests, including so-called kettling, can backfire. Such efforts to prevent or prosecute a few isolated, relatively minor infractions can result in widespread violence or property damage (Maguire 2016; Perkel 2017). Finally, tackling public health violators has reverberating effects; if law enforcement diverts significant resources to enforcing such measures, it becomes harder to counter complex cybercrime and the most dangerous, deliberate extremism or terrorism.

Thus, deliberate choices must be made, starting with politicians who allocate resources down to agency leaders who help set the agenda for deploying those resources. This exercise should not take place under the cloud of an emergency. Rather, Canada must take advantage of the lessons learned during the pandemic to better plan its enforcement going forward, both in terms of broader social and criminal trends (see problem 1, above) and with a view to providing an institutional bulwark against a repeat of these systemic deficiencies should another emergency arise. A review of government priorities and resources with the goal of internal reflection and improvement, coupled with a sustained effort to prioritize how and when police make arrests and where prosecutors expend resources, would thus be well-advised post-pandemic.

To be clear, deliberate prioritization of resources is not *only* about procedurally identifying trends in criminal behaviour and risks to society and its institutions; it is also about identifying which resources should be reallocated. The idea of "doing more with less"—too often the solution in large organizations and government bureaucracies—is not the solution here, or is at least far from the only solution. A significant source of reallocation could come from moving a portion of Canada's investigative and prosecutorial resources away from so-called administrative offences (e.g., bail violations) (Wade and Zhang 2013; Department of Justice 2017; Beattie, Solecki, and Morton-Bourgon 2013) and low-level drug activity. The Public Prosecution Service of Canada (PPSC) announced it was taking such steps during the COVID-19 pandemic (Tunney 2020).

Administrative offences alone consume a massive amount of court resources. A 2013 study found that these types of cases made up 25 per cent of those tried in criminal court in Canada, costing taxpayers an estimated $807 million per year (Wade and Zhang 2013). These resources could instead go to prosecuting crimes that have a systemic impact, such as cyber scams that prey on vulnerable Canadians and extremist or foreign-influenced activities that seek to subvert not just the economy but public health, trust in institutions, and indeed the rule of law and public safety. *An Act to Amend the Criminal Code and Controlled Drugs and Substances Act*, introduced in the previous Parliament, offered an excellent example of a step in the right direction. By removing mandatory minimums (particularly for some drug crimes), promoting earlier trial resolutions, and broadening the opportunity for conditional sentences, the Act, if reintroduced, could create procedural efficiencies, cost savings, and more targeted interventions—a winning trifecta by any measure (Bill C-22 2021).

Diverting law enforcement away from mental health checkups is another source of potential resource reallocation. There is already a good deal of evidence to suggest that police are not well-suited for this role (Canadian Mental Health Association 2016). Law enforcement agencies could instead direct these resources toward white-collar crimes, organized crime, and confronting extremist groups, all of which have a significant public safety impact during emergency and non-emergency times.

Similarly, tackling systemic racism is both a moral and security imperative, as has been laid (more) bare during the pandemic. Building trust and understanding across all communities makes law enforcement co-operation and assistance more robust while simultaneously decreasing the social discord we have seen during the pandemic. Put another way, there is a need for high-level thinking, deliberate prioritizing, and *strategic budgeting* to provide a bulwark against the overstretch of Canadian enforcement institutions in the years to come. For this to work, the long-recognized, low-hanging fruit should, at minimum, be addressed in short order.

Going forward, we have also identified a second, very different need: a re-evaluation (perhaps better said, a twenty-year review) of Canada's legal framework and priorities vis-à-vis terrorism. In particular, the lack of terrorism prosecutions targeting far-right groups, coupled with widespread social unrest over unfair and/or disproportionate targeting of specific communities, has made plain a long-standing and uncomfortable dichotomy in the application of Canada's terrorism laws (Nesbitt 2021, 2019). On the one hand, Canada would seem to need to "extend" its criminal application of terrorism laws to ensure that it can and does capture the relevant actions of far-right groups or new and emerging terrorist threats (Nesbitt 2021). On the other hand, the scope of Canada's terrorism regime is already under fire for targeting almost exclusively Islamist-inspired extremism, while the Black Lives Matter movement and Indigenous protests have shone a light on so many of the dangers associated with the over-policing of specific communities. This reality has served to reinforce the need for highly circumscribed terrorism offences that are not too easily extended to new political and social groups and ideologies. This dichotomy is not unbridgeable, but it does create a genuine conundrum: How does Canada coherently define terrorist activity such that it can "expand" in a timely fashion to apply to new and emerging threats regardless of group affiliation, ideological, political, or religious motivation, and simultaneously remain properly circumscribed such that terrorism offences do not become all-encompassing political crimes attached to groups in the political or institutional disfavour of the day?

To thread this fine needle, it is beyond time to review the past twenty years of terrorism prosecutions in Canada. One clear place to start is with the definition of terrorist activity, and particularly "ideology," in the *Criminal Code* (*Criminal Code*, s. 83.01(b)(i)(B)). While Canada does not define "terrorism" in the *Criminal Code*, it does define "terrorist activity," which includes the nebulous requirement surrounding the need for a person or group to act with a "political" or "ideological" or "religious" motive. However, Parliament failed to define the terms "political" and "ideological" during the debates leading to the passing of Canada's terrorism offences in 2001. Not surprisingly, then, no further definition was given to the terms upon their enactment in the *Criminal Code*. Moreover, prosecutors have yet to argue for a coherent definition of either term at trial or offer policy explanations for how these terms will be treated, for example, in the PPSC Deskbook (2020). Finally, although proving political, religious, or ideological motivation is an element of various terrorism offences that must be proven in court, courts themselves have yet to define the terms in any judgment. Unfortunately, the definitions offered outside the legal system also look to be of little assistance. There appear to be as many different definitions of ideology as there are those trying to define it.

When Ministers of Justice then offer confusing and arguably incorrect public explanations about the scope of Canada's terrorism regime, and particularly which ideologies do or do not "count" (Mehler Paperny 2015[1]), this point of confusion becomes stark. When does a new ideology—for example QAnon—become an ideology such that if the other elements of terrorist activity definition are met, terrorism charges can be laid? Without a clear definition of what constitutes an ideology, or policy guidelines around how police and prosecutors will determine what ideologies and political groups might, in theory, commit terrorist activity, it seems inevitable that as new groups continue to arise, Canadian law enforcement will be slow to react to the (possible) terrorism threat. This hesitation may partially explain the first element of the dichotomy discussed above. In other words, it might explain why, despite years of far-right threats and numerous opportunities to do so, there are no known terrorism peace bonds or criminal terrorism convictions against far-right adherents, while examples of equivalent measures against Islamist extremism abound.

However, we should not extend this line of reasoning too far, as the inverse concern (the other side of the above dichotomy) is also well placed. Namely, if the definition of ideology—and thus the plausible application of terrorism offences—is too broad, it could easily capture new ideologies, groups, or movements that should not, in a democratic country, amount to terrorism. For example, should a protester associated with Black Lives Matter who commits a serious violent offence with the intent to coerce the government to recognize the movement (these being the other elements necessary to prove terrorist activity) bring the whole protest group into the headlights of Canada's criminal terrorism regime? There is no *legal* assurance that protest groups do not become terrorist entities the moment one person, being part of that political movement, goes criminally (and violently) rogue.

In terms of re-evaluating and defining the role of ideology in law or policy, we should start by asking what exactly the "ideological" motive requirement adds to the definition of terrorist activity that the requirement for a political or religious motive does not capture? The Crown has to prove three things to prove terrorist activity: (1) the political, religious, or ideological motive behind the crime (the "motive clause"); (2) that the offence was committed "in whole or in part with the intention of intimidating the public, or a segment of the public, with regard to its security ... or compelling a government or a domestic or an international organization to do or to refrain from doing any act" (the "purpose clause"); and (3) that the plan or action cause death or serious bodily violence, endanger life or cause a serious risk to health and safety, cause substantial property damage, etc. (the "consequence clause") (*Criminal Code*, s. 83.01(b)(i)(B); Nesbitt and Hagg 2019, 608–13). So, the question posed herein is: When is a motive "ideological" but not "political" or "religious"? It is tough to conceive of a limited definition of ideology that would not already neatly fall into the political or the religious. At the same time, applying a broad conception of ideology that is neither political nor religious (a personal idea or goal driving a crime, for example) almost certainly takes terrorism into the territory of the mundane or the everyday. Put another way, if the act of serious violence is neither politically nor religiously motivated, it is hard to imagine why it should constitute terrorism and thus why the reference to ideology is needed at all.

The above question is not merely theoretical or posed to suggest a harmless redundancy between ideology and political/religious motivations; for, as noted above, at the investigative stage the ideological requirement is arguably causing confusion (including for ministers of justice) when new extremist groups arise and the state must come to terms with their ideologies (see the confusion around the decisions not to charge Minassian, Bourque, Bissonnette, Baine, Souvannarath, as but some examples) (Nesbitt 2021). If this analysis is correct, then the term "ideology" results in delays in moving quickly against new and dangerous extremist movements while offering little to limit the scope of terrorism or help explain to the Canadian public why some acts count as terrorism and others do not. If this is true, it is time for a high-level legislative and policy review of this proposition.

A further, perhaps more fundamental question flows from the above analysis: If one proves an intent to intimidate the public or compel a government to take action (the purpose clause), as well as the consequence clause, then what role is played by the motive clause at all, whether it be ideological, political, or religious?

The reality is that Canada is twenty years into its experience with its criminal terrorism regime, and some cracks are showing. Canada has been (arguably) too slow to respond to emerging extremist threats, too muddled in its public explanations of what is and is not terrorism in Canada, and has done too little to assuage concerns from minority groups that they will not be disproportionately targeted. A re-evaluation of Canada's criminal terrorism regime should be done deliberately and in the abstract rather than through reactionary incrementalism. Given the increase in various forms of extremism that coincided with the pandemic, Canada needs to engage in this discussion urgently before the next emergency brings with it a new extremist threat.

Problem 3: Increased and New Forms of Criminality (Problem 1) and Extremism (Problem 2) Layered Over an Already Overstretched Criminal Justice System

The closing of courts due to the COVID-19 pandemic placed a significant burden on an already strained system. Canadian courts have yet to transition to a fully virtual method of record-keeping, complicating the sudden shift to virtual trials (Puddister and Small 2020). There are concerns that this closure will impact the justice system for years to come, even doubling the amount of time taken to process an accused (Graveland 2020). Currently, the nationwide number of backlogged cases created by the pandemic can only be estimated; however, at the time of writing, provinces such as Ontario are believed to have about thirty thousand delayed cases (Stefanovich 2020).

One of the main questions that has yet to be answered is whether the Supreme Court of Canada's landmark 2016 decision in *R v Jordan*, which sets time limits on bringing a case to trial, will continue to apply to cases delayed during this or a subsequent emergency (*R v Jordan* 2016; Brady, Rosenberg, and Courtis 2016). Justice Minister David Lametti expressed complete confidence in the system's ability to deal with these cases. The *Jordan* principle already provides for "exceptional circumstances," which allow courts (and the state) to extend the so-called *Jordan* timelines beyond the eighteen months allowed for provincial court trials and thirty months to finish in superior court (Connolly 2020). Nevertheless, Minister Lametti proposed the introduction of new legislation to provide a guideline for what constitutes "exceptional circumstances." There is, however, concern that a legislative interpretation may capture cases down the road never intended to be encompassed by this legislation (Stefanovich 2020). Without further guidance on how exactly the pandemic will be interpreted as an exceptional circumstance—or better yet, how we should view exceptional circumstances at all—the courts could begin to throw out hundreds of cases for violating the *Jordan* principle (Azpiri and Daya 2020).

More broadly, any emergency—the COVID-19 pandemic included—brings with it a risk of perpetuating the cycle of backlogged cases (Statistics Canada 2021b) in the Canadian court system (Senate Committee on Legal and Constitutional Affairs 2016). There were already eighteen judicial vacancies across Ontario courts at the beginning of the pandemic (Smith 2020). Similar shortages exist across the nation. Coupled with the economic blow from the pandemic, the courts are not equipped to deal with the influx of cases expected once the dust of COVID-19 settles.

Engaging with *Jordan* timelines and system delays only in response to the pandemic emergency is like bailing water out of a canoe when one has the tools to plug the leak. *Jordan* itself was a judicial response to an overstretched criminal justice system (*R v Jordan* 2016, para 3) that saw trials being delayed by years due to lack of resources, including the timely appointment of judges, physical court resources (buildings, etc.), staff, the availability of both federal and provincial prosecutors, and other factors (Smith 2020). In *Jordan*, the court sought to address the overall complacency that had developed in the criminal justice system, including "unnecessary procedures and adjournments, inefficient practices, and inadequate institutional resources [that] are accepted as the norm and give rise to ever-increasing delay" (*R v Jordan* 2016, para 40). The case dates from 2016, but there have been few meaningful legislative responses in the years since. The idea driving the *Jordan* decision was always to force Parliament to do its job and take a broad look at the funding, workings, and efficacy of the criminal justice system and to make the necessary changes. Instead, the courts have been further strained post-*Jordan*. Not only are we witnessing system and trial delays (Azpiri and Daya 2020), but some courts in Canada still cannot even access the tools necessary to hold remote court appearances to perform basic functions. As the pandemic exacerbates these systemic problems, it is a reminder that politicians need to act now and not count on the Supreme Court to "legislate" by judgment when Parliament fails to take action (*R v Jordan* 2016).

Parliamentary and bureaucratic responses should not, however, be viewed simply as system upgrades. Creating efficiencies now will provide a *marge de manoeuvre* within the system to allow the criminal justice system to better counter extremism in the future. Additionally, parliamentary responses could create or reinforce innovations necessary to make all prosecutions more efficient and effective, terrorism cases perhaps most of all. A commendable example of this is Bill C-23, which seeks to formally implement many of the technological and efficiency upgrades introduced in criminal law practice during the pandemic (Bill C-23 2020).

Still, the government response must be careful to consider the criminal justice system as a whole rather than merely treat the courts as surrogates for the entire system—and thus the sole object of reforms. For example, during the pandemic, prosecutors accessed files from home that required security that remote-access systems through government and courts do not necessarily allow. In this way, federal prosecutors are similarly placed and require the same technological support as many other government employees who handle sensitive information. Simply put, upgrades should be prioritized not as a matter of preference or convenience but of security.

Finally, prosecutors must also contend with external systems that feed into the justice system. Such feeder systems come from institutions on both the top and bottom of the prosecution sandwich, including provincial courts and associated individuals on the top half and investigative agencies like the RCMP and provincial and local police forces on the bottom half. Some prosecution offices and evidentiary disclosure processes have not moved to an electronic filing system, slowing the process down before files ever get to court.

It is beyond time for the above systems and procedures to move from antiquated to innovative. The ultimate success of Canada's criminal justice response to extremism depends on such innovation, and the federal government is best placed to recognize the needs of federal prosecutors and the system as a whole. Adopting more innovative and secure technology will have up-front costs but will reap downstream savings. It will also significantly improve access to justice for the very public this system is meant to serve.

Conclusions

We now have preliminary evidence that intuitively aligns with what one might assume will happen during a global pandemic: new threat vectors emerge while old ones morph in scope, capacity, and application; new criminal actors take advantage of the situation while other forms of (largely opportunistic) crime fade; and an already strained system will be stress tested under the weight of new and shifting demands and priorities coupled with greater economic constraints. Though the result of the story told in this chapter is not surprising, it is stark. There is every reason to imagine that government agencies must prepare themselves for a repeat performance during the next emergency, perhaps with an even more strained economy. As a result, the time to act is now.

Of course, the question is how should we prepare? The problems seem insurmountable, ever-shifting, and resource-based at a time when resources are already stretched to sustain the economy and people's livelihoods. Although the specifics will have to be negotiated in the years to come, we offer three recommendations.

First, a deliberate strategy must be in place to prioritize criminal investigations and prosecutions. Such a strategy will allow decisions to be made in a clear-headed, prospective fashion, and not under the fog of an emergency. Deliberate prioritization should include critical thinking about emerging threats and training for the investigation and prosecution thereof, which is sure to focus on online criminality, financial crimes, fraud, and the likely spread of mis- and disinformation. Crime itself tends to be opportunistic (Clark 1995; Wilcox and Cullen 2018), and as we move increasingly online, an increase in such crimes is inevitable (Statistics Canada 2019).

Second, Canada needs to think deeply about extremism and terrorism in terms of scope, application, and deterrence, particularly during a pandemic or subsequent emergency. This includes identifying law enforcement priorities and budgeting accordingly. Prosecutorial prioritization is also needed that deliberately considers when public health violations are enforced compared with other criminal laws, and how extremist fallout is best prioritized and targeted during both emergency and non-emergency times. Similarly, it is time to revisit the *Criminal Code*'s terrorism regime, particularly the definition of terrorist activity. After twenty years of largely successful prosecutions, a look back at what has gone well and what has caused problems is in order. In this regard, a close look at the role of the motive requirement of "terrorist activity" is necessary.

Third and finally, during the pandemic, the effects of a lack of physical, technological, and monetary investment in the justice system became more pronounced. Such systemic challenges must be viewed, in part, through the lens of security. If prosecutors do not have safe and accessible methods to access and share files from home, if courts are not prepared for the electronic future (or present), and if system constraints go unaddressed, then surges in the system during times of emergency may lead to blackouts. It is time for Parliament to take steps now to address *Jordan* delays and innovate and upgrade the system from investigations to prosecutions to courts. The pandemic has shown that repairing the series of small cracks recognized half a decade ago in *Jordan* must be treated as an integral aspect of maintaining Canada's security edifice.

NOTE

1   Mehler Paperny describes a 2015 announcement by then Justice Minister Peter MacKay that a bomb plot of a mall in Halifax was not terrorism because it lacked "cultural motivation," which is not a requirement of any terrorism offence in Canada.

REFERENCES

Al Jazeera. 2020. "Far Right Seizing COVID-19' Opportunity' to Expand: Study." *Al Jazeera*, 20 November 2020. https://www.aljazeera.com/news/2020/11/20/far-right-seizing-covid-19-opportunity-to-expand-study.

Almazora, Leo. 2020. "The COVID-19 Pandemic Sparked a Cyber-Crime Boom." *Wealth Professional*, 9 February 2021. https://www.wealthprofessional.ca/news/industry-news/the-covid-19-pandemic-sparked-a-cyber-crime-boom/337643.

Amarasingam, Amarnath. 2015. "What Twitter Really Means for Islamic State Supporters." *War on the Rocks*, 30 December 2015. https://warontherocks.com/2015/12/what-twitter-really-means-for-islamic-state-supporters/.

Amarasingam, Amarnath, and Marc-André Argentino. 2020. "The QAnon Conspiracy Theory: A Security Threat in the Making?" *CTC Sentinel* 13, no 7 (2020): 37–44. https://ctc.usma.edu/the-qanon-conspiracy-theory-a-security-threat-in-the-making/.

Argentino, Marc-André. 2020. "QAnon Conspiracy Theory Followers Step Out of the Shadows and May Be Headed to Congress." *Conversation*, 8 July 2020. https://theconversation.com/qanon-conspiracy-theory-followers-step-out-of-the-shadows-and-may-be-headed-to-congress-141581.

Ashby, Matthew P. J. 2020. "Initial Evidence on the Relationship between the Coronavirus Pandemic and Crime in the United States." *Crime Science* 9, no 6 (2020): 1–16. https://doi.org/10.1186/s40163-020-00117-6.

Azpiri, Jon, and Rumina Daya. 2020. "Court Backlog Due to COVID-19 Could Put Justice in Jeopardy, B.C. Lawyer Warns." *Global News*, 8 June 2020. https://globalnews.ca/news/7042564/bc-court-backlog-coronavirus/.

Bell, Stewart. 2020. "Neo-Nazis, Extremists Capitalizing on COVID-19, Declassified CSIS Documents Say." *Global News*, 7 December 2020. https://globalnews.ca/news/7501783/neo-nazis-extremists-capitalizing-coronavirus-covid-19-csis/.

Bellemare, Andrea. 2020. "Far Right Groups May Try to Take Advantage of Pandemic, Watchdogs Warn." *CBC News*, 9 April 2020. https://www.cbc.ca/news/technology/far-right-opportunistic-covid-pandemic-1.5526423.

Bill C-22. 2021. *An Act to Amend the Criminal Code and the Controlled Drugs and Substances Act.* 2nd Sess., 43rd Parl., 18 February 20201. https://parl.ca/DocumentViewer/en/43-2/bill/C-22/first-reading.

Bill C-23. 2020. "An Act to Amend the Criminal Code and the Identification of Criminals Act and to Make Related Amendments to Other Acts (COVID-19 response and other measures)." https://parl.ca/DocumentViewer/en/43-2/bill/C-23/first-reading.

Beattie, Karen, André Solecki, and Kelly E Morton-Bourgon. 2013. "Police and Judicial Detention and Release Characteristics: Data from the Justice Effectiveness Study." Research and Statistics Division, Department of Justice. https://publications.gc.ca/collections/collection_2018/jus/J4-65-2013-eng.pdf.

Bowman, John H. IV, and Owen Gallupe. 2020. "Has COVID-19 Changed Crime? Crime Rates in the United States during the Pandemic." *American Journal of Criminal Justice* 45, no. 4 (2020): 537–45. https://doi.org/10.1007/s12103-020-09551-3.

Brady, Peter, Michael Rosenberg, and Trevor Courtis. 2016. "R. v. Jordan—The Supreme Court of Canada Dramatically Alters the Framework Applicable to the Right to a Criminal Trial Within a Reasonable Time." *Mondaq*, 18 July 2016. https://www.mondaq.com/canada/trials-appeals-compensation/510770/r-v-jordan-the-supreme-court-of-canada-dramatically-alters-the-framework-applicable-to-the-right-to-a-criminal-trial-within-a-reasonable-time.

Canadian Centre for Cyber Security. 2020. "National Cyber Threat Assessment." Government of Canada, last modified 16 November 2020. https://cyber.gc.ca/sites/default/files/publications/ncta-2020-e-web.pdf.

Canadian Mental Health Association. 2016. *Study in Blue and Grey, Police Interventions with People with Mental Illness: A Review of Challenges and Responses.* Vancouver: CMHA BC Division. https://cmha.bc.ca/wp-content/uploads/2016/07/policereport.pdf.

Canadian Security. 2020. "Cyber-Attacks Have Increased in Past 12 Months for 99 Per Cent of Canadian Organizations: Survey." *Canadian Security*, 14 July 2020. https://www.canadiansecuritymag.com/99-per-cent-of-canadian-organizations-said-cyber-attacks-have-increased-in-past-12-months-survey/.

Clark, Ronald V. 1995. "Situational Crime Prevention." *Crime and Justice* 19, no. 1 (1995): 91–150. www.jstor.org/stable/1147596.

Connolly, Amanda. 2020. "Justice Minister 'Confident' Coronavirus Court Delays Are Under Control as Second Wave Surges." *Global News*, 11 October 2020. https://globalnews.ca/news/7388961/coronavirus-court-delays-david-lametti/.

Conway, Maura. 2006. "Terrorism and the Internet: New Media—New Threat?" *Parliamentary Affairs* 58, no 2 (2006): 283–98. https://doi.org/10.1093/pa/gsl009.

Criminal Code, RSC, 1985, C-46.

Davey, Jacob, Mackenzie Hart, and Cécile Guerin. 2020. "An Online Scan of Right-Wing Extremist in Canada: Interim Report." *Institute for Strategic Dialogue*, 19 June 2020. https://www.isdglobal.org/isd-publications/canada-online/.

Department of Justice. 2017. "Criminal Court Case Processing Time." Government of Canada, April 2017. https://www.justice.gc.ca/eng/rp-pr/jr/jf-pf/2017/apr01.html

Deveau, Denise. 2020. "Fraud Related to COVID-19 Pandemic on the Rise. Here's How to Avoid Being Scammed." *CPA Canada*, 23 March 2020. https://www.cpacanada.ca/en/news/canada/2020-03-23-covid-19-scams.

Graveland, Bill. 2020. "COVID-19 Pandemic Means Court Delays and Stalled Justice System." *National Observer*, 18 March 2020. https://www.nationalobserver.com/2020/03/18/news/covid-19-pandemic-means-court-delays-and-stalled-justice-system.

Haig, Terry. 2021. "Defence Department Report Warns of Right-Wing Extremism as Pandemic Continues." *Radio Canada International*, 6 January 2021. https://www.rcinet.ca/en/2021/01/06/defence-department-report-warns-of-right-wing-extremism-as-pandemic-continues/.

Johnson, Janice. 2019. " 'State of Continual Crisis': Alberta Crown Prosecutors Overworked, Understaffed." *CBC News*, 12 December 2019. https://www.cbc.ca/news/canada/edmonton/alberta-crown-prosecutors-justice-government-1.5393024.

Maguire, Edward R. 2016. "New Directions in Protest Policing." *Saint Louis University Public Law Review* 35 (1): 67–108.

McGee, Niall. 2020. "How the COVID-19 Pandemic Fuelled a boom in Canadian Stock Promotion Scams." *Globe and Mail*, 30 December 2020. https://www.theglobeandmail.com/business/article-how-the-covid-19-pandemic-fuelled-a-boom-in-canadian-stock-promotion/.

Nesbitt, Michael. 2019. "An Empirical Study of Terrorism Charges and Terrorism Trials in Canada between September 2001 and September 2018." *Criminal Law Quarterly* 67 (1–2): 595–648.

———. 2021. "Violent Crime, Hate Speech, or Terrorism? How Canada Views and Prosecutes Far-Right Extremism (2001–2019)." *Common Law World Review*, 16 February 2021. https://doi.org/10.1177%2F1473779521991557.

Nesbitt, Michael, and Dana Hagg. 2019. "An Empirical Study of Terrorism Prosecutions in Canada: Elucidating the Elements of the Offences." *University of Alberta Law Review* 57 (3). https://doi.org/10.29173/alr2590.

Mehler Paperny, Anna. 2015. "Halifax Plot: So What Is 'Terrorism,' Anyway?" *Global News*, 14 February 2015. https://globalnews.ca/news/1830795/halifax-plot-so-what-is-terrorism-anyway/.

Perkel, Colin. 2017. "Punishment Increased for Toronto Police Officer Who 'Kettled' Civilians in Cold Rain during G20 Protests." *Global News*, 10 November 2017. https://globalnews.ca/news/3854683/punishment-increased-for-toronto-police-officer-who-kettled-civilians-in-cold-rain-during-g20-protests/.

Press, Jordan. 2020. "Canadian Economy Posted Steepest Decline on Record as Coronavirus Struck: Statcan." *CTV News*, 28 August 2020. https://www.ctvnews.ca/business/canadian-economy-posted-steepest-decline-on-record-as-coronavirus-struck-statcan-1.5082814.

Public Prosecution Service of Canada. 2020. *Deskbook*. Ottawa: Attorney General of Canada. https://www.ppsc-sppc.gc.ca/eng/pub/fpsd-sfpg/fps-sfp/tpd/d-g-eng.pdf.

Puddister, Kate, and Tamara A. Small. 2020. "Trial by Zoom? The Response to COVID-19 by Canada's Courts." *Canadian Journal of Political Science* 53 (2): 373–7. doi:10.1017/S0008423920000505.

Quan, Douglas. 2020. "Can New Federal Unit Address Canada's 'Inconsistent Track Record' in Terrorism Prosecutions?" *National Post*, 2 January 2020. https://nationalpost.com/news/canada/can-new-federal-unit-address-canadas-inconsistent-track-record-in-terrorism-prosecutions.

Quarantine Act, SC 2005, c 20.

R v Jordan, 2016 SCC 27.

Roberts, Karl. 2020. "Policing the Pandemic: Managing the Police Response to COVID-19 Coronavirus." *Blue Line*, 25 March 2020. https://www.blueline.ca/policing-the-pandemic-managing-the-police-response-to-covid-19-coronavirus/.

Russel, Andrew. 2019. "Not Just B.C.: Most Provinces in Canada Fail to Secure Convictions in Money-Laundering Cases." *Global News*, 10 February 2019. https://globalnews.ca/news/4939801/provinces-canada-fail-to-convict-money-laundering/.

Smith, Dale. 2020. "Losing Ground on the Backlog." *Canadian Bar Association National Magazine*, 29 April 2020. https://nationalmagazine.ca/en-ca/articles/law/hot-topics-in-law/2020/losing-ground-on-the-backlog-(1).

Statistics Canada. 2017. "Trends in the Use of Remand in Canada, 2004/2005 To 2014/2015." Last modified 20 January 2017. https://www150.statcan.gc.ca/n1/pub/85-002-x/2017001/article/14691-eng.htm

———. 2019. "Just the Facts: Cybercrime in Canada." 2 December 2019. https://www150.statcan.gc.ca/n1/pub/89-28-0001/2018001/article/00015-eng.htm.

———. 2021a. "Adult Criminal Courts, Cases by Median Elapsed Time in Days." Last modified 5 July 2021. https://www150.statcan.gc.ca/t1/tbl1/en/tv.action?pid=3510002901.

———. 2021b. "Labour Force Survey, January 2021." Last modified 5 February 2021. https://www150.statcan.gc.ca/n1/daily-quotidien/210205/dq210205a-eng.htm

Stefanovich, Olivia. 2020. "Justice Minister Says He's Ready to Legislate if Pandemic Delays Lead to Charges Being Tossed." *CBC News*, 15 July 2020. https://www.cbc.ca/news/politics/stefanovich-jordan-decision-covid19-cases-delay-1.5638893.

Tunney, Catharine. 2020. "Federal Prosecutors Told to Avoid Drug Possession Charges When Possible in New Directive." *CBC News*, 19 August 2020. https://www.cbc.ca/news/politics/simple-drug-possession-change-1.5657423.

UNSC CTED (United Nations Security Council Counter-Terrorism Committee Executive Directorate). 2020. "Member States Concerned by the Growing and Increasingly Transnational Threat of Extreme Right-Wing Terrorism." *CTED Trends Alert*, April 2020. https://www.statewatch.org/media/documents/news/2020/apr/un-cted-trend-alert-right-wing-extremism-4-20.pdf.

Vigneault, David. 2021. "Remarks by Director David Vigneault to the Centre for International Governance Innovation." Government of Canada, 9 February 2021. https://www.canada.ca/en/security-intelligence-service/news/2021/02/remarks-by-director-david-vigneault-to-the-centre-for-international-governance-innovation.html.

Wade, D., and T. Zhang. 2013. *The Justice System Cost of Administration of Justice Offences in Canada, 2009.* Ottawa: Department of Justice, Research and Statistics Division.

Watkins, Ali. 2020. "Violent Year in New York and across U.S. as Pandemic Fuels Crime Spike." *New York Times*, 29 December 2020. https://www.nytimes.com/2020/12/29/nyregion/nyc-2020-crime-covid.html?action=click&module=Top%20Stories&pgtype=Homepage.

West, Leah. 2020. "Dissecting the National Cyber Threat Assessment." *A Podcast Called Intrepid*, 3 December 2020. https://www.intrepidpodcast.com/podcast/2020/12/3/ep-139-part-2-dissecting-the-national-cyber-threat-assessment.

Wilcox, Pamela, and Francis T. Cullen. 2018. "Situational Opportunity Theories of Crime." *Annual Review of Criminology* 1 (1): 123–48. https://doi.org/10.1146/annurev-criminol-032317-092421

13

Untangling Deportation Law from National Security: The Pandemic Calls for a Softer Touch

Simon Wallace

Introduction

There is a significant overlap between national security law and deportation law. Non-citizens, even refugees and permanent residents, found to be terrorists, members of organized criminal groups, spies, criminals, or money launders can be declared "inadmissible" and deported from Canada (*IRPA*, ss. 34–40). For the government, deportation is a security-enforcement tool. As Public Safety Canada explains, "immigration removal is an integral part of the [Canada Border Services Agency's (CBSA)] security mandate" (CBSA 2020a).

Moreover, deportation is an often-used tool. Compared to the criminal system, immigration adjudicators are regularly called upon to grapple with terrorism cases. A recent study showed that between 2004 and 2018, there were only 15 criminal trials based on terrorism charges (Nesbitt and Hagg 2020, 597). In contrast, the Immigration and Refugee Board adjudicated 123 national security and terrorism deportation cases in 2018 alone (Immigration and Refugee Board 2021). There is a practical reason for the national security community to concern itself with what happens in the deportation space: the immigration tribunals adjudicate exponentially more national security cases than do the criminal courts.

This chapter examines how the COVID-19 pandemic impacted CBSA's ability to enforce deportation orders. Contrary to public reports and statements from government officials, I find that the pandemic significantly compromised CBSA's ability to deport people. At its core, deportation is a forceful process (Gibney 2013). Deportations happen because CBSA—using a network of jail cells, enforcement officers, and coercive tools—gets people onto planes. The pandemic, work-from-home rules, and reduced air travel all limited CBSA's ability to be coercive. As a result, it deported substantially fewer people.

However, CBSA did not "down tools" in the pandemic; it retooled. CBSA used the pandemic as an opportunity to assume a more nimble, effective, and forceful deportation posture for the post-pandemic world. Going into the pandemic, poor data-reporting practices, a large backlog of unenforced removal orders, and unclear priorities weighed down the agency (Auditor General of Canada 2020). The pandemic gave CBSA an opportunity to clean up its removals operation, enabling it to hit the ground running and resume deportations once conditions allow. What does this mean for Canada's national security community? CBSA will emerge from the pandemic with more bandwidth and more capacity.

With this framing in mind, it is apparent that Canada is staring down a crisis in the deportation space. On the one hand, inspired by a security-minded ethos, CBSA is about to be a lot more effective at enforcing the law. On the other, the pandemic produced all sorts of situations in which the regular enforcement of deportation orders would be inappropriate. Divided into two parts, this chapter asks first: What happened to deportations during the pandemic? To answer this question, I analyze the publicly available data regarding detentions, emergency court motions to stop impending deportations, and deportation file closures to assess the extent of CBSA's capacities during the pandemic and the type of work the agency was doing. Second, I ask: What is likely to happen next? As CBSA resumes enforcement operations, the agency will confront a rights crisis produced by the pandemic. Put briefly, a deportation order issued before the pandemic could not have accounted for how individual lives, and the world at large, would be impacted by COVID-19. As such, pre-pandemic deportation decisions ought to be reassessed in light of the significantly changed circumstances.

The Deportation Process

"The most fundamental principle of immigration law is that non-citizens do not have an unqualified right to enter or remain in the country" (*Canada [Minister of Employment and Immigration] v Chiarelli* 1992). This finding by the Supreme Court of Canada is the foundation for the country's deportation law and policy.

Parliament, the Court explained in *Chiarelli*, has a free hand to craft immigration policy to determine who gets to stay and who must leave. To that end, immigration legislation describes categories of "inadmissible" people who are either unwelcome to come or who, even if they come to Canada lawfully, must leave. The grounds for inadmissibility range from the administrative (e.g., failing to comply with the terms of a visa) to the exceptionally serious (e.g., engaging in terrorism).

There are multiple broad grounds of security-related inadmissibilities. For example, a person can be deported for being a member of an organized criminal group or committing a serious crime. People may also be deported for committing war crimes, being a member of a terrorist group, engaging in espionage, or being a "danger to the security of Canada" (*IRPA*, ss. 34–7). In the normal course of things, the Immigration and Refugee Board issues deportation orders. However, in rare and serious cases, the Minister of Public Safety and Emergency Preparedness and the Minister of Citizenship and Immigration may refer a security certificate to the Federal Court of Canada for adjudication (*IRPA*, Division 5 and Division 9).

When a person is determined to be inadmissible, the consequence, save for a small class of persons eligible for a form of immigration probation, is singular: an enforceable removal order. The person must leave, and if they do not, they will be deported. It is the job of CBSA to enforce deportation orders "as soon as possible" (*IRPA*, s. 48).

CBSA has a large and complex mandate, touching on all manner of border-related issues. It administers over ninety acts and regulations. The agency has its own intelligence unit, collects and ensures compliance with customs levies, and monitors cross-border traffic. In terms of immigration enforcement, CBSA officers are involved in key aspects of the migration process. They inspect people arriving in Canada, conduct in-land policing operations to find "inadmissible" persons, interview refugee claimants, administer multiple detention centres, and intervene in refugee hearings. Therefore, the expeditious enforcement of removal orders is only one part of CBSA's much larger mandate.

Despite CBSA's legal obligation to enforce removal orders expeditiously, circumstances routinely intervene to prevent their immediate enforcement. Sometimes a removal may be deferred so as not to disrupt a child's school year. In other instances, it may be delayed so a person can continue important medical treatment, or it may be pushed back to give the government time to decide a pending application for status. In 2019, for example, 1,766 requests to delay a removal were made to the CBSA, of which 689 were granted (CBSA 2020b). In rare cases, deportation may be postponed to allow for the processing of a last-ditch humanitarian and compassionate application (*Baron v Canada [Public Safety and Emergency Preparedness]* 2008). Finally, removal may also be delayed by extraneous events beyond the government's control. For example, a foreign government might not issue a necessary travel document, or a natural disaster could make deportations to a particular country impossible.

Deportations and the COVID-19 Pandemic

In January 2021, the media reported that in the previous year CBSA had enforced 12,122 removal orders (Mehler Paperny 2021). This statistic was surprising because the number represented a year-over-year *increase* of 875 deportations, even though CBSA publicly said it paused deportations for most of 2020 because of the COVID-19 pandemic (Public Safety Canada 2020b).

CBSA was one of the first government organizations required to respond substantively and publicly to the COVID-19 pandemic. As border and migration policy evolved, CBSA was required to adapt frequently. In January 2020, officers began to screen all travellers from Hubei province in China. On March 4, screening expanded to include travellers from Iran and then, on March 12, from Italy. On March 16, the Prime Minister urged all Canadians abroad to come home, leading to the sudden return of thousands of individuals at Canada's airports. On March 17, the government postponed all scheduled removals from Canada. On March 18, borders were closed to foreign nationals, except for various forms of essential travel, requiring CBSA officers to make important decisions about whether someone's travel was essential (Public Safety Canada 2020c). That same day, an officer at the Toronto Immigration Holding Centre began to exhibit symptoms and was sent home to self-isolate (Durrani 2020).

CBSA explained that during the deportation postponement, the only people it could remove were people who asked CBSA to help them leave Canada and people who were inadmissible for a serious reason (terrorism, organized criminality, serious criminality, etc.) with special permission (Public Safety Canada 2020b). On 4 August 2020, the agency resumed escorted removals—deportations where an enforcement officer must travel with the person—for some serious inadmissibility cases with the approval of senior managers at CBSA headquarters. In December 2020, the moratorium was officially lifted (Public Safety Canada 2020b).

The first question this chapter asks is simple: How can we square the claim that CBSA executed 12,122 removal orders in 2020 with the fact that, for most of that year, there was a moratorium on deportation? I begin my analysis by examining the data regarding removals from 31 March 2020 to 26 November 2020. This data set is meaningful because it spans almost the entire deportation moratorium period (17 March 2020 to 30 November 2020). Table 13.1 shows that CBSA executed 7,244 orders, or approximately 905 deportations per month. While this data would suggest business as usual, this is not the case. To show what was happening, I consider each specific sub-category of removal orders in turn.

To begin, we should discount the 425 point-of-entry removals. These are not deportations but cases of exclusion at the border. For example, a point-of-entry removal order might refer to an American who attempted to enter Canada, was found inadmissible because of an American criminal record and denied entry, immediately issued a removal order, and summarily sent back. It remains noteworthy that the number of point-of-entry exclusions is down on a year-over-year basis. In 2018–19, CBSA executed 2,800 removal orders at the point of entry (Auditor General of Canada 2020). This statistic may be an important and interesting area for future research. While there is little to no publicly available data at this stage, decisions made at points of entry were undoubtedly fraught during the

Table 13.1: Removals: 31 March to 26 November 2020

Removal orders executed at the point of entry	425
Serious inadmissibility cases (terrorism, security, serious criminality, organized criminality)	147
Voluntary removals	1,331
Administrative removals	5,341
Total	7,244

Source: Public Safety Canada 2020b

pandemic: Could a family reunite? Was someone's work essential? Who was ultimately allowed in or denied access to Canada?

Serious inadmissibility removals were also down significantly. In 2018–19, the agency executed approximately 1,250 removal orders based on serious inadmissibilities (e.g., organized criminality, terrorism, security, etc.) (Auditor General of Canada 2020).[1] Following the first wave of pandemic lockdowns, the agency deported 147 people for serious inadmissibilities. The data is consistent with CBSA's description of its pandemic deportation program (Public Safety Canada 2020b). Given that CBSA stated that it was prepared to remove some people inadmissible for serious reasons, deportations in this category were expected. Nonetheless, the rate of deportation dropped significantly. In 2018–19, there were 104 removals per month for serious inadmissibilities. During the pandemic deportation moratorium, the number of removals dropped to 18 per month.

The next category is "voluntary removals." The agency describes voluntary removals as those initiated when the subject person "approach[ed] the CBSA with a request to leave voluntarily" (Public Safety Canada 2020b). The question here is whether this is an accurate account of what happened.

TABLE 13.2: Motions to stay a scheduled deportation decided by the Federal Court of Canada

	Jan	Feb	March	April	May	June	July	Aug	Sept	Oct	Nov	Dec
2019	61	44	53	38	32	21	31	26	14	33	23	12
2020	26	33	17	0	0	2	1	0	0	0	6	4

Table 13.2 shows how many times the Federal Court of Canada decided motions for an interlocutory stay of removal in the past two years.[2] In lay terms, a person facing deportation may apply to a judge for an order to stop a deportation. These motions are a good barometer of how contentious the deportation program is because they are brought on an emergency basis and always decided with reference to a scheduled deportation. In other words, a case cannot be brought and decided until a deportation date is set and the person decides that they want to challenge their removal. Therefore, if CBSA attempted to force many people out of the country who did not want to leave, we would expect at least some percentage of those people would try to stop their deportations before the orders are executed.

Beginning in March 2020, there was a significant drop in the number of stay motions brought and decided by the Court. This decline shows that fewer people went to court to try and prevent their removals from Canada as the deportations pause started. These statistics are compelling corroborative evidence that the CBSA has accurately described voluntary removals as voluntary. If this were not the case, the Federal Court of Canada data would show deportees bringing motions to stop scheduled removals.

Likewise, a review of the data regarding immigration detention shows that the deportation program became markedly less coercive during the pandemic. The primary purpose of immigration detention is to secure a person's body to ensure their availability for removal. When CBSA establishes that a person is unlikely to participate in their deportation, it can obtain an order for their detention (*IRPA*, s. 58). In this way, detention and the act of deportation are connected: it exists to enable the machinery of removal. A deportation program that makes a point of removing people who do not want to go will necessarily make greater use of detention facilities.

As table 13.3 shows,[3] CBSA made substantially less use of the detention power in the first two quarters following the implementation of the deportation pause. The average daily detainee count and the aggregate number of days spent in detention dropped by almost two-thirds during the moratorium. Recent research shows that detention adjudicators acknowledged that the pandemic was making all detention cases uncertain because CBSA was unable to explain when, how, or if a deportation would happen (Arbel and Joeck 2021). Together, the data reveals a substantively less contentious and coercive deportation program. Fewer people went to court to challenge and contest their deportations, and CBSA detained fewer people pending their removal from Canada.

The final category of removal order are the administrative removals, of which there were 5,341. This category makes up 74 per cent of CBSA's reported deportation work during the pandemic. On an annualized basis, administrative removals are up almost five times, from 1,657 in 2019 to 8,215 in 2020 (Mehler Paperny 2021).

It is necessary to address a particular accounting problem that previously plagued CBSA databases to understand administrative removals. Often people who are the subject of a deportation order leave Canada without advising CBSA. In these cases, their deportation file remains open because the order is technically unenforced. As CBSA explained, "even when sufficient information exists to indicate to the CBSA that the person is no longer in Canada, the case remains open because there is no explicit regulatory authority that allows for the removal order to be administratively enforced" (Public Safety Canada 2018).

This problem, combined with others, began to impair CBSA's ability to manage its workflow and properly account for its work. A spring 2020 report from the Auditor General of Canada found that poor data quality, poor file management, and general disorganization substantively hampered CBSA's ability to enforce removals. The average time to enforce a deportation order ranged from four years for asylum claimants to eleven years for persons with criminal records on immigration warrants (Auditor General of Canada 2020).

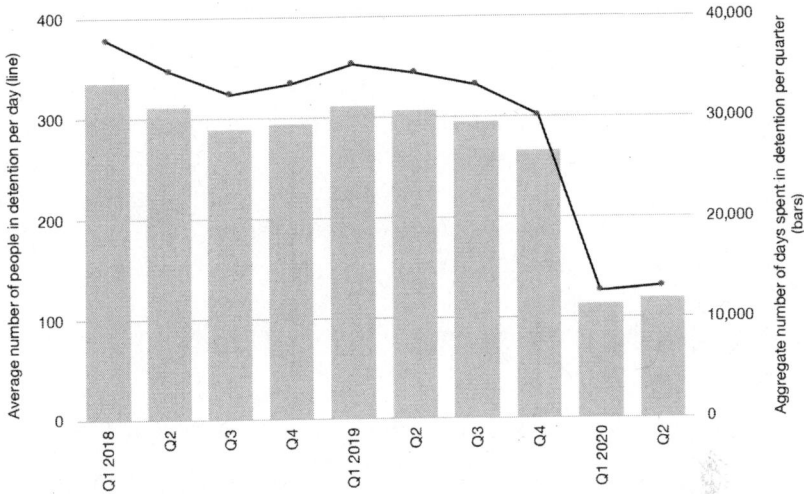

FIGURE 13.1: Immigration Detention and COVID-19

In 2018, the government enacted a new regulation to address this problem. Now, when CBSA has compelling evidence that the person under a deportation order has left Canada, their removal may be administratively enforced (*IRPR* s. 240(3)). Essentially, CBSA obtained the power to administer desk closures and address data-integrity problems in its databases.

As CBSA employees were not actively removing people from Canada during the pandemic, the agency had time to process administrative removals. As the agency explained, these "can be conducted by officers working from home in light of pandemic response measures and will contribute to additional removal statistics during the period of COVID-19 measures" (Public Safety Canada 2020a). As a result, administrative removals increased almost sevenfold between 2019 and 2020. It is not that Canada deported more people during the pandemic, but rather that in 2020 CBSA could finally count and account for self-deportations from years past.

The bottom line is that contrary to public reports, the deportation moratorium was real. CBSA did not deport thousands of people during the pandemic. In fact, it appears that the people against whom the agency executed deportation orders were not interested or able to challenge their removals. The number of emergency deportation hearings dropped to negligible numbers and resort to immigration detention, the essential coercive power that makes deportation work, dropped precipitously. Nevertheless, CBSA did not sit idle. The agency worked to clear backlogs and data blockages identified by the Auditor General of Canada in keeping with the government's pre-pandemic commitments to step up immigration enforcement and deportations.[4]

Looking Forward: The Resumption of Deportations

On 30 November 2020, CBSA announced that it was resuming its general deportation program but explained that "removal volumes will continue to be significantly reduced for some time" (Public Safety Canada 2020b). While it is difficult to anticipate when global conditions will allow for the deportations to resume at scale, and even though the project of deportation has lost a year, it appears that CBSA will be ready to hit the ground running. This posture is in keeping with the pre-pandemic objective "to improve case identification and to ensure cases are processed in a timely and efficient manner" (Auditor General of Canada 2020).

Expeditious and efficient enforcement could, however, be problematic from a rights perspective. When the day comes, and CBSA is ready to scale up its operations, how comfortable should Canada be deporting people post-pandemic on the strength of pre-pandemic deportation orders? It is possible to fear that concerns about national security and law enforcement will have distorting effects on the post-COVID-19 deportation space. As long as deportation is conceived of as an integral part of CBSA's mandate, national security concerns may eclipse an important reality: security cases are a small percentage of all deportation cases and it can be inappropriate to generalize a strict law enforcement approach to all cases. Scholars have long recognized that security-based thinking can warp Canada's immigration program and can inappropriately rationalize a more mean-spirited and sharp immigration policy (Dauvergne 2016). Rather than tighten our grip on deportation, the pandemic's conclusion necessitates a softer touch.

In the pre-pandemic world, the Federal Court of Canada explained that a large part of the reason CBSA could be called upon to strictly and diligently enforce removal orders is that the law countenances a range of mechanisms for a "person's interests" to be "assessed" before deportation (*Baron v Canada [Public Safety and Emergency Preparedness]* 2008). In other words, the law already gives people a range of opportunities to obtain status before an order is enforced. Once CBSA finally issues an order, the agency can safely enforce it because every person's case will have already been fully assessed and adjudicated. Parliament, of course, could never have anticipated the pandemic nor imagined how COVID-19 would reshape the world, let alone how it would impact people's relationship with the immigration process.

There is currently nothing in the law that provides a means of revisiting deportation orders issued before the pandemic that CBSA has not yet enforced. It remains too early to know how people's lives have changed during the pandemic. If nothing else, at least some people have since become entrenched in Canadian life and, for others, return to some parts of the world is no longer viable. For example, Canada should not deport someone with serious underlying health conditions to a part of the world where COVID-19 is not entirely under control. Moreover, there should be a way to account for and recognize that some people and their families just spent more than eighteen months further establishing themselves in Canada, and deportation from here could cause new hardships.

As such, it would be unfair and inappropriate for CBSA to resume deportations as if the pandemic were a temporary blip that only impacted the agency's operations and not the lives of people subject to removal. It would be a mistake to say that the law should be enforced in the same way after the pandemic as it was before. Deportations are severe enough when they are "timely and efficient," but they may be altogether inhumane at the tail end of a global pandemic.

The law, and the protections built into it, never countenanced this level of disruption. What should government then do? Even if CBSA can hit the ground running, it should walk first. Instead of looking at each deportation order as a law enforcement problem, the agency should recognize that the pandemic may, for some people, have produced a new compelling case to stay. In practical terms, when an officer encounters someone whose deportation was delayed because of the pandemic and who wants to stay, that person's deportation case should be moved to the bottom of the enforcement pile so that they can make a last-ditch compassionate application for status. Instead of crediting CBSA for meeting targets, this is the time to credit CBSA for making the fair and generous decisions that account for the scope of the pandemic's disruptions.

NOTES

1   CBSA does not identify the number of different types of misconduct under the heading of serious inadmissibility. However, a review of Immigration and Refugee Board case files shows that these are overwhelmingly cases of criminality, as opposed to, for example, terrorism or espionage. For example, in 2019, 78 per cent of all serious inadmissibility (serious criminality, organized criminality, terrorism, or security) removal orders issued by the board resulted from a conviction of a criminal offence.

2   To obtain this data I reviewed all motions to stay a deportation reported on CanLii. For 2020, I additionally reviewed publicly available Federal Court of Canada dockets. Given the nature of these motions, settling on exact figures is more a matter of art than science. For example, for strategic reasons a lawyer may bring multiple motions regarding one person that are argued simultaneously but reported separately. Similarly, some motions may be summarily dismissed by the judge even before a hearing and no decision will be reported. To the extent that I have been able to identify outlier cases, this chart reflects the number of motions finally decided by the Court regarding a single person or family unit.

3   The data regarding detentions is reported quarterly at CBSA (2019).

4   In October 2018, CBSA set an internal target of 15,500 deportations in 2022 (IRC 2020).

REFERENCES

Arbel, Efrat, and Molly Joeck. 2021. "Immigration Detention in the Age of COVID-19." In *Research Handbook on the Law and Politics of Migration*, edited by Catherine Dauvergne. Northampton: Edward Elgar Press. https://papers.ssrn.com/sol3/papers.cfm?abstract_id=3653452.

Auditor General of Canada. 2020. *Reports of the Auditor General of Canada to the Parliament of Canada, Spring 2020: Report 1: Immigration Removals*. Ottawa: Office of the Auditor General of Canada. https://www.oag-bvg.gc.ca/internet/english/parl_oag_202007_01_e_43572.html.

Baron v Canada (Public Safety and Emergency Preparedness), 2008 FC 341.

CBSA (Canada Border Services Agency). 2019. "Quarterly Detention Statistics. Fourth Quarter (Q4)—2018–2019." Government of Canada, last modified 20 August 2019. https://www.cbsa-asfc.gc.ca/security-securite/detent/qstat-2018-2019-eng.html.

———. 2020a. "COVID-19: Appearance before the Parliamentary Standing Committee on Health (31 March 2020)—Removals and detentions." Government of Canada, last modified 29 July 2020. https://www.cbsa-asfc.gc.ca/pd-dp/bbp-rpp/hesa/2020-03-31/removal-detent-renvoi-eng.html.

———. 2020b. "2019 Deferral of Removal Requests, A-2020-10346 / JBROD." Accessed through ATIP request; in possession of the author.

Canada (Minister of Employment and Immigration) v Chiarelli, 1992 CanLII 87 (SCC), [1992] 1 SCR 711.

Dauvergne, Catherine. 2016. *The New Politics of Immigration and the End of Settler Societies.* Cambridge: Cambridge University Press.

Durrani, Tebasum. 2020. "Why Immigration Holding Centres Could Become COVID-19 Hot Spots." *TVO*, 30 March 2020. https://www.tvo.org/article/why-immigration-holding-centres-could-become-covid-19-hot-spots.

Gibney, Matthew. 2013. "Is Deportation a Form of Forced Migration?" *Refugee Survey Quarterly* 32 (2): 116–29.

IRC (Immigration, Refugees and Citizenship Canada). 2020. "PACP—Parliamentary Context PACP Appearance: OAG Report 1 on Immigration Removals." Government of Canada 24 November 2020. https://www.canada.ca/en/immigration-refugees-citizenship/corporate/transparency/committees/pacp-nov-24-2020/pacp-parliamentary-context-pacp-appearance-oag-report-immigration-removals-nov-24-2020.html.

Immigration and Refugee Board. 2021. "Admissibility Hearings Finalized by Type of Allegation." Accessed 23 March 2021. https://irb-cisr.gc.ca/en/statistics/hearings/Pages/AdmHAlle.aspx

IRPA (Immigration and Refugee Protection Act), SC 2001, c 27.

Nesbitt, Michael, and Dana Hagg. 2020. "An Empirical Study of Terrorism Prosecutions in Canada: Elucidating the Elements of the Offence." *Alberta Law Review* 57 (3): 595–645.

Mehler Paperny, Anna. 2021. "Canada Deporting Thousands Even as Pandemic Rages." *Reuters.* 22 January 2021. https://www.reuters.com/article/us-health-coronavirus-canada-deportation-idUSKBN29R1EL.

Public Safety Canada. 2018. "Canada Gazette, Part I, Volume 152, Number 20: Regulations Amending the Immigration and Refugee Protection Regulations." Government of Canada, 19 May 2018. https://gazette.gc.ca/rp-pr/p1/2018/2018-05-19/html/reg4-eng.html.

———. 2020a. "Binder for the Minister of Public Safety and Emergency Preparednes—Committee of the Whole: Removals." Government of Canada, 5 August 2020. https://www.passengerprotect-protectiondespassagers.gc.ca/cnt/trnsprnc/brfng-mtrls/prlmntry-bndrs/20201201/012/index-en.aspx.

———. 2020b. "Removals." Materials prepared for Minister of Public Safety and Emergency Preparedness (PS-2020-2-QP-0014). Government of Canada, 1 December 2020. https://search.open.canada.ca/en/qp/id/ps-sp,PS-2020-2-QP-0014.

———. 2020c. "Timeline—CBSA Border Measures." Government of Canada, last modified 4 September 2020. https://www.publicsafety.gc.ca/cnt/trnsprnc/brfng-mtrls/prlmntry-bndrs/20200724/003/index-en.aspx.

National Security Lessons Regarding the Disproportionate Impact of COVID-19 on Migrant and Refugee Communities in the United States and Canada: A Bilateral Approach

Adham Sahloul and Diana Rayes

Introduction

The COVID-19 pandemic has illuminated the public health, economic, and political challenges facing minority communities. These challenges are particularly pronounced in high-income countries that are home to large migrant and refugee communities, such as the United States and Canada. Evidence revealing the disproportionate impact of the COVID-19 pandemic on migrants worldwide and the historic, cultural, and economic ties between the United States and Canada, the world's deepest bilateral relationship, presents opportunities to address this regional dynamic through unique channels of bilateral co-operation. Using a comparative approach, this chapter first examines how COVID-19 has disproportionately impacted migrant and refugee communities in the United States and Canada. We then assess how these outcomes could have been mitigated with higher-quality data, and how data can be integral to preventing future national and global security threats. We conclude by proposing enhanced bilateral co-operation when it comes to addressing health disparities among migrant communities.

Background

Migrant populations, refugees, asylum-seekers, and other foreign-born ethnic and racial minorities comprise one-seventh and one-fifth of the US and Canadian civilian populations, respectively. However, Western national security discourse overtly or unintentionally marginalizes these populations, with an overemphasis on the threats of terrorism and inter-state conflict, resulting in a misallocation of political, financial, and personnel resources away from addressing economic, climate, and human security (Hathaway 2020). Evidence-based, democratic national security frameworks prioritize the challenges facing migrants in times of calm and in national or global crises. While the US intelligence community's 2019 assessment of threats to US national security had dedicated space to human security issues such as public health, displacement, and climate, this paradigm shift has been catalyzed at a political and societal level by the reality of the COVID-19 pandemic (Coats 2019). The relationship between the United States and Canada is uniquely special in terms of how the migration policies of the two countries have shaped the societies, economies, and shared future of North America. How the United States and Canada each handle the COVID-19 pandemic bears heavily on their respective migrant communities, but also on the international community's ability to support migrants and refugees through and beyond the pandemic. As such, it is critical that US and Canadian policy-makers evaluate the national security implications of the COVID-19 pandemic's impact on migrant and refugee communities to develop sound and inclusive national security policies.

Characteristics of Migrant Populations in the United States and Canada

As of 2019, the United States was home to at least 44.9 million migrants, comprising 13.7 per cent of the population (Migration Policy Institute n.d.b). While 24 per cent of this total are unauthorized migrants, the majority of legal immigration to the United States is via family reunification and is largely represented by individuals from Latin America and Asia (Batlova 2021; Migration Policy Institute n.d.a). Historically, the United States has also hosted a robust refugee resettlement program that has

TABLE 14.1: Comparison of foreign-born populations in the United States and Canada

	US (% of total population)	Canada (% of total population)
Total population	328 million**	37.5 million**
Migrants	44.9 million (13.7%)	7.8 million (21.5%)
Unauthorized migrants	11 million***	28,000***
Refugees & asylum-seekers	46,500**	58,338*

Sources: World Bank 2019a, 2019b; Batlova 2021; OECD 2020a
* 2020
**2019
***2018

resettled a total of 3 million refugees since 1975. However, the Trump administration's politically charged administrative assault on legal forms of immigration, including the US refugee resettlement system, has resulted in the lowest refugee resettlement rates since the passage of the *Refugee Act of 1980*, a fact especially notable following the announcement of a record-low refugee admissions ceiling of 15,000 for 2021 (Wolgin 2018; Batlova 2021). In 2020, a total of 11,800 refugees were resettled in the United States, representing only 66 per cent of the refugee admission ceiling of 18,000 set by the Trump administration for 2020 (UNHCR n.d.; Batlova 2021). In comparison, Canada, a country whose population is around 11 per cent of the United States', accepted 320,000 migrants in 2018, the majority of which were economic migrants and their families. About 21.5 per cent of Canada's total population are migrants with permanent residence—this includes humanitarian migrants or refugees, who comprise nearly 14 per cent of the total immigrant population (OECD 2020a). The Canada Institute at the Wilson Center in Washington, DC illustrates the difference between the two systems: in 2017, Canada admitted 57 per cent of its legal migrants via economic immigration, while the United States admitted 68 per cent under family reunification (Sanders 2020). It is worth noting that this difference in scale and immigration patterns, in addition to the larger proportion of undocumented immigrants in the United States, portends divergent socio-economic priorities between the two countries' migrant health policies.

Financial, Economic, and Travel Impacts of COVID-19 on Migrant Populations

Migrants form an integral component of global and national economies. For example, migrants make up about 17 per cent of the US workforce and about a quarter of the Canadian workforce (Budiman 2020; OECD 2019). The impacts of COVID-19 on migrant communities illustrate the consequences for human security, but also the vital role these communities play in the post-pandemic global recovery (OECD 2020a; Tastsoglou 2020). According to the OECD, the United States and Canada are among the few countries where foreign-born populations experienced an increase of more than 4 per cent in unemployment rates in comparison to native-born populations following the onset of the pandemic. That these members of the workforce filled "essential worker" roles across sectors during the pandemic should be a reminder to policy-makers that they are essential to the economy and society beyond periods of crisis.

Statistics from the UN Department of Economic and Social Affairs also demonstrate that travel restrictions in response to the pandemic have shrunk global migration figures. In fact, the lifting of travel restrictions has resulted in return migration to countries of origin among tens of millions of migrants with few options in pandemic-stricken host countries (Le Coz and Newland 2021; UN News 2021). Addressing the travel-related impacts of COVID-19 will therefore be a key part of any successful global economic recovery. Just as challenging as repatriating, quarantining, and reintegrating migrants to countries of origin in line with the 2018 Global Compact for Safe, Orderly, and Regular Migration will be accounting for and ultimately replacing the economic vacuum caused by migrant labour flight.

The global economic suffering caused by the pandemic is compounded by migrants' relative inability to send critical remittances to family members in their countries of origin. The World Bank found that global remittances to low and middle-income countries (LMIC) will shrink by 14 per cent through 2021, a loss of $78 billion (World Bank 2020a). This is nearly three times the decrease in remittances witnessed at the nadir of the 2009 global financial crisis (NPR 2021). In 2018, US remittance outflows were at $68.5 billion, while Canada's outflow was $6.6 billion (World Bank 2020b). This bears consequences for human security at home and abroad. In addition to migrants who have taken a financial hit and are unable to keep their families afloat, the lack of remittances will deepen cycles of poverty, as access to food, health care, and education in LMIC countries are affected, while maintaining a financial burden on migrants in the United States and Canada.

Public Health Impacts of COVID-19 on Migrant Populations

In the United States alone, there have been over 42 million reported cases of COVID-19 and over 681,000 associated deaths reported as of September 2021 (Johns Hopkins University 2021). Among these are a disproportionate number of ethnic minority groups, including Asians, Hispanics, Blacks, and Native Americans and Alaskan Natives—who have faced an unequal burden in COVID-19 incidence and mortality rates relative to the US population. Notably missing from demographic data breakdowns regarding COVID-19 impacts are data on migrant populations, including refugees, asylum-seekers, and undocumented migrants living in the United States (OECD 2020b). This is the case even though approximately 46 per cent of the Hispanic community are considered foreign-born migrants (OECD 2020b). This is also despite the fact that migrants to the United States comprise a significant portion of the essential workforce and have therefore been at greater risk of exposure to COVID-19 as well as pandemic-related job losses and slower rates in job recovery (Chishti and Bolter 2020). According to the OECD, migrants in the United States make up 30 per cent of workers in the security and cleaning sectors, 24 per cent in the hospitality sector, 17 per cent in the health sector, and 15 per cent in retail trade (2020b).

TABLE 14.2: Cases of and deaths from COVID-19 in the United States and Canada (as of 23 September 2021)

	United States	Canada
Cases	42,552,758	1,598,109
Deaths	681,253	27,596

Source: Johns Hopkins University 2021

The impact of COVID-19 on refugee and migrant populations in Canada is also not represented holistically through data at the federal level. Trends reported by provinces, such as Ontario and Quebec, have revealed greater risks of COVID-19 in neighborhoods with higher numbers of refugee and migrant populations (Guttman et al. 2020). The City of Toronto identified higher rates of COVID-19 cases among socio-economically disadvantaged households, as well as among individuals who identified as members of racial or ethnic minorities (Guttman et al. 2020).

Migrant populations in Canada also make up a significant proportion of the essential workforce, including 31 per cent of workers in the hospitality sector, 30 per cent in security and cleaning services, 28 per cent in retail trade, and 27 per cent in the health sector (OECD 2020b). As unemployment rates have climbed in both the United States and Canada following the onset of the pandemic, the OECD notes that the lack of retention schemes (which are available in Europe) have led to potentially higher rates of unemployment among migrants in both countries.

This has both short- and long-term implications for the labour market integration of migrant populations in both countries. Immigrants tend to work in the service sectors that have been most heavily impacted by the pandemic, resulting in significant risks of migrants losing access to their livelihoods as well as increased risk for exploitation or potential deportation. These trends will also reinforce disparities and disadvantages faced by these populations.

TABLE 14.3: Breakdown of migrants employed per service sector

	United States (%)	Canada (%)
Hospitality	24	31
Health	17	27
Retail	15	28
Security and cleaning services	30	30

Source: OECD 2020b

COVID-19 Data Disparities and Inequities: Implications for At-Risk Communities in the United States and Canada

In both Canada and the United States, health-care disparities have shed light on pre-existing health inequities for minority communities, particularly among migrants and refugees. These disparities have been made worse by the multiplicative impacts of the pandemic on the livelihoods and futures of these populations. Among these are socio-economic disparities, including higher rates of poverty and poor housing conditions among immigrant populations (OECD 2020b). In Canada, for example, more than half of all domestic service workers are migrants. Access to culturally and linguistically sensitive health-care services are another hurdle facing migrant communities; refugees in Canada are reported to experience challenges in accessing interpreters or securing eligibility for health insurance (Clarke et al. 2020). Researchers in Canada have highlighted the fact that, despite access to universal health care, migrant populations have historically experienced significant challenges when it comes to actually accessing that health care. This led to a call to address the structural racism and discrimination that underlie the Canadian health system and "reinforce inequities faced by racialized communities" as a key part of the COVID-19 response (Tuyisenge and Goldenberg 2021). In the United States, health-care access is complicated by eligibility criteria based on immigration status, which is particularly challenging for those who rely on employer-provided insurance coverage and are at risk of unemployment (Capps and Gelatt 2020).

As Hacker and Hathaway (2020) note, the costly nature of the US health-care system is a national security threat in its own right, due to the effect on human security across communities—and especially minority communities—and due to high health-care expenditures coming at the expense of other items in the national budget critical to national security. The employment-based nature of US health care—that is, the lack of a universal health-care system—has meant that historically and statistically, underprivileged communities have had less coverage and have therefore lacked access to preventative health care. Structurally, the legacies of discriminatory housing, labour, and education policies have disproportionately affected minority communities. The lack of health-care coverage among such communities was made even more dire as more of the US workforce lost their jobs during the pandemic.

As the COVID-19 pandemic was spreading in North America, so too was the realization that particular communities were being disproportionately impacted by the disease. Traditionally, policy-makers were able to rely on federal data to capture trends regarding at-risk communities to inform smart decision-making and strategic resource allocation, especially during a crisis. However, the unavailability of ethnic and racial demographic breakdowns of COVID-19 incidence and mortality data has been a pervasive issue throughout the pandemic. These data disparities have had dangerous consequences for policy-making during and in anticipation of national security crises. In fact, policy-makers have noted that, had they had earlier access to data on COVID-19 disparities, many deaths could have been prevented (Keating, Ariana, and Florit 2020).

In the United States, this is best demonstrated by data reported to and by the US Centers for Disease Control and Prevention (CDC) regarding demographic trends of COVID-19 cases and deaths (CDC 2021). As of September 2021, age and sex breakdowns are made available for between 98 and 99 per cent of COVID-19 cases and deaths reported to the CDC by various states. In stark contrast, race and ethnicity data, which are sorted into five ethnic and racial group categories—not including migrants—is only available for 52 per cent of cases and 74 per cent of deaths (see tables 14.1 and 14.2). Disparities in racial and ethnic data are largely attributable to shortcomings in data collection at the state level when it comes to identifying the racial and ethnic background of individuals at risk for COVID-19.

Data reported by the CDC continues to demonstrate that those most at risk for COVID-19 are white and/or Caucasian populations. However, as more attention was being paid to the disproportionate impact of COVID-19 on minority groups, the CDC was forced to reconcile with these data gaps. On 4 June 2020, during a committee hearing before the House of Representatives, CDC director Robert Redfield acknowledged that data disparities were "an inadequacy in our response" and promised to work toward improving socio-demographic data. On 1 August 2020, the reporting of race and ethnicity data for each COVID-19 test became a requirement across all states (Goldstein 2020). As of September 2021, 51 out of 56 states and US territories report on race and ethnicity data—almost double the number of states that were reporting ahead of the CDC mandate (COVID Tracking Project 2021). While the CDC acknowledges the increased risk of COVID-19 among refugee, immigrant, and migrant populations, there is no indication of what proportion of these populations are represented in the racial and ethnic surveillance data (HHS 2020; CDC 2020).

Most importantly, what are the implications of these data disparities? The lack of quality data with which to quantify the risks for vulnerable populations, which include migrants and refugees, provided policy-makers little direction as to how to manage already limited resources, including testing, access to health care, and regulations regarding social distancing. Another implication was that the data failed to identify underlying disparities leading to a disproportionate impact, including access to health care, the density of households, rates of unemployment and types of employment among communities of colour, as well as pervasive discrimination within the US health system, including access to insurance for most immigrant and refugee populations. It also failed to capture the nuances of potential barriers to COVID-19 care, including mistrust and fear, limited access to up-to-date and quality information, potential for vaccine hesitancy, and the lack of access to culturally and linguistically sensitive health care. More recently, the consequences of early disparities in data collection have had a significant impact on vaccine rollout. For example, federal- and state-level data as of September 2021 has already demonstrated that Black and Hispanic populations have received smaller shares of vaccines in comparison to the proportion of COVID-19 cases and deaths identified in these groups; however data reveals that shares of vaccination are increasing with time (Ndugga et al. 2021).

These disparate impacts on racial and ethnic minorities in the United States led to increased pressure on local officials to understand similar disparities within the Canadian population. However, federal agencies, such as Statistics Canada, did not track impacts on particular racial and ethnic ("racialized") or socio-economic groups early on in the pandemic (McKenzie 2020). This drew criticism from researchers who claimed that Canada failed to provide an equitable response to racialized groups throughout the pandemic, including by identifying risk factors that may have exacerbated COVID-19 rates in these populations (McKenzie 2020). Moreover, Canadian officials, including from the Public Health Agency of Canada, identified research gaps when it came to COVID-19 impacts on ethnic minorities in Canada relative to their US and UK counterparts (Public Health Agency of Canada 2020a, 2020b). As such, researchers opted to combine publicly available COVID-19 trends with census data to identify key geographic areas that were particularly vulnerable to the pandemic. One such study, conducted by Choi et al. (2020), studied the social determinants of COVID-19 in what the authors refer to as a "data vacuum" and the potential increased risk among marginalized communities. This analysis discovered that Black communities in Canada have been disproportionately impacted by COVID-19, and it provided explanations for why places like Montreal, with large numbers of Black migrants, have emerged as epicentres of COVID-19 (Choi et al. 2020). It also revealed that immigrant communities in Canada, of whom 90 per cent settle in cities with high population densities, are also particularly vulnerable to COVID-19.

These statistics led to a national reckoning across Canada, relating not only to COVID-19 disparities, but also the underlying inequities within the health system more broadly. In October 2020, for example, the Chief Public Health Officer of Canada acknowledged that COVID-19 has had an unequal impact on particular communities and proposed a health equity framework that explicitly mentions the importance of increasing Canada's capacity to conduct and publish rigorous data and research on this topic (Public Health Agency of Canada 2020c). Also embedded in the framework was a broader call to reduce stigma and discrimination against minority populations and to adopt an awareness-shifting approach in order to change underlying values and attitudes regarding health inequities.

National and Bilateral Security Implications

Despite systemic differences in US and Canadian migration and healthcare policy, the deep bilateral relationship—which is receiving critical attention with the new working relationship between the Biden administration and Trudeau government, each of which view global health and migration and refugee policy through a similar lens—is an opportunity for coordination on issues of shared public health, economic, and social concern. This has already been observed: the February 2021 Roadmap for a Renewed US-Canada Partnership provided a joint framework for bilateral coordination on the COVID-19 response and called for addressing global migration and systemic racism in the post-pandemic economic recovery (White House 2021). Partnerships between the US Department of Health and Human Services, and particularly the National Institutes of Health, with Health Canada and the Public Health Agency of Canada on funding research and resource gaps on health disparities is an achievable lift for what has been identified as a shared challenge.

The Biden administration's National Security Adviser, Jake Sullivan, outlined a US national security and foreign policy "for the middle class," and the Biden administration has sought to put racial equity at the centre of its economic and COVID-19 policies. In theory, this would include a focus on human security and racial equity for the American middle class, of which the migrant community is a central pillar. US-Canada trade, which was valued at $718.4 billion in 2019, will naturally be affected by supply and demand in both countries (USTR n.d.). The health of the North American economy, integral to global economic recovery in the post-pandemic period, is affected by the human security of migrant consumers, workers, and taxpayers. The economic impact of the pandemic affects the foreign policy priorities of both the United States and Canada, and particularly foreign aid and development assistance. It also impacts resource allocation and strategic planning, as well as the domestic political band-width available to leaders in Washington and Ottawa for important, but not urgent, matters of national security and foreign policy. Additionally, the Biden and Trudeau governments, along with the relevant legislative, oversight, and regulatory bodies in each country, should stand poised to make human security a pillar of the implementation of the USMCA/CUSMA (US-Mexico-Canada Agreement, the revised North American Free Trade Agreement), which went into effect during the pandemic on 1 July 2020, particularly in managing drug pricing and in ensuring labour and environmental protections—facets of the trade framework that disproportionately affect communities of colour.

The shared challenges and opportunities of enacting public health and economic policies in a federal system provide another opportunity for bilateral coordination among the two neighbours. Moreover, the need for deepened public health and social policy diplomacy between US states and Canadian provinces and territories, as well as municipal governments, is less contingent on political tides in Washington and Ottawa. The Pacific NorthWest Economic Region, an organization of regional US states and Canadian provinces, for instance, directs policy working groups across shared priorities and provides an appropriate regional platform through which to address systemic challenges to public health access and COVID-19 recovery among migrant communities.

Importantly, the COVID-19 pandemic has spurred a conversation about racial disparities and human security. This has provided a larger opening for national security and foreign policy professionals to align their work on public health and domestic policy, and vice versa. This positive breaking of the "wall" between domestic and foreign policy is most pronounced in the personnel decisions of the Biden administration, which, for instance, named Ambassador Susan Rice, most recently the Obama administration's National Security Adviser, as chair of the Domestic Policy Council. US government leadership stands to benefit from its allies in breaking the policy wall; in Canadian and European contexts, the rotations of ministerial portfolios at the political level are far from novel.

REFERENCES

Batlova J., M. Hanna, C. Levesque. 2021. "Frequently Requested Statistics on Immigrants and Immigration in the United States." *Migration Policy Institute*, 11 February 2021. https://www.migrationpolicy.org/article/frequently-requested-statistics-immigrants-and-immigration-united-states-2020#refugees-asylum.

Budiman, Abby. 2020. "Key Findings about U.S. Immigrants." *Pew Research Center*, 20 August 2020. https://www.pewresearch.org/fact-tank/2020/08/20/key-findings-about-u-s-immigrants/.

Capps, Randy, and Julia Gelatt. 2020. "Barriers to COVID-19 Testing and Treatment: Immigrants without Health Coverage in the United States." *Migration Policy Institute*, May 2020. https://www.migrationpolicy.org/research/covid-19-testing-treatment-immigrants-health-insurance.

CDC (US Centers for Disease Control and Prevention). 2020. "COVID-19 Case Investigation and Contact Tracing among Refugee, Immigrant, and Migrant (RIM) Populations: Important Considerations for Health Departments." Last modified 4 December 2020. https://www.cdc.gov/coronavirus/2019-ncov/php/rim-considerations.html.

———. 2021. "Demographic Trends of COVID-19 Cases and Deaths in the US Reported to CDC." CDC COVID Data Tracker, accessed 23 September 2021. https://covid.cdc.gov/covid-data-tracker/#demographics.

Chishti, Muzaffar, and Jessica Bolter. 2020. "Vulnerable to COVID-19 and in Frontline Jobs, Immigrants Are Mostly Shut Out of U.S. Relief." *Migration Policy Institute*, 24 April 2020. https://www.migrationpolicy.org/article/covid19-immigrants-shut-out-federal-relief.

Choi, Kate, Patrick Denice, Michael Haan, and Anna Zajacova. 2021. "Studying the Social Determinants of COVID-19 in a Data Vacuum." *UCLA CCPR Population Working Papers*, 11 April 2021. DOI: 10.31235/osf.io/yq8vu.

Clarke, Sarah K., Gayathri S. Kumar, James Sutton, Jacob Atem, Anna Banerji, Mahli Brindamour, Paul Geltman, and Najah Zaaeed. 2020. "Potential Impact of COVID-19 on Recently Resettled Refugee Populations in the United States and Canada: Perspectives of Refugee Healthcare Providers." *Journal of Immigrant and Minority Health* 23:184–9.

Coats, Daniel. 2019. "Worldwide Threat Assessment of the U.S. Intelligence Community." Senate Select Committee on National Intelligence, 29 January 2019. https://www.dni.gov/files/ODNI/documents/2019-ATA-SFR---SSCI.pdf.

COVID Tracking Project. 2021. "Racial Data Dashboard." Accessed 23 September 2021. https://covidtracking.com/race/dashboard.

Goldstein, Amy. 2020. "Race, Ethnicity Data to Be Required with Coronavirus Tests Starting Aug. 1." *Washington Post*, 4 June 2020. https://www.washingtonpost.com/health/race-ethnicity-data-to-be-required-with-coronavirus-tests-starting-aug-1/2020/06/04/402fc58a-a68f-11ea-b473-04905b1af82b_story.html.

Guttmann, A., S. Gandhi, S. Wanigaratne, H. Lu, L. E. Ferreira-Legere, J. Paul, P. Gozdyra, T. Campbell, et al. 2020. "COVID-19 in Immigrants, Refugees and Other Newcomers in Ontario: Characteristics of Those Tested and Those Confirmed Positive, as of June 14, 2020." ICES, September 2020. https://www.ices.on.ca/Publications/Atlases-and-Reports/2020/COVID-19-in-Immigrants-Refugees-and-Other-Newcomers-in-Ontario.

Hacker, Jacob, and Oona Hathaway. 2020. "Universal Health Care Is a National Security Issue." *Just Security*, 12 March 2020. https://www.justsecurity.org/69130/universal-health-care-is-a-national-security-issue/.

Hathaway, Oona. 2020. "COVID-19 Shows How the U.S. Got National Security Wrong." *Just Security*, 7 April 2020. https://www.justsecurity.org/69563/covid-19-shows-how-the-u-s-got-national-security-wrong/.

HHS (US Department of Health and Human Services). 2020. "CDC's Collection and Use of Data on Disparities in COVID-19 Cases and Outcomes." Office of the Inspector General, US Department of Health and Human Services, accessed 28 February 2021. https://oig.hhs.gov/reports-and-publications/workplan/summary/wp-summary-0000493.asp.

Johns Hopkins University. 2021. COVID-19 Dashboard by the Center for Systems Science and Engineering at Johns Hopkins University, 23 September 2021. https://coronavirus.jhu.edu/map.html.

Keating, Dan, Eunjung Cha Ariana, and Gabriel Florit. 2020. " 'I Just Pray God Will Help Me': Racial, Ethnic Minorities Reel from Higher COVID-19 Death Rates." *Washington Post*, 20 November 2020. https://www.washingtonpost.com/graphics/2020/health/covid-race-mortality-rate/.

Le Coz, Camille, and Kathleen Newland. 2021. "Rewiring Migrant Returns and Reintegration after the COVID-19 Shock." *Migration Policy Institute*, February 2021. https://www.migrationpolicy.org/sites/default/files/publications/mpi-covid19-return-reintegration_final.pdf.

McKenzie, Kwame. 2020. Race and Ethnicity Data Collection during COVID-19 in Canada: If You Are Not Counted You Cannot Count on the Pandemic Response." *Royal Society of Canada*, 12 November 2020. https://rsc-src.ca/en/race-and-ethnicity-data-collection-during-covid-19-in-canada-if-you-are-not-counted-you-cannot-count.

Migration Policy Institute. n.d.a. "Regions of Birth for Immigrants in the United States, 1960–Present." Accessed 26 March 2021. https://www.migrationpolicy.org/programs/data-hub/us-immigration-trends#source.

———. n.d.b. "U.S. Immigrant Population and Share over Time, 1850-Present." Accessed 26 March 2021. https://www.migrationpolicy.org/programs/data-hub/us-immigration-trends.

NPR (National Public Radio). 2021. "Pandemic Hits Global Poor: World Bank Projects Drop in Remittances." NPR, 6 February 2021. https://www.npr.org/2021/02/06/964893542/pandemic-hits-global-poor-world-bank-projects-drop-in-remittances.

Ndugga, Nambi, Olivia Pham, Latoya Hill, Samantha Artiga, and Noah Parker. 2021. "Latest Data on COVID-19 Vaccinations Race/Ethnicity." *KFF*, 23 September 2021. https://www.kff.org/coronavirus-covid-19/issue-brief/latest-data-on-covid-19-vaccinations-race-ethnicity/.

OECD. 2019. "Context For Labour Migration to Canada." In *Recruiting Immigrant Workers: Canada 2019*." Paris: OECD Publishing. https://www.oecd-ilibrary.org/sites/184a3868-en/index.html?itemId=/content/component/184a3868-en.

———. 2020a. "Executive Summary." In *International Migration Outlook 2020*. Paris: OECD Publishing. https://www.oecd-ilibrary.org/sites/ec98f531-en/index.html?itemId=/content/publication/ec98f531-en.

———. 2020b. "What Is the Impact of the COVID-19 Pandemic on Immigrants and Their Children?" OECD, 19 October 2020. http://www.oecd.org/coronavirus/policy-responses/what-is-the-impact-of-the-covid-19-pandemic-on-immigrants-and-their-children-e7cbb7de/.

Public Health Agency of Canada. 2020a. "Social Determinants and Inequities in Health for Black Canadians: A Snapshot." Government of Canada, 8 September 2020. https://www.canada.ca/en/public-health/services/health-promotion/population-health/what-determines-health/social-determinants-inequities-black-canadians-snapshot.html.

———. 2020b. "COVID-19 and Ethnicity: What Is the Evidence?" *Canada Communicable Disease Report*, 46, nos. 11–12. //www.canada.ca/en/public-health/services/reports-publications/canada-communicable-disease-report-ccdr/monthly-issue/2020-46/issue-11-12-november-5-2020/covid-19-ethnicity.html.

———. Publica Health Agency of Canada 2020c. *From Risk to Resilience: An Equity Approach to COVID-19. Chief Public Health Officer of Canada's Report on the State of Public Health in Canada 2020*. Ottawa: Public Health Agency of Canada. https://www.canada.ca/en/public-health/corporate/publications/chief-public-health-officer-reports-state-public-health-canada/from-risk-resilience-equity-approach-covid-19.html#a2.

Sanders, Richard. 2020. "A Layered Look at Canadian and U.S. Immigration." *Wilson Center*, 21 July 2020. https://www.wilsoncenter.org/article/layered-look-canadian-and-us-immigration.

Tastsoglou, Evangelia. 2020. "Immigration Is the Key to Canada's Survival and Recovery after COVID-19." *Open Democracy*, 1 December 2020. https://www.opendemocracy.net/en/pandemic-border/immigration-is-the-key-to-canadas-survival-and-recovery-after-covid-19/.

Tuyisenge, Germaine, and Shira M. Goldenberg. 2021. "COVID-19, Structural Racism, and Migrant Health in Canada." *Lancet* 397 (10275): 650–2.

UNHCR (United Nations High Commissioner for Refugees). n.d. "Refugees in America." Accessed February 28, 2021. https://www.unrefugees.org/refugee-facts/usa/.

UN News. 2021. "Pandemic Curbs Trend Towards Ever-Increasing Migration." *UN News*, 15 January 2021. https://news.un.org/en/story/2021/01/1082222.

USTR (US Trade Representative). n.d. "Canada: U.S.-Canada Trade Facts." Accessed 21 April 2021. https://ustr.gov/countries-regions/americas/canada.

White House. 2021. "Roadmap for a Renewed U.S.-Canada Partnership." Briefing Room, Statements and Releases, 23 February 2021. https://www.whitehouse.gov/briefing-room/statements-releases/2021/02/23/roadmap-for-a-renewed-u-s-canada-partnership/.

Wolgin, Philip. 2018. "Family Reunification Is the Bedrock of U.S. Immigration Policy." *Center for American Progress*, 12 February 2018. https://www.americanprogress.org/issues/immigration/news/2018/02/12/446402/family-reunification-bedrock-u-s-immigration-policy/.

World Bank. 2019a. "Population, Total—Canada." Accessed 21 April 2021. https://data.worldbank.org/indicator/SP.POP.TOTL?locations=CA.

———. 2019b. "Population, Total—United States." Accessed 21 April 2021. https://data.worldbank.org/indicator/SP.POP.TOTL?locations=US.

———. 2020a. "COVID-19: Remittance Flows to Shrink 14% by 2021." Press release, 29 October 2020. https://www.worldbank.org/en/news/press-release/2020/10/29/covid-19-remittance-flows-to-shrink-14-by-2021.

———. 2020b. "Tabulation of Data from the World Bank Prospects Group. Annual Remittance Data." Accessed 26 March 2021. www.worldbank.org/en/topic/migrationremittancesdiasporaissues/brief/migration-remittances-data.

Conclusion

Thomas Juneau

This short conclusion draws out some of the key themes that emerged in the chapters throughout this edited volume. In particular, it highlights:

- the extent to which the national security and intelligence community was ready—or not—to face the pandemic;
- how the threat environment changed during the pandemic;
- how the community adjusted; and
- the longer-term implications for the community going forward.

Preparedness

When the pandemic hit Canada in March 2020, how ready was the national security and intelligence community? In answering this question, it is important not to set an impossible standard. To some extent, the pandemic has been a unique and unprecedented crisis for which no government could have been reasonably expected to be fully prepared. Nevertheless, security agencies understand that the world is unpredictable, and it is undeniably appropriate to expect them to plan for a range of contingencies.

Not surprisingly, therefore, when the pandemic struck, many agencies and departments were ready to implement business continuity plans that they had already prepared. However, as meticulous as these plans might have been, they did not survive unscathed from their first contact with the virus. As Carvin explains in her chapter, such plans were often helpful in allowing senior officials to rapidly identify critical missions that had to continue, even with reduced staffing levels. Still, they were of less use to guide more tactical decisions, notably on sanitary procedures.

The Department of National Defence and the Canadian Armed Forces (DND/CAF) had a detailed counter-pandemic contingency plan, which, once activated, became Operation LASER. This preparation is not surprising given that the CAF's very nature demands that it be ready to operate in crisis environments. As Cox explains in his chapter, there have been two aspects to this operation: the first focusing on force protection, integrity, and effectiveness, and the second providing military support to civil authorities. According to Cox, this preparedness allowed the Defence Intelligence Enterprise to adapt rapidly and, after important adjustments, to meet its priority intelligence requirements.

The national security and intelligence community was ready—to some extent—to face the pandemic. Rayes and Sahloul argue, however, that the pandemic has shone a light on the specific public health, economic, and political challenges facing minority communities, including migrants and refugees, in the United States and Canada. In their view, governments were not prepared to understand the disproportionate impact the pandemic would have on these communities, notably because of the unavailability of ethnic and racial demographic breakdowns of COVID-19 incidence and mortality. Without such data, governments cannot build a more holistic view of the security challenges facing these communities.

Turning to the legal system, Nesbitt and Hansen identify in their chapter three systemic challenges in criminal law that the COVID-19 pandemic exposed. First, they argue that Canada's criminal justice system has been stress tested by the pandemic, notably due to increases in certain types of criminal behaviour and the introduction of new public health regulations. Second, they write that Canada saw a rise in ideologically motivated extremism, especially of the far-right type, and conspiracy-driven threats like QAnon (discussed below). Third, this shift occurred in the context of an already overstretched criminal justice and national security apparatus. In other words, Nesbitt and Hansen argue that an already strained criminal justice system has had to respond since March 2020 to increased security threats while operating with fewer resources because of the imposition of pandemic-related public health measures.

Threats

One of the main themes that emerges from the chapters in part 1 is that the pandemic did not so much lead to the emergence of new security threats as foster conditions that allowed pre-existing threats to intensify.

Conspiracy theories often thrive in times of crisis, and the recent pandemic has been no exception. Early on, various theories—concerning 5G technology, the accusation that vaccines include microchips, or, more broadly, that the pandemic is a vast conspiracy to establish a new global order—emerged and have since multiplied. Their spread was already a concern before March 2020. Yet the pandemic (and more specifically, measures taken by governments to limit its spread) contributed to an unprecedented rise in conspiracy theories and the merging and blending of different conspiracies. As Argentino and Amarasingam explain, there may be no better example of this trend than the QAnon movement, which grew in popularity partly because it rode the wave of COVID-related conspiracies. Until 2020, the Canadian government rarely looked at conspiracy theories through the prism of national security. This approach, however, is changing as the risk increases that conspiracy theories will motivate domestic extremists to commit violent acts. The problem has attracted significant attention in the United States, most visibly with the 6 January 2021 insurrection at the Capitol in Washington, DC. But, as Argentino and Amarasingam note, Canada has not been immune from the phenomenon.

Similarly, Babb and Wilner explain that the pandemic has emboldened terrorist and extremist groups worldwide, providing them with new opportunities. Far-right groups, in particular, have taken advantage of the COVID-19 pandemic to aggressively promote their cause in cyberspace and on social media. As with the spread of conspiracy theories, this is not a new trend but it intensified after March 2020. It has also been a global phenomenon, with direct implications for Canada. Yet as Babb and Wilner explain, as much as the trend is worrying, the concrete national security implications of these online activities are still poorly understood. Like the pandemic, the online threat environment is fast evolving in unpredictable ways, making it a constant challenge for Canada's national security agencies to keep track and do more than react. The authors, moreover, expect these trends to continue: malicious actors mobilized and emboldened after March 2020 will need to adapt as the pandemic subsides, but they will not disappear.

The pandemic has also opened additional space for threats to Canada's economic security. As with the spread of conspiracy theories and the mobilization of far-right groups, these threats predate the pandemic, but events since March 2020 have allowed them to intensify. As Momani and Bélanger argue in their chapter, the long-standing shift by the Canadian economy and society toward the digitalized world has rapidly accelerated during the pandemic, forcing the national security and intelligence community to be even more vigilant about foreign and domestic cyber attacks on critical infrastructure. Indeed, there has been a significant increase in cybercrime and more advanced attacks since the start of the pandemic. Critical infrastructure, according to Momani and Bélanger, is the "soft underbelly" of Canada's cybersecurity defences. The health-care system, in particular, has been the target of ransomware attacks, both in Canada and elsewhere in the world. The situation is especially complicated in the Canadian context because critical infrastructure has steadily shifted from public to private ownership and control. As a result, efforts to shore up defences involve a growing number of actors at all levels of government and in the private sector.

Similarly, as Carvin and a group of her students from the Infrastructure Protection and International Security Program at Carleton University explain, Canada's supply chains, especially in the food and personal protective equipment sectors, experienced difficulties during the pandemic. Again, this was not a new phenomenon: concern about the security of supply chains in strategic sectors predates the pandemic. Events since March 2020, however, have demonstrated how weaknesses in critical supply chains can have negative economic consequences that can quickly spill over into the security realm. In their chapter, Carvin and her students thus identify five reasons why Canada's supply chains experienced difficulties during the pandemic: a lack of domestic manufacturing and production capacity, short time frames, non-diversified sources for materials and consumers, vulnerabilities to global disruptions, and a lack of redundant systems in place.

Adjustment

The pandemic forced the national security and intelligence community to adapt in new and unforeseen ways. However, a consistent finding throughout this edited volume is that the pandemic also accelerated changes already taking place inside the community. It has forced departments and agencies to hasten their adoption and use of certain technologies, change their management of human resources, and engage with new partners both inside the federal government and beyond.

The community, most obviously, had to revise expectations of what it could and could not do, both upward with its political masters and downward with staff. It then had to target its suddenly limited resources toward critical priorities in what is labelled in Carvin's chapter a "ruthless" exercise. The community's leaders had to make difficult choices at every stage of the intelligence cycle. Collection, analysis, and dissemination of intelligence could not continue at a normal pace, and less essential activities had to be abandoned or slowed down. Moreover, it rapidly emerged that this re-prioritization exercise could not merely involve the reduction of resources dedicated to less critical activities; it also had to include the commitment of additional resources to new priorities as they emerged.

The precise impact on the community's departments and agencies varied. In his chapter, Wallace explains how deporting unwelcome migrants is, like prosecutions discussed in the chapter by Nesbitt and Hansen, a critical tool for the federal government to fulfill its national security mission. Wallace emphasizes that before the pandemic, the Canada Border Services Agency (CBSA) regularly initiated terrorism and security inadmissibility proceedings. Unlike the limited use of criminal prosecutions for terrorism or other national security offences, this is a power that the government in Canada uses widely. Wallace finds, however, that the pandemic negatively impacted CBSA's ability to enforce deportation orders, notably because of remote working conditions and reduced air travel. Yet he argues that the pandemic also created conditions that permitted CBSA to reform its deportation posture, which will allow it to emerge, once normal life resumes, with more capacity.

The COVID-19 pandemic also imposed adjustments on the CAF. They have had, in particular, to engage in more operations on the domestic front, notably by deploying to long-term care facilities in Ontario and Quebec and by assisting with vaccine distribution. Interestingly, Saideman, von Hlatky, and Hopkins note in their chapter that the impact on international operations has not been evenly distributed. Maritime and air operations only required modest changes. Land operations, however, often had to be curtailed, especially when they involved a capacity-building component, since training foreign troops presents a higher risk of COVID-19 transmission.

Cox's chapter details how the Defence Intelligence Enterprise conducted this re-prioritization exercise. On the analytical side, risk management decisions within the Canadian Forces Intelligence Command were delegated down to mid-level managers. These managers then determined which strategic intelligence products were essential—and therefore required that analysts come into the office to work on classified systems—and which ones could be delayed.

Human resources thus became an urgent preoccupation. As Cox explains, managers in the Defence Intelligence Enterprise have tried to strike a complex and constantly shifting balance between evolving intelligence priorities, sanitary measures which capped the number of employees in the office, and the needs of employees, many of whom had children at home. Similarly, Robinson analyzes in his chapter how the Communications Security Establishment (CSE) managed to balance the need to maintain a fast operational tempo in a highly classified environment with its obligation to protect its workforce.

The pandemic has also imposed an unexpected burden on the community's IT staff as thousands of employees suddenly started working from home, creating an enormous surge in demand for various services. As Robinson explains, CSE's Canadian Centre for Cyber Security, in particular, played a critical role in supporting the efforts of Shared Services Canada (the federal department responsible for the public service's communications systems) to provide secure and reliable access for online work for federal employees.

In recent years, the intelligence analysis community in Ottawa has slowly but steadily grown more comfortable with incorporating more open-source information into its work. Even if some resistance remains, analysts and their managers have increasingly understood that the best analysis is based on both classified and openly available sources. Here again, the pandemic accelerated this pre-existing trend. In her chapter, Carvin explains how various analytical units, notably the Intelligence Assessment Secretariat in the Privy Council Office and the Intelligence Assessment Branch in CSIS, had to adjust to the reality of a proportion of their analysts working from home—first by consuming more open-source information and then producing more unclassified reports.

A final trend that predates the pandemic but has intensified since March 2020 is the level of co-operation between the national security community and non-traditional partners. In recent years, the community has had to significantly ramp up its co-operation with other departments and agencies in the federal government such as Elections Canada and Innovation, Science and Economic Development to deal with emerging threats such as foreign electoral interference and foreign investments of concern. It has also had to learn to work more closely with actors in other levels of government and the private sector. CSIS and CSE, for example, have expanded their ability to work with universities and private companies to warn them against the growing threat of economic espionage.

The pandemic has led to a rapid intensification of the national security and intelligence community's efforts to expand its ties with non-traditional partners. Robinson's chapter, for example, explains how CSE's Canadian Centre for Cyber Security, in addition to its standard activities in support of the rest of the federal government, has increasingly provided cybersecurity advice and services to public and private health institutions, notably those involved in vaccine research and development. Similarly, in her chapter, Carvin reports that CSIS's Academic Outreach and Stakeholder Engagement branch gave threat briefings to more than 400 private-sector entities in 2020.

Finally, just like other sectors of the workforce, the national security and intelligence community has had to deal with significant mental health and well-being challenges for its personnel, as discussed by many authors in this volume. Like everyone else, national security personnel have had to deal with the anxiety caused by having children at home because of school closures and the possibility of family members falling sick. Those who had to continue physically showing up at the office also struggled with concerns regarding workplace safety. Many struggled with the additional work pressures stemming from having to do more with less. For managers, this has represented an additional burden as they have had to juggle the new demands created by the pandemic with the genuine emotional stress of a large proportion of their staff.

The Future

The pandemic forced the national security and intelligence community to make many adjustments. Some of those changes will undoubtedly revert to the pre–March 2020 *status quo ante* eventually. Should some of those adjustments be retained, even if only partially? What lessons, more broadly, can the community learn from its experience during the pandemic?

An early question the community will have to ponder is the issue of remote work. A few chapters in this volume suggest that at least some employees might want to keep the option of working from home, even if only on a part-time basis, once the pandemic subsides. For many employees in the national security and intelligence community, this is an option that, at most, they can only adopt on a very partial basis since much of their work requires access to classified material and spaces. Nevertheless, even in their case, events since March 2020 have shown that, with some planning, many employees can organize their week to use a specific day to focus on unclassified work at home. Certainly, the frequency of remote work could be higher for other employees less dependent on access to classified material and spaces. For many employees, this can bring significant benefits, notably for mental health and avoiding commuting.

Beyond human resources issues, the national security and intelligence community will face a series of questions regarding its mandate, how it conducts operations, and the nature of its co-operative relationships with partners and stakeholders.

Looking ahead, the most important high-level debate for the community might be the place of health intelligence in its work. Should the collection and analysis of health intelligence be given greater priority than before 2020? Should analytical units deliver more products focusing on threats to health security? In theory, answering these questions in the positive is appealing, but in practice, this would lead to difficult choices. In a context of scarce resources and with agencies' collection and analytical capacity already stretched by the diversification of the threats Canada faces, calling for more focus on health intelligence is far easier said than done. Would CSIS, CSE, and others receive budget increases to support a greater focus on health intelligence? This funding might be unlikely in the difficult economic and fiscal context that will follow the pandemic. Without additional resources, what other priorities would the agencies downsize to allow for a greater focus on health intelligence?

At the very least, what does seem clear from many chapters in this volume is that the core members of the national security and intelligence community will need to strengthen and institutionalize some of the links they have built with non-traditional partners since March 2020. Outreach by CSIS and CSE with private- and public-sector research, particularly discussed in chapters by Carvin and Robinson, offers a valuable model for the future—in the health intelligence realm and perhaps beyond.

More broadly, as Davis and Corbeil assess, the pandemic has shown the value of improving co-operation and information sharing between the national security and intelligence community and various other sectors of government—in health, but also in the social and economic spheres. These channels of communication and governance structures had been improving and diversifying in the years before the pandemic; one can only hope that this maturation and institutionalization will continue. As Davis and Corbeil emphasize, Canada, like its allies and partners, learned the hard way that a public health emergency such as a pandemic has profound national security consequences. The answer, according to them, is for the actors involved to learn to better work together and share more information.

Beyond the issue of mandates, the pandemic offers lessons at a more granular level of the tool kit the federal government has at its disposal. In her chapter, West argues that existing legal authorities and emergency legislation in Canada do not allow the federal government to collect the personal information of Canadians (like location data) for public health purposes. Where authorities do allow for collecting or analyzing data necessary to trace the spread of communicable disease or enforce public health measures, it is only in very narrow and specific circumstances that are not necessarily sufficient in a pandemic. Whether a future government will want to give themselves greater authorities is another important question to ponder.

Another tool in the federal government's portfolio to deal with public health crises is the military. As Saideman, von Hlatky, and Hopkins highlight in their chapter, some in the CAF leadership already lamented the high pace of domestic operations before the pandemic. However, events since March 2020 have shown the value of calling on the Forces to deploy in assisting civil authorities during public health crises, be it to help out in long-term care facilities or to lend their logistical expertise to support vaccine distribution. Saideman, von Hlatky, and Hopkins therefore argue that one of the main lessons of the pandemic, from the military's perspective, is that requests for assistance to civil authorities are unlikely to decrease in the future, especially if—or when—other public health crises emerge. Therefore, as the government considers the future of defence policy, it is essential to reflect on the balance between domestic and international operations. This calculation, of course, has significant implications for procurement, force structure, doctrine, human resources, etc.

The COVID-19 pandemic has also highlighted the importance but also the limits of warning. In their chapter, Lee and Piper explain how effective surveillance, monitoring, and reporting are essential for early warning of outbreaks. Efforts to strengthen Canada's ability to face future public health crises must therefore strengthen and renew the capacities that used to reside under the Public Health Agency of Canada, especially the Global Public Health Intelligence Network. Here again, the devil will be in the details: What should be the precise objectives of such a warning function? What specific skills should its staff possess? What should be its relationship with other partners in the federal government, in other levels of government, with private sector and civil-society actors, and with international partners? In their chapter, Davis and Corbeil emphasize that such a health intelligence warning capability needs to be able to work more closely than in the past with the national security and intelligence community. Yet as students of warning intelligence understand well, Davis and Corbeil also caution that a better warning capability is far from a guarantee of future success: timely and accurate warning is a necessary first step in mounting an effective response, but getting political leaders to act, and act on incomplete and fragmentary information, is, here again, easier said than done.

Finally, the pandemic has forced the community to think hard about burden-sharing with allies and partners. As Cox discusses in his chapter on the Canadian Forces Intelligence Command, before 2020, members of the Five Eyes partnership (Australia, Canada, New Zealand, the United States, and the United Kingdom) already often agreed to a certain division of labour for specific collection and analytical tasks (although little is known publicly about the details of these arrangements). However, given the constraints of the pandemic, they agreed in some cases to divide their work even further, notably on assessments and daily briefs, and to rapidly share the products of this burden-sharing. In this context, it will be interesting for Canada and its closest national security and intelligence partners, especially in the Five Eyes, to reflect on how this type of burden-sharing could be further broadened and routinized post-pandemic.

Canada's national security and intelligence community, in sum, has faced unprecedented stress since March 2020. Its many departments and agencies had contingency plans in place, but the intensity of the pressure it was suddenly under meant that large parts of these plans were inadequate to face the system-wide shock caused by the COVID-19 pandemic. With a combination of hard work, trial-and-error adaptation, and ruthless re-prioritization, the community modified its human resources management practices, assessed the evolution of the threat environment, and adjusted its operations. As the pandemic steadily subsides, the next set of challenges for Canada's national security and intelligence community—and for its allies and partners—will be to carefully read the post-COVID threat environment and ensure that it learns and applies the appropriate lessons.

Index

Figures and tables indicated by page numbers in italics

Canadian Armed Forces (CAF), 145–55; introduction and conclusion, 5, 145, 154–55, 161, 266; adaptations for COVID-19, 147, 161, 164–67; air force, 150–51; counter-pandemic contingency plan (Operation LASER), 146, 163–64, 173, 262; COVID-19 contagion within, 147–48; CSE's SIGINT operations and, 133; domestic operations, 146–47, 148–49, 155, 156n15, 270; expeditionary operations, 149–54, 165–66; land forces, 151–54; maritime operations, 149–50; readiness, 148; recommendations, 10, 155, 270; training delays, 171–72. *See also* Defence Intelligence Enterprise

Canadian Centre for Cyber Security: accelerated change at, 121; on critical infrastructure risks, 74–75; cybersecurity operations, 129–32; on cyber threat actors, 42; establishment, 128; IT services at, 113; new partners and clients, 116, 267; support for Shared Services Canada, 266; Traffic Light Protocol, 118–19, 122; workplace protection, 136–37. *See also* national security operations

Canadian Charter of Rights and Freedoms, 196, 197–98, 203, 206, 207

Canadian Food Inspection Agency (CFIA), 58, 59

Canadian Forces Information Operations Group, 134, 135–36

Canadian Forces Intelligence Command (CFINTCOM), 167–73; introduction and conclusion, 162, 163, 173; adaptations during COVID-19 lockdown, 169; Canadian Forces Intelligence Group, 170–71, 172–73; command issues, 171; co-operation with intelligence allies, 170, 271; medical intelligence, 168–69; organization of, 168, *168*; return to normal, 172–73; role and responsibilities, 167; training delays, 171–72; workplace protection issues, 169–70

Canadian Forces Intelligence Group, 170–71, 172–73

Canadian Forces Joint Imagery Centre, 170, 172

Canadian Forces National Counter-Intelligence Unit, 170, 172

Canadian Forces School of Military Intelligence (CFSMI), 171–72

Canadian Rangers, 147

Canadian Security Intelligence Service (CSIS): Academic Outreach and Stakeholder Engagement branch, 117, 118, 121, 267; authorities to collect information, 126n2, 198–99, 207; business continuity, 110; on COVID-19 online disinformation, 140; CSE's SIGINT operations and, 133; cybersecurity and, 42, 130; GPHIN and,

187; health intelligence and, 96; intelligence from, 90; IT services, 113; managing stress and anxieties, 112; new partners and clients, 269; new products, 117; openness and public outreach, 121; open-source intelligence, 118; staffing, 110; workforce protection, 136. *See also* national security operations

Canadian Security Intelligence Service Act (*CSIS Act*), 197, 198–99, 206, 207

Carignan, Jennie, 152

Centers for Disease Control and Prevention (CDC), 252–53

Centre for International Governance Innovation (CIGI), 121

certification, manufacturing, 54, 56

Charter. See Canadian Charter of Rights and Freedoms

Chayer, Marie-Hélène, 164–65

Chiarelli, Canada [Minister of Employment and Immigration] v [1992], 233

China, 54–55, 56, 76–77, 92–93, 98, 121, 195

Choi, Kate, 254

climate change, 64, 92, 93

Collins, Ben, 28n1

Collins, R v [1987], 203

command, military, 171

Communications Security Establishment (CSE), 127–41; introduction and conclusion, 4–5, 127–28, 139–40, 266; accelerated change in, 121; active and defensive cyber operations, 132; assistance mandate, 9, 130–31, 207; authorities to collect information, 200; cybersecurity operations, 129–32; future considerations, 140–41; GeekWeek conference, 138; new partners and clients, 115–16, 269; openness and public outreach, 121; open-source intelligence, 119; roles and responsibilities, 127; SIGINT operations, 132–35; workforce protection, 135–39. *See also* Canadian Centre for Cyber Security; national security operations

Communications Security Establishment Act (*CSE Act*), 128, 130, 140, 200

computer network attack, 132

conspiracy theories, 15–28; introduction and conclusion, 3, 15–16, 28, 263; characteristics of, 18; COVID-19 and, 17–19, 20–21; history of, 17; national security threats and, 25–27; problem of evil and, 18; proportionality bias and agency panic, 20; QAnon movement, 19–21, 21–25, *22*, *24*; recommendations, 7

co-operation, with allies and partners, 63–64, 115–16, 170, 267, 269, 271

Cossette-Trudel, Alexis, 26–27

Counter-Terrorism Committee Executive Directorate (UN), 39

COVID-19 pandemic: cases and deaths in Canada and US, *250*; vaccine distribution, 147. *See also* Canada's intelligence and national security community and COVID-19 pandemic

COVID Alert (app), 131–32, 195–96

Criminal Code: authorities to collect information, 196, 198, 199, 207; on terrorism, 218, 224; on trade secrets, 205, 208n3

criminal justice system, 211–25; introduction and conclusion, 5–6, 211–12, 223–24, 262–63; comparison to deportation, 231; and extremism and terrorism, 215, 217–21, 224, 225n1; need for modernization, 223, 224–25; need for prioritization, 215–17, 224; overstretched system, 221–23; public health violators and, 215–16; recommendations, 9, 224–25; shifts in criminal offences and, 212–14; systemic racism and, 217

crisis informatics, 35

critical infrastructure: conspiracy theories and, 27; supply chain disruptions and, 52

critical infrastructure, and cyber attacks, 73–82; introduction and conclusion, 4, 73, 82, 264; attack impacts, 75–76; COVID-19 and, 78, 80–81; need for multi-stakeholder coordination against, 77–78; protection challenges, 78–80; recommendations, 7, 82; risk assessment of, 74–75; state responses, 76–77; vulnerability to, 74, 77. *See also* cybersecurity; cyberspace, and malicious non-state actors

CSE Act (*Communications Security Establishment Act*), 128, 130, 140, 200

CSIS Act (*Canadian Security Intelligence Service Act*), 197, 198–99, 206, 207

cyber attack operations, 132

Cyber Centre. *See* Canadian Centre for Cyber Security

cybersecurity: common threats, 129; COVID-19 challenges, 114–15; CSE operations, 127, 129–32. *See also* critical infrastructure, and cyber attacks; cyberspace, and malicious non-state actors

Cybersecurity and Infrastructure Security Agency (CISA), 76

cyberspace, and malicious non-state actors, 33–44; introduction and conclusion, 4, 33–34, 44, 263–64; Canada's national security and, 42–43; delegitimation activities, 36–38; inciting violence and intimidation activities, 40–41; increase in extremist activities, 214–15; recommendations, 6–7; recruitment activities, 38–40; threats overview during

COVID-19 pandemic, 35–36. *See also* critical infrastructure, and cyber attacks; cybersecurity

D

Daesh. *See* Islamic State of Iraq and Syria (ISIS)

data: disparities for COVID-19 and racial and ethnic minorities, 252–54; Global Public Health Intelligence Network (GPHIN) and, 186–87. *See also* surveillance apparatus and data collection

Defence Intelligence Enterprise (DIE), 161–74; introduction and conclusion, 5, 161–63, 173–74, 266; adaptations for COVID-19, 164–67, 262; Canadian Forces Intelligence Command (CFINTCOM), 162, 167–73; counter-pandemic contingency plan, 163–64, 173, 262. *See also* Canadian Armed Forces; Canadian Forces Intelligence Command; Department of National Defence

Defense Information Systems Agency, 76

Defense Production Act (US), 56

defensive cyber operations (DCO), 132

delegitimation, 36–38

Democratic Republic of the Congo, 152–53

Denmark, 52, 76

Department of Defense (US), 76

Department of Health and Human Services (US), 255

Department of National Defence (DND): adaptations for COVID-19, 161, 164–67; counter-pandemic contingency plan, 163–64, 173, 262; CSE's SIGINT operations and, 133; health intelligence and, 96; officer biographies, 156n2. *See also* Defence Intelligence Enterprise

deportation, 231–42; introduction and conclusion, 6, 231–32, 265–66; 2022 deportation target, 242n4; administrative removals, 238–39; COVID-19 impacts on, 234, 235, 239–40; motions to stay, 237, *237*, 242n2; process of, 233–34; recommendations on resuming post-pandemic, 240–42; serious, inadmissibility removals, 236, 242n1; voluntary removals, 236–38

de Wilde, Jaap, 98

disinformation, definition, 45n1. *See also* conspiracy theories; cyberspace, and malicious non-state actors

diversity, in supply chains, 54–56, 59

Domestic Policy Council, 256

Dosanjh, Ujjal, 179

Duarte, R v [1990], 197

Dubajic, Daniel, 41

Integrated Terrorism Assessment Centre (ITAC), 136

intelligence: in Canada, 90, 96; collection challenges during COVID-19, 113–14; definition, 90; open-source, 118–19, 122, 267. *See also* Canada's intelligence and national security community and COVID-19 pandemic; health intelligence; national security operations

Intelligence Assessment Branch (IAB), 118, 267

Intelligence Assessment Secretariat (IAS), 2, 90, 113, 117, 118, 169, 267. *See also* national security operations

International Health Regulations (IHR), 177, 180, 182

Internet. *See* critical infrastructure, and cyber attacks; cybersecurity; cyberspace, and malicious non-state actors

Investment Canada Act, 53

Iran, 75, 152

Islamic State of Iraq and Syria (ISIS), 37, 38–39, 40

Israel, 94, 95–96, 97, 98, 99, 194

IT services, 112–13

J

Jamieson, Kathleen Hall, 17

January 6, 2021 US Capitol attack, 7, 16, 21, 35, 40, 263

Joint External Evaluation of Canada Self-Assessment Report (2018), 186

Joint Meteorological Centre, 170–71, 172

Jones, Scott, 131

Jordan, 152, 156n12

Jordan, R v [2016], 221, 222

K

Kallas, Jessica, 27

Kaplan, Alex, 23

Kosovo, 152

L

Laforest, Eric, 153

Lamberty, Pia, 17

Lametti, David, 221

Latvia (NATO Enhanced Forward Presence), 151–52, 153–54, 155, 166

Lebanon, 152, 156n12

lessons-learned exercise, 9–10

location data, 193–94, 198–99, 200, 204–6

long-term care facilities (LTCFs), 146–47, 148, 154

M

MacFarquhar, Neil, 38

MacKay, Peter, 225n1

Maersk, 76

malicious non-state actors. *See* cyberspace, and malicious non-state actors

manufacturing and production, 53–54, 58

Mapping and Charting Establishment, 171, 172

maritime operations, 149–50

Mayer, Anna, 206

McInerney v McDonald [1992], 204

medical intelligence (MEDINT), 168–69

Medicom, 54

Mehler Paperny, Anna, 225n1

Melley, Timothy, 20

mental health: law enforcement and mental health checkups, 217; in workplace during COVID-19, 111–12, 170, 267–68. *See also* workplace protection

Mexico, 37

Microsoft Teams, 81

migrant and refugee communities: introduction and conclusion, 6, 245, 262; background, 246; in Canada, *247*, 247–48; COVID-19 financial, economic, and travel impacts, 248–49; COVID-19 public health impacts, 249–50; disparities in racial and ethnic data, 252–55; employment per service sector, 250, *251*; and national and bilateral security opportunities, 255–56; recommendations, 8–9; socio-economic disparities, 251–52; in US, 246–48, *247*

misinformation, definition, 45n1. *See also* conspiracy theories; cyberspace, and malicious non-state actors

Multinational Force and Observers (Sinai), 152

N

National Center for Medical Intelligence (NCMI), 93–94, 97

National Consortium for the Study of Terrorism and Responses to Terrorism (START), 16

National Cross Sector Forum: 2018–2020 Action Plan for Critical Infrastructure, 78–79

National Defence Headquarters (NDHQ), 162, 164–67, 172. *See also* Defence Intelligence Enterprise

National Emergency Strategic Stockpile (NESS), 56–57, 65

National Institutes of Health, 255

National Research Council, 183

national security. *See* Canada's intelligence and national security community and COVID-19 pandemic; national security operations

National Security Agency (NSA), 134, 136, 138

National Security and Intelligence Advisor, 10, 167